OLUSEGUN OBASANJO

PASSING

THE

TORCH

By

Albert Omotayo

Published by:

The Teacher Gospel Ministry

: +234 704 37 09 402; GSM: +234 806 33 22 663.

E-mail: gospelteacher2008@yahoo.com

The author is wholly responsible for the views expressed in this book, its ultimate design, content and editorial accuracy.

Table of Contents

Acknowledgements

My gratitude goes to our Lord Jesus Christ, the Giver of all gifts, under whose grace I live and function. All the glory and the honour go to Him.

I thank His Excellency, Chief (Gen.) Olusegun Obasanjo, GCFR, who graciously permitted me to make him the case study in this work and also granted me interview over and over again.

I thank my best friend, my wife, Mrs. Titilayo Omotayo, for creating in our home a consistently favourable atmosphere for the exercise of my God-given gift.

I thank my good friend of over fifty years, Maj. Gen. Simeon Kayode Oni (rtd.), who provided the materials and data for a substantial part of this work.

I also thank Dr. Ona Soleye, a childhood friend of Chief Obasanjo and Mr. Charles Igbodo, a pioneer member of staff of Obasanjo Farms as well as a host of other members of staff of Obasanjo Farms, for the interviews they granted me in spite of their busy schedule.

Dedication

To my beloved country, Nigeria and her illustrious sons and daughters past, present and future, whose lives and hard-earned achievements offer inspiration and hope for the realisation of a truly great Nigeria.

Foreword

Greatness gets on our nerves. It generates more envy than praise, more criticisms than congratulations. Three of the greatest men I know in Atlanta: President Jimmy Carter, Architect John Portman and CNN Founder Ted Turner, are little loved and often criticised for any little non-conforming action or opinion. But they make powerful impact on our city, the nation and the world.

It is nothing new. Few political leaders have faced the ridicule, scorn and derision of Thomas Jefferson the 3rd U. S. President, Abraham Lincoln and Franklin Roosevelt and his wife Eleanor most of all.

When it was asserted in WW II that black men could not fly an airplane, she personally visited Tuskegee, Alabama and invited a black pilot to fly her in a series of deft but difficult manoeuvres, which forced her husband, the President to launch the Tuskegee Airmen, who emerged as one of the most distinguished flying squad in both North Africa and Europe.

Greatness is visionary and courageous and it reminds more cautious and cowardly men to look for something to criticize rather than face their own lack of bravery and insight. Great men, somehow, forget themselves and worry about the needs of others. I first noticed this about Olusegun Obasanjo while he was in prison. When I asked what could I send him to help through his unjust imprisonment, all he wanted was a large print Study Bible and clothing for his fellow inmates so that they need not be discharged and have to return to their families and cities in humiliating prison clothes.

As I began to try to understand Nigeria's development and its important role in African problems, I found that since 1960, as Lieutenant in the peacekeeping force of the UN in Zaire under Dr. Ralph Bunche, Obasanjo was not only present but recognised by Dr. Bunche as a reliable leader and a young leader of great potential because of his boundless energy and leadership of a well-disciplined force of peace keepers.

For the past 50 years, there has been almost no African issues or conflict in which Obasanjo has not become a major factor – often behind the scenes but always in the midst of the action.

This book is about the story of Africa's longest serving, broadest contributing and most active and faithful leader. The world knows of Mandela because of his release from prison and his brilliant leadership in a new democratic

South Africa. But few remember that it was Obasanjo that acted fearlessly against Britain's military and economic power with Nigeria's moral power by enforcing a threatened boycott of British products and contracts, including expelling Conoco Oil for shipping Nigeria's oil to South Africa in contravention of UN and OAU sanctions.

Prime Minister Margaret Thatcher hurriedly dispatched Lord Carrington to Nigeria to apologise and seek a solution to the conflict. The result was the Eminent Persons Committee led by Australia's Prime Minister, with Obasanjo seated there as an implied presence of Nigeria's moral and economic power. This could not be compromised, with the ANC prisoners release and a commitment to free and fair elections with "one person, one vote". Immediately, this set a standard for the democratization of the majority of Africa's nations. These are personal observations from my personal friendship over the past 40 years and of my close watch over the African scene.

Shortly after winning the Nobel Peace Prize in 1964, Martin Luther King, Jr. was asked to consider a mediating role in Nigeria's civil war and I was asked to study the situation but he determined that we didn't know enough about Nigeria to get involved. Once they start it's almost impossible for well-intentioned outsiders to intercede until the conflicting sides were exhausted by conflict or bloodshed. Fortunately, Nigerians not only survived their civil war but also created a lasting peace, which has survived for several generations of peace and democracy. While far from perfect, the will of the majority has emerged victoriously and power shared among 36 States has created a fairness formula, which should be considered by other nations of the world.

Now a very successful farmer, this African patriot remains involved in the world over, though his vision, courage and uncompromising frankness still keep us ordinary leaders uncomfortable. You never know what he will say and to whom he will say it, but be assured, he speaks the truth as he sees it and does what he feels in Nigeria's, Africa's and World's best interest. "You shall know the truth and the truth shall set you free." It also might make you mad if you are looking at only personal short-term interest.

Our Native American Tribal Elders came to visit me as the U. S. Ambassador to the United Nations to remind me of the wisdom of their heritage: "Leaders must make wise decisions for seven generations, yet unborn." Absolutely true, but much of our short-term political options are challenged by this wisdom.

Olusegun Obasanjo is an African Patriot, who understands, appreciates and acts on this wisdom; whether we like it or not. I'm sure future generations will understand, appreciate and be thankful that at least one man stood tall enough to see a peaceful, prosperous, free and democratic Nigeria.

Andrew Young

Chairman, Good Works International.

Former U. S. Ambassador to the United Nations.

Introduction

Many well-meaning Nigerians are becoming increasingly less hopeful of our country ever becoming a truly great country that our founding fathers dreamt of. Corruption is growing with more pernicious roots each day in our public life, in spite of intimidating legal and institutional arrangements to achieve the contrary. Public utilities are dying. Nigeria is notoriously referred to as the darkest country in the world. Our public service has practically become an institutional cult for graft and personal enrichment of a few privileged public officers. Hard work, integrity and sacrifice are considered old fashioned, if not foolish. Everybody is literally in a rat race to consume today as much as the nation can give today and even tomorrow.

Unfortunately, there is no short cut to greatness. In order to achieve national greatness, we must all work hard in our different callings, we must love our nation, and we must individually uphold probity as well as make necessary sacrifices. The easy money from oil that we presently rely on is unsustainable and cannot make our nation great. As we have seen, it only lines the pockets of a marginal group of individuals, while the nation is left to wallow in an ever-deeper morass of underdevelopment. Ironically, this grim Nigerian situation does not bear out the achievements and the sacrifices of our founding fathers as well as the contributions of even some contemporary citizens. Could we have forgotten their labours, sacrifices and ideals?

We had Herbert Macaulay, Nnamdi Azikiwe, Obafemi Awolowo, Aminu Kano, Sardauna of Sokoto, Anthony Enahoro, Prof. Oritsejolomi Thomas, Prof. Taslim Elias, Chief Rotimi Williams, Justice J. I. C. Taylor, Prof. Kodilinye, Gen. Murtala Mohammed, Gen. Olusegun Obasanjo, Mrs. Funmilayo Ransome-Kuti, Mrs. Margret Ekpo, Prof. Kenneth Dike, Prof. Bolanle Awe, Prof. Wole Soyinka, Prof. O. Akinkugbe, Prof. J. F. Ade Ajayi, Prof. A. Lambo, Prof. Ben Enwowu, Sir Kashim Ibrahim, Simeon Adebo, Jerome Udoji, Allison Ayida, Arc. Fola Alade, Hogan Bassey, Thunder Balogun, Hubert Ogunde, Rex Lawson, Victor Olaiya, Fela Anikulapo-Kuti, and more. These great Nigerians, some of who are still alive, in their times and different callings, took the name of Nigeria, and indeed the name of Africa, to enviable heights. Their inspiring achievements, which were by dint of hard work, sacrifice, and commitment, made us proud and remain a legacy that can be passed on to future generation.

These illustrious Nigerians are however, regrettably in character, orientation and service, a sharp contrast to many of our present day leaders. Our contemporary leaders do not seem to be interested in achieving anything spectacular or in leaving a good legacy for posterity. They are somehow bereft of any traits of the ideals and character of our past heroes. This may not be unconnected to the fact that present day Nigerians have only a hazy idea of the great men and women that Nigeria has produced. This robs the nation of the pedigree of our past successful men and women.

In the absence of a pedigree and a culture, our present day leaders are left to set their own subjective standards in their callings. In addition, the lack of pedigree also makes our leaders anonymous. They have neither name nor standard to protect or project. They have only the selfish desires from their base instincts to pursue. They did not have tutelage in ethics and proper behaviour. They climbed the ladder of leadership outside an entrenched leadership culture. It is not any surprise then that they are so unfamiliar with acceptable leadership character orientation.

This is typified by the extremely low performance of the last National Assembly (2007 – 2011). In the face of unprecedented unemployment rate, falling standard of education, diminishing health care delivery facilities, failed infrastructures, general insecurity, widespread poverty and general hardship, these 'honourable' members, in a cruel display of legislative power, used their sacred position to fix for themselves, salaries and allowances that were far ahead of the national economy. They pushed through this callous desire in spite of public outcry and then adopted a lifestyle that was, in its opulence and meretricious vulgarity, a sharp contrast to the general frustration and sobriety that pervaded the nation.

It is however not out of place to think that if the members of the National Assembly in question had any ethical tutelage in the form of a thorough exposure to the patriotism, hard work, sacrifices and accomplishments of our past leaders, they would most probably have behaved better. They would most probably have chosen to place service above easy fortune and strive to match or surpass the standards of their chosen role models among our past illustrious political leaders.

On the other hand, we all share the blame because we don't consciously document and teach those coming behind the struggles, the sacrifices and the achievements of our past leaders. They therefore do not know our past and can claim that they met nothing to build upon. God instructed the children of Israel to publish, distribute and teach their children from generation to generation, as well as celebrate yearly, all His acts in their lives. This was to enable them build a culture that would guarantee the preservation of the standards and ideals divinely instituted for them.

In sharp contrast, we do not want to have anything to do with our past; let alone use it to build a culture to support and foster future progress. Corporate greatness does not happen by accident. It is earned by building the appropriate culture that gradually, over a period of time, ushers it in. Therefore, in the pursuit of national development, there must be pedigree and an ingrained culture of patriotism that holds together our national struggles.

The great nations of Europe and America took the giant leap that propelled them to global scientific and technological prominence on the platform of their cultures, which they had built over many centuries. They painstakingly wove into the daily life of their citizenry an irrepressible culture of freedom, investigation and the feats of their past great men and women. Every new government continues as a matter of course the good work of the preceding administration.

Ours is sadly different, so different that we stand out in the world as the country with the largest number of abandoned projects. Every new administration starts off with a rabid, yet jejune, hatred for the preceding administration and all it did. Everything that came from, or initiated by, the preceding administration must therefore be obliterated or abandoned. This attitude goes beyond mere political puerility; it is a grave, if not deadly, abnormality in the national psyche.

Let me therefore seize this opportunity to pay particular tribute to patriots like Prof. Akinjide Oshuntokun, Dr. Femi Ogunsanwo, Prof. Wole Famuyiwa, Tunde Olusunle, Kelechi Anosike, Adinoyi Ojo Onukaba, and a few others. They deployed their talents and other resources to dig up and publish for the benefit of the present and coming generations, the treasures of ideas and transferable principles of achievement that had been buried with our past. It is in their footsteps that I am attempting by this humble work to look at the extraordinary achievements of another great contemporary Nigerian, Chief (Gen.) Olusegun Obasanjo.

As shall be shown in this work, Chief Olusegun Obasanjo broke the bounds of stifling challenges in all his careers to record extraordinary accomplishments that make him a great asset to our dear fatherland. He is also still a player in many regional and global endeavours, where he continues to set standards that make him a pride to Nigeria and the entire black race.

Our problem is certainly not the dearth of good and beautiful people, into whose shoes present day leaders could step to successfully accomplish their missions and move the nation forward. One prominent Nigerian lamenting the death of Chief Awolowo said of the latter: "the best President Nigeria never had." What a shame!

We need in this millennium to consciously outgrow petty envy, which we hide under 'politics' and take due advantage of the great human resources that God has graciously deposited in our nation. If we acknowledge and build upon the achievements of our past great men and women, we surely will be able to build the appropriate culture for the realisation of our collective aspiration and redirect our nation to the path of true greatness. This is the message of this work.

An Excellent Soldier!

Chapter 1: Preparation For Military Achievement

Chief (Gen.) Olusegun Obasanjo started life disappointing observers at every turn. The period of his educational career was characterised by abject poverty that led him to do menial jobs to keep in school. There was nothing about him that suggested greatness. He moved from one lower class to a higher one amidst uncertainty and fear in some minds that it might be his last class because the finances of his parents did not improve. Although he could not pay his fees, he was nonetheless very brilliant. At the beginning of each year, those who had thought at the end of the previous year that he would not find the means to come back to school were disappointed. He came back, though still struggling but moving on. His poverty was so bad that it hid the promise of greatness held by his academic brilliance.

His school contemporaries could rationalise his brilliant performance. He had no means for the enjoyment of social life; he must therefore necessarily be studious and do well in his examinations. There was nothing particularly extraordinary in that. If by any miracle he finished and got a job, his social life would pick up and his flair for studies would correspondingly wane. On the other hand, he might find his way into the University but they reasoned: "where will the money for that come from?" Eventually, Obasanjo got to the class where he felt that he could sit for the General Certificate of Education (GCE) examination and he did so as a private student. He passed the examination and observers, who by the reason of his poverty, thought that he would not attain the School Certificate standard, again were disappointed.

He then went to Ibadan to take up a stipendiary job. The optimists among his friends and school contemporaries were expecting to find his name on the list of those who passed the Concessional Entrance Examination to the University of Ibadan or one of the then Nigerian Colleges of Arts and Science. However, not only did Obasanjo's name fail to appear where it was popularly expected to appear, it did where they never expected to find it. His name was found on the list of army cadets. What a wrong person to go to the army! He was too brilliant for that. Perhaps it was mere coincidence of names. In any case, the person, whose name was found on the list of army cadets turned out to be the same Olusegun Aremu Obasanjo, that dour, bare-footed, serious, bookish, boy from Baptist Boys' High School, Abeokuta. It was a disappointment to school contemporaries and friends. Some of them even feared that he might have developed a kind of personality disorder.

They wondered, why he thought that he was a right material for the Army. He never drank alcohol, which used to be the distinguishing mark of the kind of soldiers that most people in Abeokuta at that time were familiar with. He was not particularly active in any sports or games. He was not athletic whether by practice, physical build or psychological inclination. Nothing, except his brilliance, taciturnity and poverty, drew attention to him. He however joined the Army on 5 March 1958 and he was among the set of cadets sent for training at the Regular Officers Special Training School, Teshie, Ghana.

This was a military institution established in 1953 for the recruitment and training of officer cadets in the colonial army stationed in West Africa. It was called the West African Frontier Force. The period of training lasted six months. It was essentially a foundational course that consisted of Weapon Handling, Elementary Battle Craft, War Operations, Physical Drills and Staff Duties. The set of Nigerian officer cadets sent to Teshie along with Olusegun Obasanjo and who succeeded after the initial six months, included Benjamin Adekunle, Patrick Amadi, Jacob Esuene, Henry Igboba, Humphrey Chukwuka, Samuel Adegoke, Foluso Sotomi and Emmanuel Udeaja. At the end of the course, Olusegun Obasanjo was among those selected to continue their military training with another six-month course at the Mons Officers School in Aldershot, United Kingdom.

While in Aldershot, two things not directly related to his course happened that sounded loud suggestions of Obasanjo's future greatness. The first was the premature death of his mother. His mother was in the circumstance of the poverty that engulfed the family, the family's life wire. She and her husband, Olusegun's father, had relied on wisdom and expediency to withdraw their second child, a female, from school so that Olusegun could have education and be equipped to break the bondage of poverty that hung over the family. This act shows the depth of love that they had for their son and his position in their priorities. The death of such a devoted mother was, expectedly a big blow and it was further compounded by Olusegun's anxiety over his sister, who at this time desperately needed his brother to share the sorrow with her. It was a trying time for Olusegun, who was absent in faraway United Kingdom.

The second thing that happened to him was his enrolment in Aldershot Polytechnic for a course that led to the award of a Diploma in Engineering. He repeated the Baptist Boys' High School feat, when he sat for the Society of Engineers' Professional Examination at the end of his first session in this Polytechnic and passed. Olusegun Obasanjo therefore did not consider it needful for him to continue with the

Diploma programme. This was because the ultimate attainment of the entire training, whether at the Diploma or Degree level, was the professional certificate, which he now had. The professional Certificate was what commended an engineer to the public as one who could be relied upon to offer engineering services.

These two events were critical in that they could have truncated the military career of Olusegun Obasanjo if he did not manage them well. He was not in doubt that his mother died in the struggle to make her two children, Olusegun and Adunni success stories. He was equally certain that the Army held the promise of empowerment for him to give a comfortable life that was well deserved by a loving mother like his mother. He also did not forget that his sister, Adunni, was withdrawn from school to make it easier for their parents to cope with his own educational demands. The cooperation of Adunni to make such a sacrifice for her brother undoubtedly deserved Olusegun's appreciation in the form of attention and care.

With their mother dead, Olusegun, who was far away in England, also agonised about the loneliness into which Adunni was unavoidably thrown. All these naturally disturbed Olusegun and caused confusion in his mind. He could have resolved this inner confusion by rushing back home. The temptation to rush back home was increased by his British Training Officer, who offered to permit him to go back home but Obasanjo turned down the gesture. He chose to bear his grief as quietly as he could, while he committed his sister into God's care for the best in the meantime.

His enlisting in the Army was in the first instance, his own idea. It was not well received among his kith and kin, when he made it known to them. Had he gone back to Nigeria at this time, anything could have happened. Would he have been unaffected by the immediate and looming suffering and deprivation of Adunni and his father, who was actually the chief mourner? Would he be able to disengage from them and return to England to continue his course? Although being on a military assignment might provide a shield, but he certainly had to fight the natural pressure welling up inside him to return home and be a part of the sorrow and funeral ceremonies.

On the other hand, his decision to stay back in England was not escapist. It was the first test of his capacity for accomplishments and greatness; whether he knew it or not. While mum was alive, the economic condition of the family was bad enough. The only hope that the family had of a better future hung on no other person than Olusegun. He had, by enlisting in the army, started to follow the right path towards achieving the family objective. He was in

England at this critical period because he knew that he had a mission to accomplish. Olusegun regarded with utmost seriousness the expectation of his mother that if he received education, he would lift the other members of the family out of poverty. As far as he was concerned, nothing must stand in the way of the realisation of this expectation. It was the only way to uphold what mum stood, suffered and died for. The career that he was pursuing was also for him a closer walk to that realisation.

Therefore, rather than be weighed down and lose focus on account of this tragedy and the dejection that it threw up, Olusegun Obasanjo saw it as the compelling reason to succeed in his course. This determination rapidly unfolded, when a few hours after he heard the news of the tragedy, his training officer decided to choose him as the company commander in the exercise that immediately followed. Notwithstanding the sorrowful state of his mind, he carried out the assignment satisfactorily.

Unfortunately, some observers wrongly believe that the death of his mother rendered him indigent of any true love for a woman. They argue that Olusegun Obasanjo has since the death of his mother seen the women in his life as usurpers, who came to reap, where they did not sow. This opinion certainly does not reflect the familiar characteristic of Obasanjo. He loves and respects his friends but he does not submit his goodwill to those, who see him as a cheap means to their private ends. He sees such people as exploiters and parasites. He instead prefers to build an enduring system from which everybody, whether friends or foes, can benefit.

Secondly, his success in the Professional Engineering examinations was quite consistent with his secondary school academic performance. It was therefore not a surprise to him or to anybody watching him. However, for a man, whose primary calling was to deliver his family from the clutches of absolute poverty, the expediency of financial reward in an engineering career would make the precarious life of military service less appealing. At this time the Nigerian Army had only an Engineering Squadron and Olusegun Obasanjo was training to become an infantry officer.

The decision to continue his military course after the attainment of a professional qualification in engineering, when the Army did not offer much prospect in that profession, speaks a lot about Obasanjo's courage and foresight. Poverty in a family is usually a source of intense pressure that drives some people into desperation. The way such desperation is expressed differs from one individual to the other. Some seek short cuts that end up defeating their own ends and leading such people back to where they were running away from or even to worse situations. Others, in the attempt to fast track their liberation from poverty, slip into criminal activities and so ruin their lives without achieving their goal. There are also others, who get enmeshed in the pursuit of shadows, which leaves them ultimately becoming a part of the problem that they set out to solve.

As for Olusegun Obasanjo in the case in question, he calmly carried out a deep reflection on his situation. He ended up brushing aside the inner pressure and sentiments that surrounded him and set his mind on what brought him to England in the first instance. He viewed his current success and the tempting opportunities it offered as mere enrichment to the primary cause. He therefore decided to face his military career, although the full benefit was yet in a hazy distant future. He showed commitment to his decision, when he returned home and transferred to the Engineering Squadron. He was with Mike Okwechime, who had been there before him, a pioneer in the Squadron.

This decision of Olusegun Obasanjo to leave the established and predictable infantry corps to be a co-pioneer in the Engineering Squadron that was regarded at that time as a dead end, made many of his course mates wonder how queer he must be. However, with time, his foresight paid off. What was just a squadron at the time later grew to become an Engineering Corps that Olusegun Obasanjo ultimately commanded. In retrospect, one could ask what would have happened if there was no civil war that bloated the size of the entire Nigerian Army to the advantage of the small units of those days such as Engineering, Reece, Signal, Intelligence, Artillery, Military Police and Ordnance? Would they have remained mere squadrons?

The life of officer cadet Olusegun Obasanjo in Aldershot showed him as one, who strives to know and understand the heart of the matter in any situation. This is the ability to separate the wheat from the chaff or make a distinction between the substance and the shadow. Many people fail in life; not for the want of physical and financial resources but for the inability to sift surrounding issues and voices competing for attention and identify the right one to hold.

Olusegun Obasanjo was rated above average in his course at Aldershot. This success was not a surprise but what really marked him out was the way he handled the personal issues that conflicted with his military career at the time.

This attribute also saved him from the hands of hostile Congolese soldiers, when he was on peacekeeping operations in that country. He went on a reconnaissance to alert the nuns, whom he had orders to evacuate to safety, to prepare them for the evacuation. He had barely finished talking with the nuns, when two

Congolese soldiers accosted him, put him in the boot of their car and drove him off to be executed. This however did not happen as the soldiers were ordered by their superior officer to release him immediately. The point in the drama was the possibility of his acting in self-defence but he instead stuck to his instructions to avoid a clash. He quietly endured the indignity and the discomfort of this experience and in return gained his life. In his own words:

"I suffered no shock or physical harm except for a minor bruise on my right shoulder in the boot of the car. When we were at the cement factory, there were four soldiers with me and only two were armed. For one moment my mind flickered over the thought of gunning down the four of them in self-defence. I was lucky or perhaps they were lucky that the thought did not persist for too long, before I remembered my order." - Olusegun Obasanjo: Nzeogwu, Spectrum Books, 1987, p. 65.

The pistol and ten rounds of ammunition that he had on him at that time was enough for him to gun down his four captors but would he have outlived the reprisal by the rest of the Congolese soldiers in that area? His ability to restrain himself and avoid overreaction in the name of acting in self-defence, in spite of the seeming advantage, saved his life.

The Nigerian Army in which Olusegun Obasanjo enlisted was one bound by deep esprit de corps, genuine nationalism and a collective desire for a professional Army that was competent to defend the nation against any kind of aggression. This desire was partly realised through the training of officers. Olusegun Obasanjo took full advantage of all the training opportunities that were made available to him. He strove to excel in internal examinations such as the Captain-to-Major examination, in which he came first, both in the mock and actual examinations.

Olusegun Obasanjo returned from the Congo with his mind made up on a military career in the Engineering Squadron. He was therefore in 1962, immediately after his promotion to the rank of Captain, sent to the Royal College of Military Engineering at Chatham, England. It was another opportunity for Captain Olusegun Obasanjo to repeat the previous academic excellence and this time, he earned the distinction of "the best Commonwealth student ever". He returned to Nigeria to take up the command of the Nigerian Army Field Engineering Squadron. After eighteen months at home, he was on his way to India again to attend the Indian Staff College and thus became the first non-infantry officer in the Nigerian Army to attend Staff College. At the end of the course, he was rated "the best officer who was sent up till now from that country (Nigeria) to Wellington".

While in India, he also attended the Indian Army Engineering School at Poona for a familiarisation course, in which he also excelled.

Apart from his brilliant performance in the courses, which he attended while in the Army, Obasanjo's readiness to be trained for every responsibility also shows an inner understanding of the supremacy of knowledge in any endeavour? This emphasises the fact that the path of success can be trodden only with the feet of knowledge and humility. Knowledge can be gained only when it is sought. A person who is seeking knowledge can only do it in humility because seeking knowledge is at the same time confessing one's ignorance in the area of knowledge in question. This explains why the Bible declares that only the humble can receive from God. In the case of Olusegun Obasanjo, we shall see how his humility handsomely paid off in his future endeavours.

Major Obasanjo returned to Nigeria from India on the eve of the outbreak of the politico-military crisis that started on January 15 1966, when the army took over the reins of government in Nigeria. The crisis was in various quarters described as a mutiny, a putsch and a coup d'etat. In any case, Olusegun Obasanjo was not involved in the crisis. It marked the beginning of a sad and painful national journey, which ended in a thirty-month-long fratricidal hostility that almost led to the demise of the federation. This war put into a very tough test the level of our post-colonial political development as a nation. It also above all, put to equally tough test the quality of our armed forces in general and the professional quality of each military officer in particular.

Sadly, no military officer was prepared for such test. In fact, the military officers, who executed the January coup showed egregious naivety, as they had no plausible answers to the questions of ethnic interest and personal ambition raised by the method of their action and the particularity of the victims of their action. The consequence was that wrong overtook wrong, as the government that emerged also mishandled the already bad situation thrown up by the January coup. The mishandling by the Ironsi administration of the aftermath of the January coup, in turn provoked a counter-coup. The counter-coup was from all intents and purposes a reprisal against Ibo officers and men by officers and men of Northern Region origin. This is because the Northern officers saw the January coup as an Ibo agenda, aimed at foisting Ibo domination upon the country. From that moment began a political crisis that got increasingly worse everyday.

In the end, the Eastern Region of the country, which had a preponderant Ibo population, and for that reason bore the brunt of the reprisal of July 1966, seceded under the leadership of Col. Odumegwu Ojukwu, who was at the time the Military Governor of Eastern Nigeria. What followed was a civil war that was bitterly fought for thirty months. The Federal Army was made up of three divisions: First Division, Second Division and Third Marine Commando Division.

In the third year of the war when the hope of a Federal military victory over the rebels was becoming increasingly more elusive, Col. Obasanjo was appointed as the General Officer Commanding the Third Marine Commando. Within about six months of taking over, Col. Obasanjo led his Third Marine Commando Division to bring the rebels to their knees. He obtained from the rebel military leadership the Instrument of Surrender that brought the civil war to a permanent close. I was in my second year in the University of Lagos, when this happened. The question that was on the lips of all of us, students then was: ***"Obasanjo? How did he do it?"***

The same question was asked with amazement within the larger population. While the entire populace was pleasantly surprised to hear that the war had ended, it was however more surprised that it came unexpectedly and by the hand of an obscure officer called Olusegun Obasanjo. Again, on the lips of everybody was 'how did he do it?' I met Brig. Olusegun Obasanjo for the first time five years later, when the latter was the Federal Commissioner for Works and Housing and I was an Assistant Secretary in the same Federal Ministry of Works and Housing. I could not resist asking the same question. I said to Brig. Olusegun Obasanjo:

"Sir, when you were appointed the GOC Third Marine Commando Division, I became less hopeful of a Federal victory but you finally ended the war. How did you do it?"

Brig. Obasanjo responded with a humble smile that hid an inner strength of character and the prospect of yet greater victories.

Figure 1 - A Family Event in 1979

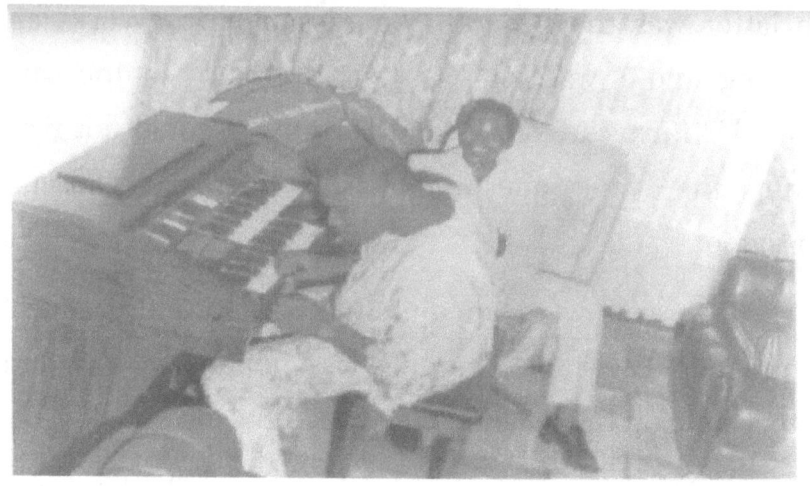

Figure 2 - Obasanjo Playing Piano in Ibogun Country Home 1979

Figure 3 - Wedding Day

Chapter Two: The Outbreak of the Nigerian Civil War

The generality of Nigerians at the time of this story, except those, who served in the colonial army during World War II, had never experienced war before. Although there had been civil disturbances in some parts of the country, the police was usually sent to quell such disturbances. There were very few instances, such as the Tiv riots in the mid-sixties, when the Government resorted to military force to quell a civil disturbance. The Federal Government actually approached the onset of the civil war with a police action because nobody, including the military, expected the war to last longer than six months. In fact, Col. Olusegun Obasanjo and late Col. I. D. Bisalla sat together to write the appreciation and operational order of the war. They predicted that the war would end within six months. The Federal Government also wanted to avoid an action that would aggravate the bitterness of the Ibos and make post-war reconciliation impossible. It therefore started the war with a police action. The reality of the war however forced the contrary.

In 1968, almost two years into the war, Federal troops made so much progress in the war against the rebels that it was predicted that the war would end in that year. This was however not to be the case, largely because of the human and material resources made available to the rebels by France as well as internal maladministration and mismanagement of operations among the Federal military leadership. This enabled the rebels to recapture from the Federal Army, strategic areas such as Owerri and Oguta, within a not-too-distant range from Port Harcourt. The situation was made worse by the diplomatic recognition accorded the rebel regime by Cote d'Ivoire, Tanzania, Zambia, Gabon and Haiti. What the Federal Government got instead of a quick victory over the rebels in 1968 was therefore a protracted war going into its third year. At the end of the second year of the war, the general situation of the war could, at best be described as a stalemate.

As the war dragged into its third year, its concomitant destruction of lives and property also persisted. There was furthermore the ill prospect of more international recognition for the rebel regime. These made the Federal Government expectedly desperate. The rebels too, having by now succeeded in creating a stalemate became increasingly bolder and more hopeful of victory or a negotiated settlement, if they could hold on longer. While the military leadership was battling with the reverses of Federal troops at the war front and the increasing internationalisation of the war, the public too was becoming less patient. They began to say openly that Biafra had come to stay and should be allowed to stay. The Nigerian Government therefore needed her best hands on deck to speedily bring the war to an end unconditionally in favour of the Federal Government. Unfortunately, things did not seem to be working too well for the Federal Government.

As earlier mentioned, there were three military divisions fighting the war. The three Divisional Commanders were responsible to Army Headquarters, from where they received their Operational Orders and logistic support. At the Army Headquarters were the Service Chiefs and their Staff Officers, who drew out the Operational Plans. They also handled procurement and allocation of human and material resources such as weapons, ammunition, transport and personnel. At the very apex was the Commander-in-Chief of the Armed Forces, who was also the Head of State. He coordinated the entire war effort. The most important thing in the war effort therefore was the esprit de corps among all those who were involved, from the apex to the very base; that is, from the Commander-in-Chief to the troops fighting at the battlefront.

Espirit de corps refers to the relationship that exists among officers and men of a fighting force. In practical terms, it is found in the love, camaraderie and trust that characterise official and non-official relationship within the force. Therefore, when an officer commands his men to take a particular action, say, advance, retreat, shoot or any other command, the troops obey promptly. The prompt obedience of the troops is based essentially on the trust they have in their officer that his order is in the best interest of the common cause and also in their own interest. This is what distinguishes a military organisation from any other kind of organisation. The suspicion and insensitiveness commonly found in non-military organisations are ordinarily not found in military organisations. This is what makes fighting and winning a war possible. On the other hand, when a fighting force loses its esprit de corps and morale is low, reversals become inevitable.

A deathblow was dealt on the esprit de corps of the Nigerian Army, when on January 15 1966 some young army officers decided to carry out a coup d'etat against the elected civilian Government. The civilian Government in question had Sir Abubakar Tafawa Balewa as the Prime Minister and Dr. Nnamdi Azikiwe as the President. Not only did the coup fail, the coup plotters also, by the selectivity of the victims of their violence, left observers with the irresistible conclusion that they were merely pursuing an Ibo ethnic agenda. This was because most of the officers, who planned and executed the coup were of Ibo extraction and most of the victims were non-Ibo. Most unfortunately, the military government of General Ironsi thrown up by the ill-fated coup did not help matters.

General Ironsi, while accepting that the January coup was a rebellion, did not take appropriate action as demanded by the law against the plotters. By his inaction over the January coup, Ironsi made it irresistible to regard him at best as sympathetic to the coup, and at worst as being an active collaborator. Besides, by some political indiscretion, he promulgated Decree 31 of 1966, which abolished the Federal system and established instead a unitary system of administration in the country. This action was received with anger and bitterness in the Northern Region, where most of the military officers and political leaders killed in the failed coup came from. The promulgation of the decree seemed to confirm the growing fears in the Northern Region that the coup plotters and the new government of General Ironsi were one and the same group, whose ultimate goal was Ibo ethnic hegemony.

The political and military leadership of Northern Region responded with a counter-coup that was not only very bloody but also unmistakably directed at Ibo officers and men within the Army. Unfortunately, what started as a military outburst soon deteriorated into a complete breakdown of law and order, as the carnage spread to the civilian Ibo population beyond military barracks. A large number of Ibos, especially those residing in the Northern part of the country, were either killed or maimed during the crisis. The socio-economic consequence of this crisis was colossal. Its political implication was the bitterness and distrust, which provoked the civil war that almost destroyed the unity of the country.

More important for the future of the Army however, was the death of esprit de corps and normal discipline among the officers and men of the Nigerian Army. It was so bad that the war was largely seen at its onset as a military confrontation between the Northern Hausa-Fulani and the Eastern Ibos. This was made worse by the fact that the class fighting the war, the military class, was at the same time the class ruling the nation. The strain of having to combine a political role with directing a war soon started to manifest in the relationship that grew among the Commander-in-Chief, the Staff Officers, who had responsibility for the appreciation and planning of the war and the Field Commanders.

It must also be remembered that the Commander-in-Chief was a product of the counter-coup, in which he most probably did not play any critical role beyond mere connivance. He therefore owed his position to the Northern officers, who executed the counter-coup, particularly the leaders of the counter-coup. The January-July crises thus inexorably killed esprit de corps and military discipline and replaced them with ethnic and social cleavages within the Army.

This made it possible for some officers and men to get away with acts of indiscipline or blatant disobedience, even in wartime. Some of them even became a law unto themselves. Such officers were audacious enough to do what they chose to do and ignore whatever else remained, regardless of the order from their superior officers. At a certain time, it became unclear to whom some officers and men gave their loyalty. Thus, not only was esprit de corps destroyed, discipline was also destroyed.

Gen. Gibson Jallo, in a recorded interview commented on esprit de corps and general discipline at this time:

"There were switches of loyalty; at the end of it, before 2 Division even finished, Akinrinade even left 2 Division. There were a lot of switches dislocating the Army because everybody wanted to go and look for where his man or his friend was. There was that disloyalty among officers moving from office to office or from unit to unit. Some of our Northern officers found themselves with 2 Division. There was a lot of disloyalty. You wanted to fight alongside the man you like or you trust.

The general effect, as far as I am concerned, was complete chaos, disorganisation, and poor general followership. If the general followership were not poor, it wouldn't have been possible for somebody to leave his area and get accepted elsewhere." Gen. G. S. Jallo (Rtd.), The Nigerian Civil War 1967-1970, History and Reminiscences, ed. Maj-Gen. Momoh, Ibadan, Sam Bookman Publishers, pp. 628-629.

Col. Murtala Muhammad demonstrated most the anti-climax of the crack within the army, when he carried his grievances to the point of openly criticising the Commander-in-Chief and accusing him of ineptitude. He later abandoned his command and dared the Army to discipline him. When nothing happened, he offered to resign his commission. Instead of calling him to order in the appropriate manner, emissaries were covertly sent to beg him to rescind his decision. This degree of indiscipline within the Nigerian Army expectedly produced a general decline in morale and lack of commitment to the war effort across the entire army. There were also some officers, who concentrated on the opportunities offered by the war to feather their own nests. They watched with unconcern, when their troops engaged in looting and other unprofessional acts that seriously undermined the cause of the war.

As for the Field Commanders, they engaged in prolonged grudge against the Staff Officers at Army Headquarters over what the former perceived as a deliberate starving of their divisions of needed supplies and munitions. On the other hand, the Staff Officers accused the Field Commanders of lack of prudence in the use of the supplies made to them. Furthermore, instead of operational cooperation among the Field Commanders, there was bitter rivalry that led to one laughing when the other had a setback. The situation was further compounded when the Commander-in-Chief got married during the war in a style that was completely out of tune with the restraint normally dictated by a war situation. Some officers reacted to this by deciding to remain inactive, while some others took advantage of the slightest opportunity to abandon the war front. The circumstances described above partly explain why decisive victory eluded the Federal side for so long.

The reversals that the Federal troops experienced at this time spoke more eloquently about the crack and weaknesses that bedevilled the Nigerian military Government and the military hierarchy. However, Army

Headquarters did not look the other way but tried to do what they could to renew the fighting spirit of the troops at the war front. Army Headquarters rightly felt at a certain stage that the Divisional Commanders, having stayed continuously at the war front for upwards of two years, needed some rest. This, they argued, would allow them the opportunity to appoint new Commanders that were capable of injecting a new spirit into the war effort. This was eventually agreed upon by Army Headquarters, which accordingly thereafter on 12 May 1969 announced the appropriate changes. By the changes, Col. I. D. Bisalla took over the command of the First Division from Col. Mohammed Shuwa, Col. Gibson Jallo took over the command of the Second Division from Col. Mohammed Haruna and Col. Olusegun Obasanjo took over the command of Third Marine Commando Division from Col. Benjamin Adekunle.

The Operational Instructions issued to the new Commanders were as follows: First Division was to take over from the Second Division in Onitsha Area. The Division was also to advance to Nnewi and beyond and thereafter capture Orlu and explore forward. The Second Division was to defend the Mid-West and hold defensive position along River Niger in order to prevent rebel infiltration across the river into the Mid-West. The Third

Marine Commando Division was to stabilise and straighten its defensive line, recapture Owerri and explore forward. The Division was also to recapture Oguta and explore forward.

The Army Headquarters probably knew the truth about the deteriorating situation in the area of operations of the Third Marine Commando Division. In fact, Col. Abisoye, at that time the Rear Commander of Third Marine Commando Division, not long before this time visited Bonny. He took advantage of his visit to Bonny to also visit the war front in order to assess the war situation in the operational area of his Division. He returned to write a Situation Report that gave ominous warnings about the imminent loss of Aba, Owerri, Owaza oilfield and Port Harcourt except a drastic action was taken. This earned him the appellation of 'a prophet of doom' and he was even almost officially chastised for the Report.

Col. Abisoye was seen as mischievously creating problems for his friend and forward commander, Col. Adekunle. Col. Abisoye was however satisfied that he had done what was his duty to do. He left the rest to those, who were saddled with the duty of taking the final decision. Within a few weeks after submitting the Report, events at the war front proved Col. Abisoye absolutely accurate, as the Federal troops lost Owerri. In addition, the rebels were advancing

47

Albert Omotayo

towards Port Harcourt while Aba was also badly threatened.

Notwithstanding the truth known by Army Headquarters, it was not expedient to wash the dirty linen of the Army in the public. All that it could do was to go ahead with the decision to change the Field Commanders. This was not at that time as easy as it might appear, largely because of the popular, but not necessarily accurate, interpretations given to official decisions by both the uninformed, and sometimes mischievous, members of the public. It was therefore necessary for the Government, in dealing with any of the Field Commanders, to be seen as fair to all. The Army Headquarters therefore showed sufficient sensitivity by changing at the same time all the Field Commanders, who had in any case, stayed too long at the war front and needed rest.

However, the public did not know what Army Headquarters knew and as far as the former were concerned, Col. Adekunle was the one that could prosecute the war to a victorious end for the Federal Government. Notwithstanding the conscious decision of Army Headquarters to be fair to all, some, among the Yoruba still saw the redeployment of Col. Adekunle as punitive and directed essentially against the Yoruba. The appointment of another Yoruba, Col. Olusegun Obasanjo, to succeed Col.

Adekunle however solved only part, the less important part, of the problem created by the redeployment of the latter.

According to an official Chronicle of the war:

"As 16 Brigade was withdrawing from Owerri, there was a welcome change of Command in 3 Marine Commando on 16 May 1969. Col. Olusegun Obasanjo took over from Col. Adekunle, the once famous "Black Scorpion", but now an embattled and weary commander who had lost not only many of his battles with heavy casualties, but also the confidence of his officers and men." Op cit., p.108

The more important problem was the general public pessimism that greeted the appointment of the new Commander of Third Marine Commando Division. This public pessimism was borne out of the fact that Col. Obasanjo was not known and his airport press conference on his way to assume the command of Third Marine Commando Division lacked the pep and bravado of his predecessor. In addition, many quarters reasoned that bringing in an engineer officer in war was evidence of dearth of human resources within the army. However, while the public did not know Col. Obasanjo, the Army Headquarters knew him as a distinguished officer-gentleman, who had the capability to turn the situation around.

We may now not know whether it was by divine direction or sheer accident of military posting that Col. Olusegun Obasanjo was considered to be one of the good ones, who might be able to turn the military tide against the rebels. In any case, Col. Obasanjo was in the third year of the war appointed the General Officer Commanding the Third Marine Commando Division. He succeeded the flamboyant Col. Benjamin Adekunle, who was incidentally his course mate at Teshie, Ghana.

Col. Adekunle, whether deliberately or otherwise, was surrounded with so much hype and media whitewashing that the Nigerian populace saw him as the one destined to bring the war to an end. Col. Adekunle himself also seemed to believe that he alone could bring the war to an end. This explains the general apprehension that greeted the appointment of Col. Obasanjo as the GOC of Third Marine Commando Division. However, the taste of the pudding is in the eating; so, the populace waited.

Col. Obasanjo was actually not a stranger to the war at the time of his appointment as GOC Third Marine Commando Division. He had been the Commander of the Second Area Command with its headquarters at Ibadan. He was actively involved in the routing of the rebel troops that infiltrated into the Western Region through the Mid-West Region shortly after the outbreak of the war in 1967. Besides, as the

Commander of the Engineering Corps, he constantly visited the war zones to ensure that the Army Engineering units operating with the various divisions properly acquitted themselves in the support that they were required to give to the troops.

When Enugu was liberated and somebody was needed to administer the liberated areas of the East Central State, Col. Obasanjo was instrumental to the appointment to that position of Mr. Ukpabi Asika, a lecturer at the Political Science Department of the University of Ibadan. In fact, Col. Obasanjo played more than a passing role in the appointment of Asika. The Commander-in-Chief had his mind for that office on a military officer on the Federal side or a politician from the East. Col. Obasanjo however argued that the situation in the East then called more for a civilian administrator of Ibo extraction than for a military officer on the Federal side. His reason was that a civilian administrator would more likely give the required confidence to the large population of displaced persons than a military administrator. Col. Obasanjo was therefore immediately saddled with the task of finding the right person. The result of his effort was the appointment of Ukpabi Asika as the Civilian Administrator of the liberated areas of the East Central State. Although Col. Obasanjo was at the time of his appointment as Commander of Third

Marine Commando Division very familiar with the war, he would however henceforth go beyond the phase of familiarity to facing the fire of the war.

Figure 4 - High School Days in the 1950s (BBHS). Obasanjo (Standing) Extreme Right

Figure 5 - Successful Cadet in the UK

Figure 6 - Cadet Obasanjo (left) at Regular Officers' Special Training Teshie, Ghana, 1988

Chapter Three: General Officer Commanding Third Marine Commando Division

---

When Col. Obasanjo took over as the GOC Third Marine Commando Division, the full effect of the dysfunction triggered off within the military by the first coup d'etat had become manifest in all the commands. The Third Marine Commando Division was particularly bad because it added its own internal administrative maladjustment to the basic problem caused by the 1966 coup. Talking about the situation, Col. Obasanjo said in his own words:

"A day before the announcement of change of commanders, I had been called to Dodan Barracks and informed of my new appointment. I received the news without emotion and without expression. Some of the staff officers who knew the exact situation in 3 Marine Commando areas of operation expressed sympathy and fear for me. I could only thank them for their sentiments." Gen. Olusegun Obasanjo: My Command, 1999, Heinemann Educational Books, p. 61 & 63.

Following the announcement of his appointment as GOC 3MCDO, Col. Obasanjo sped to Port Harcourt after a fifteen-minute briefing by his predecessor at the airport. This was in addition to the previous briefing he received at Army Headquarters on the eve of the announcement of his new appointment. During the journey, he had to settle in his mind whether he was going to his Command to build a media image that equalled or surpassed that of his predecessor or to establish a reputation totally built on excellent professional performance in the war. It was not easy coming to a conclusion even though he is by nature not given to boasts and superficiality but those were what excited the Nigerian public.

However, flamboyance and bombastic expressions laced with myth may trigger public excitement, but when unmasked, they are often found to be nothing but a mere façade. It was a credit to Obasanjo's deeply analytic mind that he chose to pursue a professional reputation by doing the job that he was given as best as he could, with minimum exposure to the media. He then quickly reviewed what he learnt in the course of his professional training. From this review, he came to the conclusion that his most important and most pressing task was the welfare of his troops and the restoration of esprit de corps. In his own words:

"I was thinking less of the operational situation and more of how to keep the formation together as a fighting force in view of the reports of, among other things, lack of trust and confidence and in-fighting among the officers. Friendship may not be decisive in the success of other organisations, but they are absolutely imperative for the success of a military organisation in combat." Gen. Olusegun Obasanjo: op. cit. p. 66.

Col. Obasanjo arrived in Port Harcourt and went straight into the heart of the matter. Without any fuss or invocation of the instrument of official authority, he started touching the heart of his troops in a gentle but effective manner by readjusting the psychological orientation of the officers and men of his Command. First, he decided that the troops must be paid their full salaries. He however did not rule out facilitating the provision of banking services for the troops. Secondly, he rejected the room prepared for him in the house of one of his officers and chose the official Commander's house, in spite of its poor, almost uninhabitable state.

Thirdly, he was at his desk the following day at eight o'clock, something different from what the Command was used to. Until Obasanjo's first day in office, commanders of the Third Marine Commando used to resume work at 10 am. Fourthly, when he reached the Commander's office he removed the board placed on the door by his predecessor. The notice on the board read: "Enter at the pain of Death." This notice, whatever the previous Commander intended it to mean, spoke dread and fear into the mind and heart of troops and subordinate officers. Fifthly, he revived the dying team spirit among the Army and the other Services; that is, the Navy, Air Force, the Police and the Government of Rivers State, by making himself easily accessible to all. These quiet actions by Col. Obasanjo within his first forty-eight hours in his Command, signalled to all that a new dispensation of humaneness, camaraderie, cooperation and professionalism had arrived.

On the third day of his assumption of office, Col. Obasanjo held a meeting with all his Commanders, Heads of Supporting Arms and Services and Staff Officers. The purpose of the meeting in his own words was:

"The aim of my first conference was to meet as many officers of the division as possible to diagnose the ills that had affected the formation and to enunciate my principles, methods and objectives. I started the conference by asking for a one-minute silence to be observed in honour of all members of the formation who had died in the war. After paying tribute to all ranks of the division including my predecessor for their wonderful performance in the past, I went on to ask for sincere and honest comments and opinions on the ills of the division emphasising that I wanted to know WHAT was wrong and not WHO was wrong." General Obasanjo: op. cit. p. 72.

The critical issues in the new Commander's actions were his transparency and his desire to get to the heart of the problem of the Division. He left no one among his officers in any doubt that he was not going to be dragged into unprofitable recriminations and buck-passing. This saved him from what might be an instant, though silent, enmity of the loyalists of the old dispensation. The professional neutrality and adroitness that he displayed convinced everybody in the Command of the willingness of the new Commander to work with all. According to Maj.-Gen. Muhammadu Buhari in an interview:

"It was the coming of Obasanjo that time he came. Obasanjo was a more loyal officer, he was prepared to co-operate with anybody because already, those of us downstairs had already acquired experience and knew that the best way to catch Biafra was to slice it into two but Adekunle would never agree with Shuwa. Shuwa would never sit down and listen to Murtala (Mohammed)." Maj.-Gen. Muhammadu Buhari (rtd.), op. cit. p.342.

The Late Ken Saro-Wiwa had this to say about the arrival of Col. Obasanjo as Commander of Third Marine Commando Division:

"One instant effect of his (Col. Obasanjo) arrival in Port Harcourt was the immediate lowering of the temperature of military-civilian relationships. In Adekunle's last days in

Port Harcourt, civilians had been subjected to unprecedented harassment, with private vehicles being commandeered recklessly and civilians beaten and locked up "in Kampala" (jail) for the flimsiest reasons. All this was symptomatic of the desperation of 3 Marine Commando Division at that time and their discomfiture at the war front. Obasanjo put an end to all that and military relationships with the Government and the general populace took a turn for the better." Ken Saro-Wiwa, Port Harcourt, On a Darkling Plain: An Account of the Nigerian Civil War, Saros International Publishers, 1989, p. 216.

Col. Obasanjo, by this simple act, also destroyed any chance among the officers of his Command for cleavages and its ruinous effects on discipline. Besides, he presented a common cause, not himself, around which everybody rallied. They all had inputs in the cause and were therefore ready to defend and pursue its realisation together. He further created an atmosphere of freedom for all to prove their mettle in the pursuit of the common cause. Finally, by the same token, it was clear to all that discipline was to be restored in the Command and everybody therefore needed to sit up. In addition to the clear messages to the officers, the meeting also succeeded in identifying operational and human problems that had bedevilled the Division.

In order to have full knowledge of the situation in the Command, Col. Obasanjo followed up with a visit to all the Battalions and formations at the various fronts of his Command. This gave him a first-hand information, experience and knowledge of the challenges that confronted the troops of the Division. It also enabled him to know exactly how the troops felt. Moreover, his visit to the soldiers at the war front presented him as one, who identified with them and one, who would give prompt official attention to their concerns. It also revived the dying morale of the troops and created the right atmosphere for the restoration of esprit de corps.

Col. Obasanjo found that the organisation of the Division gave room for the low morale and general indiscipline that made operational failures inevitable. Soldiers were not paid their salaries under the pretext of helping them to save the salaries. In addition, some of the soldiers had been fighting for upwards of twenty-two months without any scheduled rest. They lived in trenches and had expectedly become fatigued, without anybody showing interest in their welfare. Some of them then felt that the only way to get rest was to get wounded and be evacuated from the war front. This act was so widespread that it considerably eroded the operational capability of the Division. According to Obasanjo:

"Within the first month, I had almost as many casualties as I had reinforcements and more than fifty per cent of my casualties were self-inflicted." Gen. Olusegun Obasanjo: op. cit. p. 82.

Furthermore, some girls were recruited into the Division and christened 'Commando Girls'. They were properly recruited and given Army numbers as well as Army uniforms but with many of them, that was all. They were never trained and they formed private relationships with officers. This naturally gave them an unhealthy feeling that they were above discipline. Although the girls were almost all privates, without rank, they however often refused to obey orders given by superior and senior Non-Commissioned, Officers. They also sometimes ignored disciplinary measures taken against them because of their private and personal relationships with officers.

Another cause of indiscipline in the Division was looting that had become the pastime of both officers and men of the Division. Looting was lucrative and soon became a source of enrichment for all. This was not only diversionary but it made both officers and men so rich that it compromised their motivation for fighting. All of these acts of indiscipline were so rampant in the Division that by the time Col. Obasanjo took over its Command, the Division had been reduced to its own shadow. According to Obasanjo:

"If discipline breaks down within a formation, that formation also breaks down as a fighting unit. The level of indiscipline in the (Third Marine Commando) Division in no small measure accounted for the reverses which the Division suffered and the consequent flagging morale, the combination of which nearly marked the Division permanently as a non-effective fighting force." General Olusegun Obasanjo: op. cit. p. 83.

After this initial fact-finding exercise, Col. Obasanjo returned to carry out a proper appreciation of the war on the basis of the information that he had gathered from the meeting with the officers and men of the Division and his visit to the troops at the war front.

First, he identified the human problems, which were lack of morale and esprit de corps, as well as the total absence of discipline. All these manifested in widespread desertion, absence from duty without due permission and self-inflicted injuries among the troops. In addition, officers were in the habit of influencing the posting of their tribesmen to relatively safe assignments such as guard duties at the rear or in the officers' houses. The relationship among the officers was also laden with suspicion and rivalry. Some officers even left the Division and vowed never to return there because they believed that they were not safe as long as the former Commander remained in command. Nobody seemed to be willing to fight anymore. The fighting spirit of the Division seemed to be in a state of paralysis.

Second, he identified operational problems. The first of these was the failure of the Division to take due cognisance of the surrounding environmental factors. The Division stuck to the same operational method it used in friendly areas of the South-Eastern and Rivers States, even when it reached very hostile areas with preponderant Ibo population. The second was that the Division stuck to a lineal and road-bound advance, without any attempt to hold ground in the conventional defensive manner. These omissions explain the fluidity and high cost in men and materials that characterised the operations of the Division. Apart from fluidity and the high cost in men and materials, the Division's line of defence became uneven. This also easily exposed the troops to regular ambush by the rebels.

The third problem was the structure. He found that the command structure of the Division that started from the Battalion to Brigade to Sector and to Division was too long and wasteful of the limited resources available. The result was that most of the Commanders were too far from their men. The troops paid for this with the loss of their welfare into the pockets of their officers. This in turn generated bitterness among the troops against the Army Headquarters, which they believed, neglected them. The fourth, and indeed the most serious one, was the total absence of Reserves at all levels of the Command but it was more marked at the Divisional level. The fifth was the absence of any cooperation or coordination between the Army and the supporting Services. The sixth was that logistic support and provisioning came only occasionally in an unpredictable manner.

With steady losses on the battleground, especially the loss of Owerri, the little morale left in both officers and men of the Division evaporated. The general situation in the Third Marine Commando Division at this time was an anti-climax that debunked the much-vaunted invincibility of the Division and reduced it to a caricature of a fighting formation.

After identifying the problems confronting the Division, Col. Obasanjo went one step further by discussing widely with the officers of the Division again. The outcome of these exercises was a detailed reorganisation plan consisting of twelve steps that ultimately revived the fighting spirit of the troops and saw them through to the end of the war. The consultation that preceded the plan undoubtedly gave every officer a sense of belonging that committed him to the success of the reorganisation. This was because they were a part of the plan. They therefore saw it as their own, not the imposition of a self-conceited leadership.

The first of these twelve steps was the issue of salaries, which he had earlier on made up his mind about. He ordered the payment of the full salaries of the troops and left each soldier to manage his money the way he deemed fit. To help them however, he discussed with the Central Bank and some Commercial Banks to reopen their Branches in the areas of operation of the Division. Those who chose to save their salaries could then do so, without the so-called help from their officers.

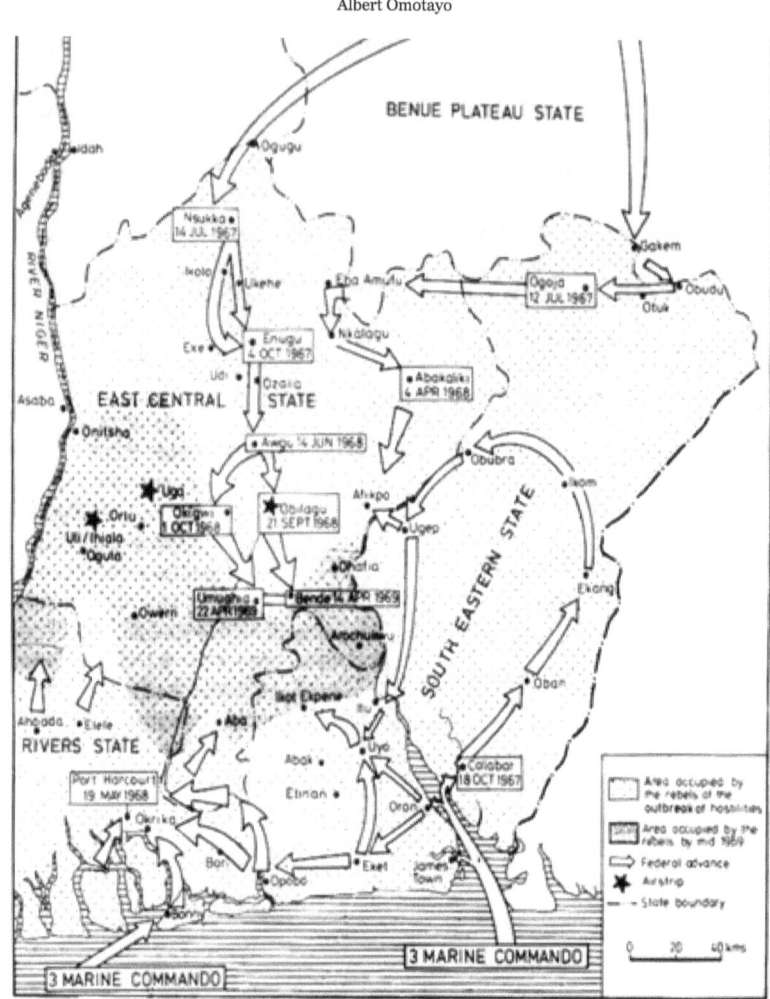

Figure 7 - The position of Federal troops as at June 1969. Source: Gen. Olusegun Obasanjo, My Command, Ibadan, Heinemann, 1981.

When he finished with this, Col. Obasanjo turned his attention to the question of organised rest for the fighting soldiers. As mentioned earlier, soldiers until this time lived in their trenches. Col. Obasanjo quickly created in Port Harcourt a well-furnished and well-staffed Rest and Recuperation Centre that had the capacity to accommodate two hundred and fifty soldiers at a time. The Centre was equipped with entertainment and recreational facilities and was administered directly by the Garrison Commander. The Centre, located at the Divisional Headquarters, was available to all the subordinate formations and units. He instructed them to work out a schedule for every soldier to have rest at the Centre for a period of ten to fourteen days at a time. This was a novel and particularly popular development in the Division.

Side by side with the arrangement for rest, Col. Obasanjo also dealt with the unprofessional conduct of self-inflicted injuries. The cases of self-inflicted injuries in the Division were in themselves a sad evidence of poor training and indiscipline that could make nonsense of the entire mission of the Division. This, if allowed to continue, would certainly cause a heavy loss of human lives. No war Commander would treat it with kid gloves because it is an act of sabotage. It must be speedily stamped out.

It is however interesting how Col. Obasanjo addressed this evil. First he identified the motivation instead of impulsively unleashing disciplinary measures. Second, when he was satisfied that the cause was largely the denial of organised rest for the troops, he made a very good arrangement for rest. Third, he organised the Division in a way that troops were well prepared, through training and provision of necessary equipment, before being launched into battle. This approach removed fear and the habit of officers influencing the posting of their tribesmen to relatively safer assignments. Fourth, he warned the soldiers to desist from inflicting injuries on themselves deliberately. He left them in no doubt that it was a grave offence that carried the capital punishment.

In spite of the Commander's new arrangement for rest and his admonition to the troops against self-inflicted injuries, there were still some, who persisted in the unprofessional act. Col. Obasanjo then on one occasion instructed the Commanding Officer of the Military Hospital to examine fresh cases of injury and bring out those that were self-inflicted. The twenty-three soldiers whose wounds were identified as self-inflicted were court-martialled. Twelve of them were convicted and sentenced to death. They were executed by firing squad after due approval of their sentence was given by the appropriate authority. This served as a lesson to others and until the end of the war only two cases of self-inflicted injury were reported.

These measures did not solve all the problems, as looting remained a pastime of almost everybody. As mentioned earlier, apart from being a tragic distraction, it also dulled their enthusiasm for the fight. They wished to go back home, whether the war was lost or won, to enjoy their newly acquired goods. Col. Obasanjo issued a Circular that spelt out adequate punishment for anybody, who engaged in looting. Thus, with organised rest, adequate training, and provision of materials as well as punishment for unprofessional acts of looting and self-inflicted injuries, general discipline was restored, the morale of the soldiers was revived and the war continued with a renewed fighting spirit.

The next problem that Col. Obasanjo dealt with was the issue of the Commando girls. These ladies, though duly recruited into the Army and carrying out useful duties as cooks, drivers and radio operators, became a problem because their presence and the way some of them conducted themselves fostered indiscipline within the Division. Discipline among a fighting force is so critical that it can make the difference between victory and defeat. The solution adopted by Col. Obasanjo however displayed an incredible ingenuity that satisfied all the interests involved.

He got the women formally discharged from the Army but they retained their positions as civilian employees. The only things they lost were their rank and the uniform. They remained employed by the same Nigerian Army, they continued to perform the duties they were performing before this reorganisation, and their salaries remained the same. Above all, they were henceforth free to have private and personal relationships with anybody but such relationships would, by the new reorganisation, cease to prejudice military order and discipline. If any of them committed an offence, she would be dealt with according to the relevant provisions of the Civil Service Rules.

Col. Obasanjo also brought budgetary discipline and accountability to the administration of the Division. The contractors and suppliers of food items in particular, who took undue advantage of the war situation to over-invoice their goods and services, were called to order. Besides, the Accounts and Supplies Unit were made to keep accurate records of expenditure. Hitherto, the Paymaster travelled to Lagos every month to collect as much as about three million pounds for the Division. The officer would then keep the cash in his house, from where he disbursed it. When the new arrangement that brought the Central Bank and the National Bank to reopen their Branches in Port Harcourt took off, the unprofessional and tempting manner of keeping funds by the Division's Paymaster stopped.

For the reason of the fluidity of the war situation and the method of recruitment adopted by the Division, it was difficult to keep accurate record of recruitment and know the actual personnel strength of the Division. This was the cause of the widespread rumour at that time that Commanders colluded with their Pay and Records unit to keep drawing the salaries of dead soldiers. Col. Obasanjo ordered the Pay and Records unit to give a monthly Return of the staff strength and nominal roll of both soldiers and civilians in the Division. He also made the production of the Return conditional for the monthly release of funds for salaries and other needs of the Division.

These administrative measures restored discipline and financial prudence in the Division. The Division henceforth drew less amount of money from Lagos to pay the salaries of more men as well as other charges. Chief Obafemi Awolowo, the Federal Commissioner for Finance at that time, did not allow this to go unnoticed. He duly acknowledged the improvement in the financial administration of the Division with a letter of commendation to the GOC, Col. Obasanjo. The reaction of Chief Obafemi Awolowo should be seen in the context of the contradiction that he had to put up with in the unrestrained profligacy of the Army under the guise of waging a war and managing the economy for national development. What marked Col. Obasanjo for commendation in this instance was the latter's capacity for restraint, orderliness and procedural propriety, even in a war situation.

After this administrative reform, Col. Obasanjo turned his attention to rebuilding esprit de corps and good inter-personal relationships among the officers in the Division. He quietly watched interactions among his officers and soon found that there was a particular officer, who made himself an agent of discord among his fellow officers. The causes of almost all the quarrel, grudge and bitterness among officers within the Division were traceable to the officer. His activities generated so much distrust that as long as he remained in the Division, it would be impossible to revive the troops' esprit de corps. Col. Obasanjo therefore requested that the officer should be posted away from the Division. He was accordingly posted away and the Division began thereafter to breathe an air of good comradeship and trust.

Col. Obasanjo then moved to reorganise the command structure of the Division. As mentioned earlier, the structure of the Division was from Division Headquarters down to Sector Headquarters to Brigade Headquarters and at the base was the Battalion Headquarters. This structure lengthened the chain of command with attendant high administrative costs, which in turn brought deprivation to the fighting troops. In spite of the obvious deficiencies of the existing command structure, Col. Obasanjo did not take a unilateral decision. He discussed the situation further with his officers to consider a review of the status quo in the face of the limited logistic and manpower resources available to the Division; particularly the inadequacy of experienced officers and non-commissioned officers. The outcome was the abrogation of the Sector. He described this in his own words:

"Again, after consulting my officers and studying the operations of the Division, the deployment on the ground, the logistics situation and manpower problems, especially the shortage of experienced officers and senior non-commissioned officers, I decided to change the command structure of the Division so that Battalions would work under Brigade Headquarters and Brigades under Division Headquarters thereby eliminating the Sector which I found superfluous." Gen. Olusegun Obasanjo, op. cit. p. 90.

The next step was the deployment of officers, which Col. Obasanjo carried out on the basis of a combination of the experience and ability of the individual officer, as well as situational dictates. In this reorganisation, Lt. Col. Akinrinade took over as General Staff Officer I, from Lt. Col. George Innih, who became the commander of 13 Brigade based at Ikot Ekpene. As GSO I, Lt. Col. Akinrinade was the second-in-command to the Commander and was in charge of Operations and Training at the Headquarters. Major Oni retained his position as the commander of 14 Brigade based at Chokocho and Capt. Iluyomade took over the command of 15 Brigade. Major Utuk took over the command of 16 Brigade, while Major Tomoye retained the command of 17 Brigade stationed at Aba. Lt. Col. Abubakar was assigned the command of 18 Brigade based at Itu and the command of the resuscitated 19 Brigade went to Major Aliyu.

This concluded the operational reorganisation of the Division into eight Brigades and two administrative garrisons stationed at Port Harcourt under Lt. Col. Ignatius Obeya and Calabar under Lt. Col. Ayo Ariyo. Capt. Okhuarobo and later, Capt. Adedayo were charged with Personnel administration while Major Tuoyo was in charge of Logistics. This reorganisation however left one officer beyond deployment because he had become frustrated and unwilling to continue. Col. Obasanjo immediately asked for his transfer and he was accordingly transferred from the Division.

In the reorganisation, 12 Brigade had three Battalions under its command, while 13 Brigade had four Battalions and 14 Brigade had three Battalions. 15 Brigade had two Battalions, 16 Brigade had three Battalions and 17 Brigade had three Battalions also. 18 Brigade had three Battalions and 19 Brigade had two Battalions. Calabar Garrison and Port Harcourt Garrison had a Battalion each. Col. Obasanjo did not leave the supporting arms and services out of this reorganisation. In line with the reorganisation, the Air Force posted Capt. Gbadamosi King to take over as the Detachment Commander. Subordinate formation commanders also keyed into this reorganisation by refurbishing their formations and units in line with the new structure and spirit.

Notwithstanding this elaborate reorganisation, there was still a critical gap created by the total absence of effective Reserves and inadequate logistic backing of reinforcements, arms and ammunition, transport equipment and materials. Reserve and Logistics are the bedrock of surprise and flexibility that are so crucial to victory in war. Col. Obasanjo therefore created a Special Task Force to serve as the Reserve of the Division.

The Task Force was a Battalion in strength and made up of experienced soldiers and specially selected young soldiers, who in addition to their training, acquired competence by operating with the experienced soldiers. The Commander took personal interest in the training, equipment and welfare of the Special Task Force, which christened itself Apollo Battalion. They chose this name because the time coincided with the American landing on the moon in 1969 in the spacecraft Apollo 11. It was a self-contained unit with its own mortar, anti-tank guns and rockets.

According to Gen. Obasanjo:

"It (the Special Task Force) operated on its own and never on frontal operations against the rebels. It moved fast on foot, with little noise and with enough food to last forty-eight hours. It was used mainly to surprise the rebels and cause panic in their midst through outflanking manoeuvres and disruption of their headquarters and line of communications thereby softening up the rebel position for the main advancing Federal troops." Gen. Olusegun Obasanjo, op. cit. p. 92.

The Special Task Force moved with such speed and style that instilled fear in the rebels. It was not designed to hold ground after a successful operation; instead, it yielded the ground gained to the formations and units meant for that. This made the Battalion easily available for decisive operations throughout the wide frontage of the Division. On every operation, they captured prisoners-of-war, who provided a lot of information for the strategic planning of subsequent operations.

Lastly, Col. Obasanjo paid many visits to Lagos to keep the Army Headquarters abreast of the situation in his Division and submit his requests for men and materials in the hope of getting adequate provision. This unfortunately was not to be the case for a number of reasons. First, Army Headquarters did not have a scientific method of procurement. This made the procurement chain defective and unable to adequately meet the demands of the fighting Divisions. Second, what was available at any given time was too small to go round the Divisions. This was the problem faced by Army Headquarters but was not known to the Field Commanders, who sent in their requests as dictated by their own needs and judgements. Third, the propaganda of the rebel government fell on sympathetic ears in the countries, from where Nigeria hoped to procure arms. Such countries shut their doors against Nigeria and so made procurement of arms and ammunition very difficult for the Federal Government.

Notwithstanding the problems faced by Army Headquarters in respect of procurement, Col. Obasanjo did not relent in making requests, as he considered necessary. Although he did not at anytime get all that he wanted, he was however within two months of taking over the command of his Division, able to slowly build stocks of weapons and ammunition to beef up all the Brigades to reasonable strength. He stockpiled enough arms, ammunition and materials to sustain a battle for forty-eight hours. He also succeeded in building a Reserve Force of two thousand and five hundred men as reinforcements, and reinforcements for battle casualties.

After he had concluded the reorganisation of the Division, he turned his attention to 'straightening the forward edge' of the Division's battle area, the first task in his Operational Order. This was necessary to avoid an encirclement battle that could eventually deteriorate into a prolonged war of attrition with no hope of early cessation of hostilities. This must be prevented in order to halt the rising cost in human and material destruction.

The frontline of the Division had become a porous zigzag that was very difficult to hold and to defend. This exposed the Division's line of defence to frequent rebel infiltration from behind. Besides, it also made its line of communications insecure and difficult to protect. This also expectedly sapped the confidence of the troops. However, with his just concluded reorganisation, Col. Obasanjo felt ready to tackle the task of straightening the frontline of his Division. He then produced a comprehensive plan that covered the entire line of the Division's defence and then held a conference with his officers to discuss the plan. The outcome was a detailed operational plan intended to be a great success and the reawakening of the Division, which the rebels, since the recapture of Owerri, had written off as the shadow of a fighting force.

Unfortunately, the plan leaked out to the rebels through civilians criss-crossing the battlefronts between the troops of Third Marine Commando Division and the rebel troops. There was also leakage through Federal soldiers captured as prisoners-of-war by the rebels, through intercepted messages and through captured documents. The consequence of the leakage was unmistakable. According to the plan, the operation was to be launched on 16/7/69 but the rebels too were preparing their 12 Division under Col. Tony Eze for an offensive to recapture Aba in the same manner that they did Owerri. They planned to advance after a successful offensive on Aba, to Port Harcourt and Calabar and so clear Federal troops out of the entire South-Eastern States of East Central, Rivers and South-Eastern. Spurred by the information at their disposal, the rebel 12 Division launched a pre-emptive attack against 17 Brigade of the Third Marine Commando along the eastern side of River Imo twenty-four hours before Col. Obasanjo's planned attack was scheduled to start.

The surprise rebel attack claimed its toll on the 17 Brigade of Third Marine Commando Division. In the bloody battled that ensued, the rebels speedily broke out behind the troops of the Third Marine Commando and overran the position of the detachment stationed at Owassa and Assa and reached the level crossing on the Port Harcourt-Aba Road. This was a very dangerous trend but with the reorganisation and the new impetus brought in by the new Commander, Col. Obasanjo, the troops of Third Marine Commando quickly regained their composure and neutralised the initial advantage of surprise, upon which the rebels hitherto rode. The Federal troops met the rebels in a determined and bloody battle that stretched for five days, after which the Third Marine Commando regained all the ground lost to the rebels during the first twenty-four hours of the battle.

Notwithstanding the success of Third Marine Commando in this operation, it was still at best, a costly distraction and at worst, a setback. The casualties were heavy on both sides and the divisional reserve of arms and ammunition was exhausted. In addition, the troops earmarked for replacement and reinforcements along the entire front were also launched into the battle against the unexpected rebel attack. After the rebels had been beaten back, Col. Obasanjo carried out a post mortem of the incident that almost made nonsense of his carefully laid out operational plan for the straightening of his Division's frontline.

The first weakness observed during the post mortem exercise was the inadequately secure management of information and documents within the Division. The clerical and secretarial staffs that were in charge of production, custody and movement of documents were particularly susceptible to breaches. This was because their duties that gave them official access to classified documents. These classes of general service workers were found to be the primary conduit, through which information passed into right and wrong hands. Col. Obasanjo therefore carried out a thorough vetting of the clerical and secretarial staffs both at the Brigade Headquarters and the Divisional Headquarters. Those who had been at the Headquarters were posted out and those coming in as replacements were thoroughly vetted. Security procedures were reappraised and communication was reviewed and improved upon. This step assured a reasonable level of security within the Division.

Ntline of 3 Marine Commando when Col. Obasanjo assumed command of the Division

Source: Gen. Olusegun Obasanjo: My Command. Ibadan, Heinemann, 1981.

In addition to the issue of security, Col. Obasanjo also reviewed the Division's method of planning and execution of operations in the context of the Division's situational peculiarities. In this respect, Gen. Obasanjo said:

"We also realised that the orthodox planning, preparation and execution were unsuited to our type of terrain and operation. We devised a modified system for planning and

preparation which we found effective throughout the rest of the war.........." Gen. Olusegun Obasanjo, op. cit. p. 97.

Thirdly, movement of civilians within the Division's area of operation particularly movement across Federal and rebel positions was controlled and closely monitored. In spite of the losses and the setback caused by this rebel onslaught, the lessons of the incident were not missed. They greatly helped the Division to achieve its ultimate objective of a decisive defeat of the rebels and the end of secession.

After the post mortem exercise and the appropriate lessons learnt, Col. Obasanjo quickly put it behind him but stuck to his original plan that leaked to the rebels. This turned out to be fortuitous in that the rebels, worsted in their spirited and well-planned pre-emptive onslaught against the Third Marine Commando Division, became frustrated and dispirited. They were therefore unable to put up any stiff resistance against the advancing Federal troops. Col. Obasanjo too started again to replenish his stock and refurbish the troops. When he achieved the level of strength that he considered adequate, he began his own attack against the rebels with great success. He personally moved with the fighting troops at a great risk of sometimes walking into rebel ambush.

In one of such unfortunate situations, he was greeted with rocket and machine gun fire. This encounter, which was for him a very narrow escape from death, left three of his escorts dead and two others wounded. He was himself wounded and he later reported at the hospital, where in spite of his wound, Col. Obasanjo seized the opportunity to inspect the whole hospital complex and visit all the wounded and sick soldiers. The inspection tour of the hospital was actually a decoy to draw away undue attention from his wound and avoid causing panic. It also turned out to be a morale booster for hospitalised soldiers, who had never seen their Commander visiting the wounded in the hospital.

Apart from this incident, the operation went very well and the Division suffered no more reverses. Col. Obasanjo achieved his objective of straightening the line of defence of his Division but he did not gloat over this success. He instead saw it as a mere stepping-stone to a decisive victory over the rebels. Gen. Olusegun Obasanjo described this stage of the war thus:

"By the end of October (1969) the defensive line of the entire Divisional front was fairly stabilised, less uneven and more defendable. The success of the operation signalled the preparation for the beginning of other operations to end the war." Gen. Olusegun Obasanjo, op. cit. p. 101.

Chapter Four: The Final Offensive and the Victory

Perhaps one thing Col. Obasanjo was never tired of doing was constantly reviewing his position in the face of situational realities in order to improve his performance. He was also never afraid of a new initiative that could improve the chances of maximum success. This is quite risky, particularly in a war situation, where a seemingly innocuous miscalculation can cause the loss of many human lives. The insurance that Col. Obasanjo had against grave errors was however God and his characteristic regular consultation with his officers. It is interesting that in a military and war setting, Col. Obasanjo still applied the democratic principles of consultation and inclusiveness to achieve success.

In the war effort to straighten the Division's line of defence, Col. Obasanjo observed that the road to victory lay in unrelenting pursuit of the rebels anytime they fled in the face of Third Marine Commando attack. He then rightly argued that a defeated formation would regroup and fight back only if it had the needed respite to do so. He therefore concluded that once the pressure on the rebel troops began, it should be sustained and increasingly intensified to ensure that the rebels had no respite and no room at all to recoup and regroup. Once again, Col. Obasanjo submitted his observation and plan to the scrutiny of his officers, who all agreed that keeping the rebels permanently on the run would exhaust them and break their fighting spirit. He said:

"I held discussions and consultations with my staff officers and subordinate commanders and they all agreed with me that our best plan of operation was to keep the rebels on the run and to keep hitting at their identified and established weak front and rear positions and by so doing cut the rebel enclave and its forces into two parts separately. We were all convinced of the soundness of the idea and the plan to bring it to fruition." Gen. Olusegun Obasanjo, op. cit. p.102.

The plan that proceeded from this idea was a four-step operation outlined as follows:

- Continue to drive the rebel soldiers northwards along the wide Aba-Ikot Ekpene front until Aba was linked with Umuahia and Ikot Ekpene was linked with Bende.

- By this, split the rebel forces into an Arochukwu-Ohafia enclave and an Owerri-Orlu enclave.

- Smash and destroy Arochukwu enclave.

- Smash and desroy Owerri-Orlu/Uli-Ihiala enclave.

When he had secured the concurrence of his staff officers and he was himself perfectly convinced that the plan was sound, practicable and achievable, Col. Obasanjo proceeded to Lagos to brief, and seek the support of, the authorities in Army Headquarters for the implementation of the plan. This was necessary because the plan in question, though dictated by the situation at the war front, differed from what was contained in the Army Headquarters' Operational Order.

The Principal General Staff Officer at the Army Headquarters, Col. James Oluleye, with whom Col. Obasanjo first discussed his Division's plan, opposed the new plan. Col. Oluleye strongly advised Col. Obasanjo to strictly adhere to what his Operational Instructions contained. Col. Oluleye's uncompromising stand was quite understandable in view of the still fresh Onitsha experience. Col. Oluleye rightly did not want a repeat of the disastrous 2 Division episode of crossing to Onitsha against the advice of Army Headquarters. In addition at that time, the desire of everybody's heart was the capture of the Uli-Ihiala airstrip because it was the only remaining rebel channel of contact with the outside world. All their goods and services came in through the airstrip and it was therefore thought that the capture of the airstrip would mean a fatal blow against the rebellion.

While Col. Obasanjo agreed that the airstrip was the lifeblood of the rebel government and the rebellion itself, he however also believed that the plan he had drawn was the easiest and fastest way of achieving that objective. He had seen that an alternative plan of capturing the airstrip as proffered by Army Headquarters would not only be costly but would also prolong the hostilities. This, from Col. Obasanjo's standpoint, was not the expedient thing to do in view of the battle realities on the ground.

There were also the unwanted likelihood of further internationalisation of the war and the mounting impatience of the public, which could turn the tide against the Federal Government if the war was allowed to drag unnecessarily. Above all, Col. Obasanjo was convinced that the execution of his plan would not produce a result similar to that of 2 Division at Onitsha. In spite of his spirited, albeit gentle, defence of his position and plan, Col. Obasanjo returned to Port Harcourt without securing the agreement of Army Headquarters. The refusal of Army Headquarters to lend support to his plan however did not dampen him. Instead, he remained unshaken in his conviction that his plan was more promising of success and a speedy end of the rebellion.

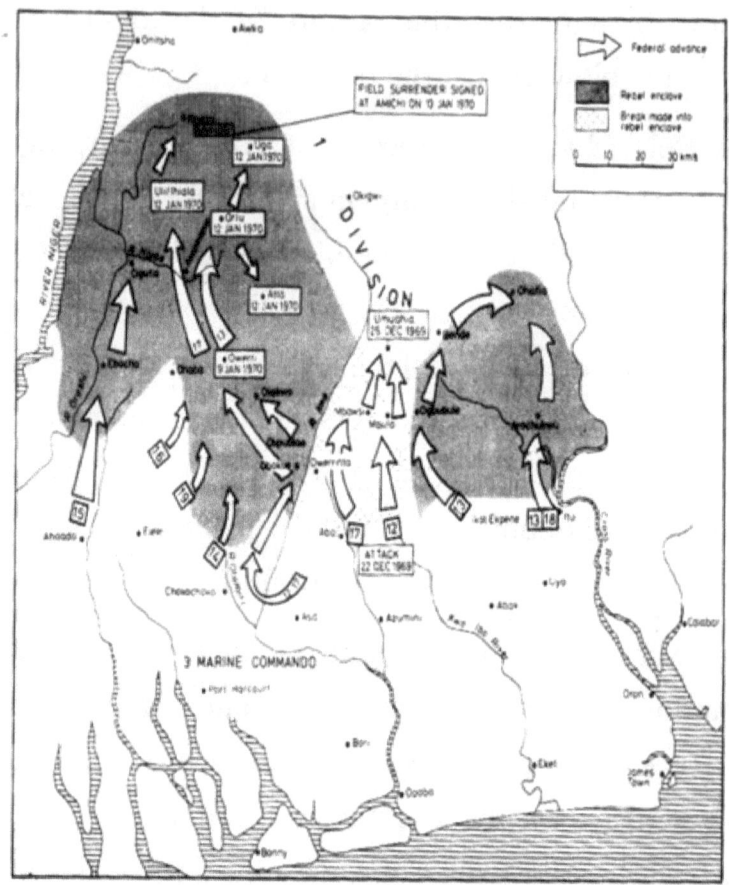

Figure 8 - Col. Obasanjo's Plan for the Final Offensive. **Source**: Gen. Olusegun Obasanjo: My Command, Ibadan, Heinemann, 1981, p.110

Col. Obasanjo left the Army Headquarters thinking of what to do. Not only did he know the basis of the apprehension of Army Headquarters, he also knew that it was a strong basis. Nobody was amused by the Onitsha episode and nobody in his right senses would want to risk any option that might lead to a similar fate. On the other hand, Col.

Obasanjo was absolutely sure that his plan held the key to a speedy ending of the rebellion. In any case, he returned to Port Harcourt with a decision to discuss his plan with 1 and 2 Divisions and seek their cooperation. Col. Obasanjo sent one of his Staff Officers to Col. Jallo, the Commander of 2 Division, while he himself travelled to Enugu to meet Col. Bisalla, the Commander of 1 Division, to discuss his plan with them.

Unfortunately at this time, 2 Division was confined to the Mid-West and had nothing other than an expression of good wishes to offer Third Marine Commando Division in the latter's plan to link up with Umuahia. Col. Obasanjo also did not meet his counterpart in 1 Division but he met his General Staff Officer I, Lt. Col. Yakubu Danjuma. Col. Obasanjo discussed his plan with Lt. Col. Danjuma and requested the Division to advance its troops ten miles south towards Umuahia, while Third Marine Commando Division troops would advance for more than thirty miles to link up with the troops of 1 Division on the outskirts of Umuahia. Such a simultaneous movement was intended to stretch out the rebels and frustrate any attempt by them to concentrate their remaining resources on the advancing troops of Third Marine Commando Division.

Lt. Col. Danjuma expressed agreement to the assumptions and expectations of the plan but he could not promise any definite support because his Commander was absent from his Headquarters then. He also did not leave Col. Obasanjo with a promise of any operational support because he knew that his GOC too was planning an offensive in the Awka-Nnewi sector. This he said might not allow 1 Division to give the operational support being requested by Col. Obasanjo. Col. Bisalla confirmed the doubt of his GSO I in his message to Col. Obasanjo, when he later returned to his Headquarters. Instead of leaving Enugu disappointed, Col. Obasanjo returned to Port Harcourt, more convinced that he was on the right path. He believed that all he needed was God, to give him the courage and determination to implement it.

Before he travelled to Enugu to solicit operational support and cooperation from 1 Division, Col. Obasanjo had chosen 17, 12 and 13 Brigades for the link-up operation and he had started a fresh and comprehensive reorganisation of the entire Division. This involved increasing, improving and strengthening the Brigades. At the end of the reorganisation, 13 Brigade gained two additional Battalions, 14 Brigade had one more Battalion, 15 Brigade gained one more Battalion, 16 Brigade also had one more Battalion, 17 Brigade had additional two Battalions, 19 Brigade received two more Battalions, while 12 Brigade and 18 Brigade were each left with three Battalions, all of which were built up to strength. While this reorganisation was going on, the Division received four new 122mm artillery pieces and Col. Obasanjo immediately started training his men on the new weapon.

The operational thrust of Col. Obasanjo's plan was to deprive the rebels any respite until final victory was achieved. He had studied the performance of the rebels and discovered their weakness, which was their unsuitability for sustained defence. He had realised that they always used to maximum advantage any opportunity they had for respite. If he was then to bring the rebels to their knees, he needed to deprive them of any respite by eliminating any gap in the series of attacks until final victory. This explains why he planned the link-up with 1 Division to be implemented in two phases, one coming immediately after the other. The three Brigades were to advance concurrently and almost side-by-side. While the first phase would start from Aba-Ikot Ekpene Road up to Mbawsi-Mbulo-Ogbuebule, the second and final phase would follow immediately without any breathing space to link up with 1 Division at Umuahia and Bende.

The operation began on 2 November 1969 and by 28 November 1969, the link-up with 1 Division had been achieved. The rebel enclave was now sliced into two with Federal troops occupying a very large area between the two rebel enclaves. This completely removed any possibility of a repeat of the Onitsha debacle. All that was left to be done was the final push to bring the rebels into surrender. It must not be forgotten that this was the same plan that failed to attract the support of Army Headquarters. Col. Obasanjo therefore decided to keep his successes secret until it spoke of itself; that is, when the rebels finally surrendered. It however did not happen that way as it somehow leaked to Lagos. An elated Commander-in-Chief, Gen. Yakubu Gowon, promptly sent to his GOC Third Marine Commando Division, Col. Obasanjo, the following congratulatory message:

"From Commander-in-Chief to Commander 3 Marine Commando Division:

I have received briefing of your latest fighting movement which resulted in heavy losses of men, equipment and ground to the rebel troops. Accept my heartiest congratulations on behalf of the nation. The movement is spectacular as a climax to many battles, halting a retreat, stabilising a dangerous forward-edge of battle area, restoration of confidence, morale building and boosting and a test operation leading to a successful debut after your appointment. After clearing your right flank, it is hoped that you will swing your guns and force to the life-line of the rebels. Early capture of the airstrips will certainly quicken the collapse of the rebel regime. Hercules be your speed. Wishing you a chain of unbroken successes. Once again heartiest congratulations to the commandos." Gen. Olusegun Obasanjo: op. cit. p. 108.

With the cat of Col. Obasanjo's success out of the bag, he travelled to Lagos after he had sent an appropriate reply to the Commander-in-Chief. He did this to personally give a situation report to the Commander-in-Chief and Army Headquarters. He assured the latter at this meeting that the war would be over within the following one month.

Col. Obasanjo returned to the war front this time with the full support of Supreme Headquarters and Army Headquarters, to launch his Division on 22 December 1969 into what he code-named "Operation Tailwind", the final offensive. By 12 January 1970, Third Marine Commando had captured Oguta, Uli-Ihiala airstrip, Atta, Orlu and Uga. With this victory, the entire Biafran nation was thrown into disarray because there was nothing left for them again to hold on to. Inexorably on 12 January 1970, Col. Philip Efiong, the rebel Chief of Defence Staff, who was at that time the person left to administer the affairs of Biafra after Ojukwu had fled, announced the surrender of Biafra.

The Chief of Staff, Army, Gen. Hassan Usman Katsina, sent the following message to victorious Col. Obasanjo:

"For Commando Chief. Fall of Uli-Ihiala Airstrip. (Rebel Port of Embarkation and Disembarkation) finally closed the chapter of fateful rebellion. The jet race to Uli was remarkable indeed. Inability to control it physically could have been one major tragedy of the operations. Accept hearty congratulations for this heroic achievement. It was an evidence of high morale generated by good command. Congratulate all subordinate commanders and troops. Message is from C-in-C. From me. Very well done." Gen. Olusegun Obasanjo: op. cit. p. 119.

Chapter Five: Humility in Victory

With the loss of Uli-Ihiala airstrip, the major towns of Enugu, Onitsha, Owerri, Aba and Umuahia, and the teeming civilian population of internally displaced persons, disconsolate, hungry, bewildered and fatigued, all compounded by the flight of Ojukwu, who lured them into the war, the rebel leadership decided to surrender. Lt. Col. Philip Efiong, the rebel Chief of Defence Staff, who was in charge of the administration of Biafra after the flight of Ojukwu, made a broadcast over Radio Biafra, where he said among other things:

"..............*I am convinced now that a stop must be put to the bloodshed which is going on as a result of the war. I am also convinced that the suffering of our people must be brought to an end. Our people are now disillusioned and those elements of the government regime who made reconciliation and negotiation impossible have voluntarily removed themselves from our midst.*

I have, therefore, instructed an orderly disengagement of troops. I am sending emissaries to make contact with Nigeria's field commanders in places like Onitsha, Owerri, Awka, Enugu and Calabar with a view to arranging armistice. I urge on General Gowon, in the name of

by the movement of population............" Op. cit., p. 122,
culled from A. H. M. Kirk-Greene, Crisis and Conflict in
Nigeria 1967-1970 (OUP, 1971), Vol. 2, pp. 451-452.

Immediately after Lt. Col. Efiong's surrender broadcast,
Col. Obasanjo sent the following message to all the Brigades
of his Division:

"From: 3MCDO (Main)

To: All Brigades

Info: 3MCDO (Rear)

*Op. Unicord. Philip Efiong today issued what amounts to
unconditional surrender. Tactical movement will continue
until every inch of 'Biafra' is physically occupied and all
rebel soldiers disarmed. Troops will not open fire unless
they are fired at. No change from ops order on treatment
of POW and refugees."* Gen. Olusegun Obasanjo, op. cit. p.
123.

The following day, 13 January 1970, after seeing off his
guest, Gen. Adebayo, who was visiting Third Marine
Commando Division at that time, Col. Obasanjo proceeded

to Owerri and then to Orlu, where he was informed that his officers, Lt. Col. Akinirinade and Major Tomoye, had made contact with the rebel officers. He set out to look for them and while doing that, he stopped intermittently to encourage the sick and the displaced persons he found on the way. He made emergency arrangements for the wounded among them to receive available medical attention. Eventually he arrived at Amichi where he met Lt. Col. Philip Efiong in Biafran Army uniform, while all other rebel Army officers there wore mufti. Gen. Obasanjo graphically described the scene:

As we drove through the gate and my escorts dismounted from their vehicles, fear and near-panic could be clearly read on the faces of the civilians standing by. I went unhesitatingly upstairs where all the officers whose colleagues we had been in the Nigerian Army stood gazing at me with fear and surprise. Obviously they were torn between saying 'Congratulations!' and 'What are you doing here?' They knew one thing – they had lost the war and 'Biafra'. But Capt. Ben Gbulie, who as a junior officer had served under me in the Corps of Engineers and who had played a significant role in the January 1966 coup, came forward unobtrusively and congratulated me saying, 'Sir that was high generalship. I feel proud of you.'

To break the ice, I put out my hand to Efiong and we shook hands warmly. I quickly followed this up by complimenting him on his good looks in his 'Biafran' Major-General's uniform. He smiled with a restrained air of pride and satisfaction. I inquired about his family and most of the senior officers on their side who were not present. I remarked that I had seen some of them outside but they had failed to enter. He explained that 'Biafran' propaganda had made everybody believe the genocide story that they were too frightened to come out. Most of them were in hiding. By now everybody in the room had relaxed as a result of my unexpectedly warm and cordial approach. I had addressed all the officers in there by their first names or their nicknames and shook hands with each of them very warmly." Gen. Obasanjo op. cit. p. 125.

Col. Obasanjo immediately followed with serious business by telling Lt. Col. Efiong in no uncertain terms that his broadcast did not go far enough. At this stage, Lt. Col. Efiong invited Col. Obasanjo to a private room to discuss that. Their respective assistants joined them in the room; Lt. Col. Akinrinade joined Col. Obasanjo, while Capt. Ben Gbulie joined Lt. Col. Efiong. There, Lt. Col. Efiong said that they were a defeated people and went further to ask what they were to do. Col. Obasanjo assured him of his personal safety and the safety of the other officers. He continued that the only two things they had to do was to formally renounce secession and accept the twelve-state structure in the context of one Nigeria. Lt. Col. Efiong promptly agreed to this.

The discussion in the room between Col. Obasanjo and Lt. Col. Efiong, with their Assistants, Lt. Col. Alani Akinrinade and Capt. Ben Gbulie respectively, turned out to be the 'negotiated settlement and final peace talk' on the Nigerian civil war. On his way from Amichi, Col. Obasanjo met Lt. Col. David Ogunewe, who was his senior and close friend, when they both served in the 5 Battalion, Kaduna before Nigeria's independence. Col. Obasanjo took him in his car to Port Harcourt, where the latter spent the night in an unexpected and rare comfort.

Before he left Amichi the previous day, Col. Obasanjo invited Lt. Col. Efiong to Owerri with his team of 'Biafran' leaders the following day. There, Col. Obasanjo discussed with them and they agreed to come with him to Lagos for the ceremonial ending of the civil war after he had formally and militarily accepted the surrender of the rebels on the field.

After this meeting on 14 January 1970, Col. Obasanjo proceeded to Obodo Ukwu for a broadcast on 'Radio Biafra':

"I, Colonel Olusegun Obasanjo, General Officer Commanding 3 Marine Commando Division, Nigerian Army, having accomplished the task given to me by the Head of State and Commander-in-Chief of the Armed Forces of Nigeria wish to make this appeal to all our brothers and sisters in the Eastern States who are in hiding to come out of hiding and settle in their respective normal places of abode.

I also, in accordance with the Broadcast of the Commander-in-Chief, Major General Yakubu Gowon appeal to soldiers who fought on the 'Biafran' side and are still in hiding to come out and surrender themselves and their weapons to the nearest Federal Troops location or Police Station. I do hereby guarantee the safety of all law-abiding citizens resident in the Eastern States,

I have ordered that tactical movements of all troops be stopped and that the Nigeria Police should take over the maintenance of law and order throughout the Eastern States.

Troops are garrisoned throughout the Eastern States and are confined to barracks. Any cases of molestation by soldiers should be reported at any Military or Police Stations for immediate action.

All officers and men of the 3rd Marine Commando send their regards and appreciation to the Commander-in-

Chief, Major General Yakubu Gowon for his support and encouragement in our arduous task.

We also thank all citizens of Nigeria for their loyal support and steadfastness and I would like to make particular mention of the cooperation and warm support we received from all the people of the Eastern States.

I hope that the magnanimity, which had been shown by the Commander-in-Chief and all our people since the beginning of the war would be strengthened by the ready and willing co-operation shown by the people of the Eastern States.

Thank you all and long live One United Nigeria." Gen. Olusegun Obasanjo, op. cit. p. 130-131.

His warmth and friendly gesture again was a very pleasant surprise to the staff of the Radio, who for the reason of Biafran propaganda had believed that they were only waiting to be slaughtered. After the broadcast, Col. Obasanjo turned the rebel Radio, to Radio Nigeria. Col. Obasanjo then returned to Owerri to prepare for the journey to Lagos with the 'Biafran' team. They left Port Harcourt later than schedule and expectedly arrived in Lagos too late for the formal surrender ceremony to take place that day. However it took place the following day and thus Col. Obasanjo went down in history as the one, who brought the thirty-month long Nigerian civil war to a victorious end for Nigeria.

One of the things that an ordinary human being finds most difficult to do is to show humility in victory. When a couple falls into an argument over an issue and the table eventually turns against one of the spouses, the other spouse seizes the opportunity to drive home the guilt of his/her partner. The innocent partner would, notwithstanding the apologies of the guilty spouse, recount the episode over and over again with vicious emphasis to make the guilty one feel more guilty and self-condemned. Successful people look down upon the less successful and the haves not only treat the have-nots with disdain, they also do all that they can to prevent those who do not have from having. Ours is a world where only the fittest survive.

The only exception is Jesus Christ, who commissioned believers to witness the love of Christ to those, who are yet to believe so that the latter too can experience the same joy and spread the good news to others. Christians are in this more faithful in words than in action in that they are less accommodating of those who are outside the Church fold. There is even now a new approach, which encourages Christians to pray what is called 'dangerous' prayers, that is, to rain deadly curses, upon known and perceived enemies.

This approach works upon the assumption that the 'enemy' is the one, who does not know Christ and who deserves to die, or perish, or be destroyed for falling out with a Christian. This is a human weakness that manifests in all forms of human interaction. In a war setting, it easily takes the form of malignant hatred for human life as the conqueror, with bestial recklessness, maims, slaughters or commits the conquered to chains. To be humble and accommodating of the weak or the conquered is therefore a virtue and in a war setting, it is much more.

It is pertinent at this stage to examine some theories of vengeful reprisal against conquered foes in a war situation. The first is the need to make the conquered pay for the destruction of lives and properties that characterise war. This theory is defective in that the conquered is not necessarily the aggressor. What determines victory in war is not causally connected to which side precipitated the war. Man has a natural inclination to strive by all means fair or foul, to retain perpetual control over the underdog. Besides, the punishment meted out for the wrongs of war, when weighed against the destructions of war, cannot be considered as equal or adequate substitutes for the destructions of war.

Moreover, both parties in a war use weapons of destruction and the damage that results from it is not selective. All the parties to a war should therefore be jointly responsible for the damage caused by the war. Before embarking on a war, the parties involved should give due consideration to the consequences; such as, disruption and dislocation of socio-economic activities, destruction of lives and properties, impoverishment, displacement and general setback, before resorting to war.

The second is the psychological theory of innate pride in the heart of the conqueror. In a war situation, this pride seeks satisfaction in a naked show of the power of life and death over the defeated people. It is meant to instil sustained fear into the heart of the conquered foe so that he never thinks again of taking up arms against the interest of the conqueror, let alone against the conqueror himself. This theory too collapses fast because the conclusion does not, in practice, follow from the premise. The destruction unleashed on a conquered person merely sows a seed of hatred that can be nursed for many years until a future, when the present conquered foe can stand up to avenge his humiliation. This theory, if pursued, merely succeeds in perpetrating hatred and an unending cycle of belligerent hostilities.

The third theory is economic. It views the liberty assumed by the conqueror to appropriate the assets and the resources of the conquered foe as sufficient motivation to go on a rampage against a weaker people. This is largely true as evidenced by the usually numerous cases of rape, looting, forced marriage and enslavement of conquered people by the victors in any war situation.

In the case of the Nigerian civil war however, Col. Obasanjo rose above all the three tendencies mentioned above. There was no doubt that his military campaign brought about the end of secession. He also received on the field the Instrument of Surrender from the rebels. However, from his attitude at Amichi to the rebel officers after the radio announcement of Lt. Col. Philip Efiong, it was clear that he did not see them as war precipitators that should be summarily dealt with. Instead, he saw them as brothers-in-arms, who needed reassurance and encouragement for reintegration into the Nigerian fold. Moreover, one of the first problems that Col. Obasanjo addressed on his assumption of the command of Third Marine Commando Division was looting and trading in the areas of operation of the Division. He issued an Instruction that spelt out stiff disciplinary measures against soldiers that indulged in looting. His stance and orders on looting remained extant, even after the war.

In addition, he displayed rare humility in victory by not approaching his former colleagues with any air or show of power. By his warm handshake and hilarious hugging of everyone in the room, where he met them, he reassured the rebel officers of a promising future in Nigeria. It was after he had achieved this primary goal that he went into the heart of the matter by telling Lt. Col. Philip Efiong that his broadcast did not go far enough. He however did not do this by issuing any threat and neither did he utter any humiliating words. Col. Patrick Anwunah, an officer of the Biafran army, had this to say about the scene:

"The point at issue here was that generally and throughout the ending of the civil war, Gen. Obasanjo and Lt. Col. Alani Akinrinade his most senior staff officer were very nice, polite and courteous, to us their Biafran military colleagues. The reunions, meetings, discussions, chats, and jokes were absolutely most friendly and cordial all round. Cold beer from Nigeria, as if it were in rear unit's officers' mess accompanied these reunions and exchanges. General Obasanjo did not humiliate any Biafran Army officers at the ending of the civil war. Even with his victory he was very happy and excited to see his friends and former colleagues." Patrick A. Anwunah, The Nigeria-Biafra War (1967-1970), Ibadan, Spectrum Books, 2007, p. 256

King Richard the Lion Heart of old England, once got lost in Sherwood Forest and Locksley, an outlaw, eventually saved his life. In his appreciation to Locksley and his band of outlaws, King Richard said:

"He who has unlimited power to do evil, but instead does good, deserves double praise."

The rebels' declaration of secession was an expression of their disenchantment with Nigeria and the rest of Nigerians. This was the cause of the war, which was bitterly fought for thirty months and ended in the defeat of the rebel Army. The defeat of the rebels did not remove their ill feelings as they were in fact throughout the war fed with the propaganda that painted Federal soldiers as bloodthirsty marauders, who had no other mission but the extermination of the Ibos. With their defeat, they were actually looking forward to nothing but mass slaughter by Federal soldiers. The Biafran populace was therefore engulfed in fright and hopelessness, when it dawned on them after Lt. Col. Efiong's broadcast that they had lost the war.

Col. Obasanjo, who led his Federal troops of the Third Marine Commando Division to this victory was therefore the man to fear immediately but wars are fought on two fronts: on the battlefield and in the heart of men. It is much easier to win at the battlefront than to win at the heart front. In the case in question, military defeat did not have any effect on the Biafran mind. To win the Biafran mind, Col. Obasanjo needed more than military victory over the rebels. As the first contact that the rebels would have with Nigeria, the country they had written off as holding no future for them, what he did would determine the course of events that would follow. How Col. Obasanjo handled this moment was therefore of paramount significance.

The Ibos needed convincing assurance that Nigeria, which Col. Obasanjo at that time embodied, had some future for them. On the other hand at this time in history, the power of Col. Obasanjo, the victorious war Commander, to humiliate, put into chains or even kill, the rebel officers, was truly unlimited. He however consciously refrained from any of the latter acts and instead, chose to cap his victory with humility, love and reassurance to the conquered people.

Thanks be to God for Gen. Yakubu Gowon, the Commander-in-Chief then, who also without question, keyed into Col. Obasanjo's gesture of true peace by declaring a no-victor-no-vanquished verdict. This facilitated and accelerated the peace efforts that followed. The Ibos returned to their friends, brothers and sisters in Nigeria to continue life without any let or hindrance. In addition, Gen. Gowon's declaration helped to put Biafra in an everlasting requiem. Both Gen. Yakubu Gowon and Col. Obasanjo deserved more than double praise for winning the civil war both on the battlefield and in the Biafran heart.

Chapter Six: Transferable Principles Of Accomplishment

The Nigerian civil war came and ended about forty years ago. It however exposed the sad superficiality of corporate Nigeria. One British magazine once described Nigerians as the happiest people on earth. Many Nigerians regarded this as an accolade but the truth is far from that. The description is more a euphemism to describe the pitiable state of Nigerians. What is mistaken for happiness is the propensity of Nigerians for superficiality and whitewashing that hide the gravity of our situation. If the people of a nation that lags behind in so many elementary indices of development, and not for the reason of inadequacy of resources, are truly the happiest people on earth, then, either happiness has assumed a strange meaning or deceit must be in the air. In the case in question, it is easy to discern the deceiver and those being deceived.

Our superficiality is typified by our attitude to the peace that followed our civil war. In all the countries of the world, war is a catalyst of national development, notwithstanding its immediate destructive accompaniment. War is the most effective gatherer and conductor of the survival instincts, gifts and talents found in a people. When the war is over, the talents and the ingenuity that sustained the war are usually not lost. They are channelled into research efforts that produce new techniques and technological inventions for rapid industrial development.

In the most recent case, Europe, America and Japan experienced phenomenal industrialisation after World War II. China too experienced a great rise in her agricultural and industrial productive capacity after the bloody, war-like Cultural Revolution. Nigeria, as happy as its citizens claim to be, now imports palm produce from Malaysia, a country assisted by Nigeria about thirty-five years ago, to start her own national palm produce project.

Bedevilled by our innate superficiality, we abandoned at the end of our civil war all the talents and ingenuity thrown up by the war and left them undeveloped and untapped. Following from this is the fact that our God is a God of purpose. Every experience whether good or bad, is expected to hold in it a beneficial divine purpose. It is however up to man to discover the purpose of God in his experiences and react to it appropriately.

Unfortunately in our case, the Nigerian civil war passed without anybody discerning the purpose of God in it. Apart from the effortless structural and political rearrangements that seemed to make secession difficult, nothing else was added to the Nigerian State in terms of development factors. Issues in the war that could positively influence our industrialisation, scientific and technological research, human development, leadership and followership were not explored at all. They were all abandoned.

The Nigerian civil war also revealed on both sides many wonderful men and women, whose special gifts and extraordinary competences could be exploited for the rapid transformation of this country to a true giant of Africa. It is sadly ironic that some of the illustrious men and women, in and outside the military, who were behind the survival feats of that time on both sides were quickly dumped and rendered irrelevant. Some have now died and those that are alive are wallowing in deep frustration.

Col. Obasanjo is one of the outstanding talents discovered by the Nigerian civil war. We have seen how he got there. We have also seen how he won not only the war against secession but the heart of the secessionists also. Col. Obasanjo was sent to the Third Marine Commando Division when the hope of Federal victory had considerably waned and the rebels were waxing stronger with the military assistance and diplomatic recognition that were pouring in from countries sympathetic to their cause. The prognosis by political and military analysts was very bad for the future unity of Nigeria. Col. Obasanjo however turned the situation around by turning the defeat staring us in the face into victory and everybody wondered how he did it.

Let us therefore look at the principles that he applied for this outstanding accomplishment. Although he applied the principles in a war situation, they are nonetheless applicable in all situations, where success is desired. There are many Nigerians that are fighting various forms of life's war. Some are fighting the war of accomplishment, some others are fighting the basic war of survival and others still, are fighting the war of personal or corporate progress. Whatever may be the form of the individual's war, the Obasanjo principles are universally applicable and will most probably produce the desired result if conscientiously applied.

The first principle is PROFESSIONAL COMPETENCE. Gen. Obasanjo was among the Nigerian Army officers, who had the opportunity of good training. All those, who have made comments on the performance of the officers that took part in the civil war eulogised the officers that joined the Army before the civil war. The reason for this is the quality of the training they received. What marked out Gen. Obasanjo was however that he was not only well trained he was also fully trained. He did not miss any training programme designed for any rank that he attained as he progressed in his career. It was from his training that he learnt the value of men in combat. It was from his training that he learnt the intricacies of warfare and it was from his training that he learnt how to lead men to fight. Col. Obasanjo's performance as the GOC Third Marine Commando Division in the Nigerian civil war clearly bore him out as a well-trained officer.

Many people shy away from training and dabble into businesses that they know nothing about. They rely on hiring those who know and the result is, more often than not, complete failure or performance that is below achievable mark. The Bible laments that people get destroyed because they lack knowledge. The source of knowledge is training and experience. Knowledge based entirely on experience is knowledge by trial and error. It makes the road to success unnecessarily long and tortuous.

Some people also run away from training because it costs a lot of money. It is however regrettable that such people fail to realise that the money spent on training is an investment that surely brings happy returns. Besides, lack of training may in the final analysis cause a life-long failure. Another objection to training is that it is appropriate only for a certain age, after which it ceases to be expedient. This is not true because training always produces knowledge and knowledge is never a waste, it instead refines the owner. In addition, there is now on-the-job training and tailor-made training programmes delivered within short periods of one day, two days, three days, and so on. We have seen the undeniable success of Gen. Obasanjo in the civil war. His training provided him a solid background that prepared him for the ultimate test and when the test came, he did not fail. Let those of us who are struggling for success in our endeavours follow the steps of Gen. Olusegun Obasanjo by availing ourselves of relevant training opportunities. It affords us competence to perform excellently in our endeavour and our career.

The second principle is MOTIVATION. The most critical issue in organisational management is how to motivate a group of people in a workplace for commitment to the attainment of a preset goal. In fact, organisational management has in the last thirty years experienced a paradigm shift to human management. This is because it has been realised that it is people who make things happen in organisations, not money and not equipment. Money and equipment have no intrinsic value. Their value derives exclusively from the use that human beings put them into. Management has therefore today become people-centred.

Many organisations suffer steady attrition and consequent collapse as a result of their inability to retain the good members of their staff. Some people think that it is all about money and equipment but the way Col. Obasanjo managed the human resources of his Division calls for our attention. He did not try to buy the loyalty of his troops with unearned money or give to anybody what the person did not ordinarily deserve. Instead, he treated everybody with due respect and gave to him according to his due as provided by extant rules and regulations. He realised that any leadership that buys loyalty with money or with undeserved and selective privileges is a corrupt leadership that would speedily become an undertaker to his organisation.

Unity among a group of people for corporate success in any endeavour; whether military, entrepreneurial or governmental, is not produced by the bestowal of undeserved and selective privileges. Unfortunately however, that is what defines a 'nice' man in our society. The truth about money is that it is a consumable item that with time will either be exhausted or lose its purchasing value. People motivated by money will therefore always demand more money. The motivation that is based on money is unsustainable and cannot be relied upon for enduring loyalty.

We cannot gloss over the fact that at the time of assumption of the command of Third Marine Commando Division by Col. Obasanjo, the Division had virtually ceased to be a fighting force. It was bedevilled by low morale, lack of esprit de corps to the extent that officers rejoiced at the failure of fellow-officers. There were in addition widespread acts of indiscipline and general unwillingness to continue to fight. The relationship of the Commander and his troops was guided more by fear than by respect and trust. Some very senior officers of the Division had even walked away.

Col. Obasanjo reorganised the Division and assigned command on the basis of training and experience, such that the right officers were given the right tasks. He equipped the troops with available weapons and those, who needed to be trained in the handling of their weapons, were accordingly trained. With the availability of equipment and relevant training, the troops no longer felt that they were being sent to their graves. Instead, their confidence was restored. They began to see their assignment not only as a call to duty but also as a call to honour.

Col. Obasanjo also ensured prompt payment of salaries to the troops. Giving the troops their legitimate dues earned the GOC the respect of his troops. Furthermore, by drawing a planned rest for every soldier, he showed empathy, to which the troops also responded with implicit trust in their Commander. He removed the organisational and structural defects that caused or worsened indiscipline in the Division, after which he meted appropriate punishment for any infringement or act of indiscipline. He removed favouritism by treating everybody equally. This enabled him to weld the officers and men of the Division together in a spirit of mutual love and trust and pursuit of the common goal of bringing the war to an end.

Col. Obasanjo also motivated his troops by an exemplary leadership. Nothing registered this in the hearts of the troops of Third Marine Commando Division more than the steps he took during his first two days in office. He had made up his mind to let his performance on the field prove his worth, instead of courting media whitewashing. He also did not come to boast of, or profess, any perfection to his troops. Instead, he acknowledged and commended the achievements of his predecessor, the fallen soldiers and the surviving troops of the Division. This acknowledgement was to the officers and men of the Division, a welcome appreciation of their efforts in the campaign and an indication that he was going to build on their achievements. This message was well taken by the troops, who at once regained the self-confidence they had by this time lost completely.

The troops were impressed by the refusal of their new Commander to witch-hunt anybody. His first address to his troops assured them that Col. Obasanjo was prepared to work with all of them. By the speech in question, he also began to blunt entrenched inter-personal animosity and hostility within the Command. He created in the troops the general frame of mind that was conducive to the growth of esprit de corps and camaraderie.

Col. Obasanjo further motivated his troops by his humility. He did not have a lifestyle that was different from that of his troops. He rejected all subtle and open invitation to an indulgent lifestyle. He also consciously brought in his officers for their active participation in the decision-making process. Furthermore, he encouraged them to show initiative and resourcefulness. All these together did not only restore esprit de corps among the troops; they also brought back the good officers, who had abandoned the Division and revived the fighting spirit of the troops.

Ken Saro-Wiwa had this to say about the revival brought into Third Division by Col. Obasanjo:

"I followed Col. Obasanjo's preparations with keen interest. When I did not have access to him, I fished information from George Innih who had also become a close friend. What I found impressive was the rebirth of confidence in the Division, the return of discipline, of a wish to prosecute the war." Ken Saro-Wiwa, Op. cit., p. 218.

Let those who are struggling to create good followership for corporate success, borrow a leaf from Gen. Obasanjo, who as the GOC, brought back the Third Marine Commando

Division to life, when it had virtually been written off as a mere pack of dry bones.

The third principle is PERSONAL ATTRIBUTE. This is the activator of gifts, talents and equipment. Negative personal attributes can make nonsense of the best talent and relegate it to dormancy, just as it can turn the best equipment into a mere white elephant. Positive personal attributes can on the other hand, expand narrow possibilities, increase capacity and multiply the fruit of one's labour.

I remember one of my school contemporaries, whom I still consider one of the most gifted individuals on earth. He ranked among the best in his class academically. He was for many years the Football captain and he won the victor ludorum cup in athletics for many consecutive years. He was an accomplished self-taught organist, guitarist and barber. He was also a fine and graphic artist. Sadly, however, he was so lazy that he barely managed a weak pass in his School Certificate Examinations. He also did not care to develop any of his gifts beyond the amateurish schoolboy's level. He retired from the public service on a middle level grade! I have gone to the details of my example because many people have the world under their feet but they lack the right personal attributes to appropriate it. Chief (Gen.) Olusegun Obasanjo is however different.

The first personal attribute of Gen. Obasanjo is his uncanny ability to speedily get to the heart of any matter that confronts him in any situation. There is no endeavour on earth that is monolithic and there are therefore always many approaches to solving a problem. When, however, one is confronted with a welter of problems, the major task is to get the lead solution that holds the solutions to the other subordinate problems and deal with the former first. This is why, in dealing with a health issue, doctors first separate the cause from the symptoms before deciding on the line of treatment. Unfortunately, and more often than not, problems do not come in black and white for easy discernment. Many people therefore adopt a trial-and-error approach, while some others go around in circles. The gifted however go straight to tackle the heart of the matter. This saves time and resources and it is more promising of success in the endeavour in question.

We saw this in young Olusegun Obasanjo, when he received the news of his mother's death and when he passed his professional engineering examination in London. In each case, he did not allow himself to be distracted. When Congolese soldiers arrested him, he saw his captors beyond their incapacity at that time and resisted the temptation of a surprise attack against them. He therefore allowed them to please themselves but ultimately, he regained his freedom. In addition, within forty-eight hours of assuming command of Third Marine Commando Division, he ordered an attack on Ohoba, a town fifteen miles from Owerri, the base of the rebels since they recaptured it from Federal troops. He ordered this diversionary attack to give him enough respite to study the situation he met at the Command. In all these instances, Col. Obasanjo identified the heart of the matter in each case and promptly dealt with it. The result was ultimate all-round success.

On the other hand, there are people struggling with failure because they do not know what to do first or later. Many people spend huge sums of money building 'befitting' offices with the resources needed for the growth and development of their enterprises. They learn too late at the end of the day that they have only put the cart before the horse. The result is inescapable failure in the enterprise. Some others invest on businesses that promise huge returns but have long gestation periods, which their capital base cannot support. The result is also speedy failure. Knowing the heart of the matter equips one with the barometer to measure progress. It helps to create a responsive organisational structure for goal achievement. It also helps to create effective supervision within the operational chain. It further helps to design appropriate staff training programme. Above all, it guides allocation of resources for maximum effectiveness in the pursuit of organisational goals.

The achievement of Gen. Obasanjo in the Nigerian civil war can be fully appreciated only if placed alongside the performance of 1 and 2 Divisions. The Second Division was confined to the Mid-West after the Onitsha debacle and did not do any more serious fighting. The First Division was early in the war at the threshold of decisive victory over the rebels but it did not see what Col. Obasanjo saw. Col. Obasanjo saw that the rebels often made excellent use of any respite they had, to fight back with greater determination. The result was that the rebels either regained lost ground or succeeded in creating a stalemate that prolonged the war.

In contrast, Col. Obasanjo penetratingly studied the battle trend and discovered the rebels' operational pattern and its characteristic weakness. He quickly changed the conventional approach of 'beat the enemy back, occupy and dig in' because it gave the enemy ample time to recoup and launch a counter attack. While the advance of 1 Division was steady, it was nonetheless so slow that it also allowed the war to drag with obvious cost implications. On the other hand, Col. Obasanjo quickly saw, and went straight to, the heart of the matter, which was to deprive the rebels of any respite. The consequence was the speedy and decisive conclusion of the war by his troops.

The other personal attribute of Gen. Obasanjo relevant to this work is his single-mindedness. We saw this in him when he passed his Professional Engineering Examinations, while undergoing military training. He could have abandoned the course and seek an appropriate job that would provide money immediately for the family he left behind in Nigeria. He did not do that but he carried on with his military assignment. He waited for a likely opportunity in his military career for the exercise of his engineering knowledge. Col. Obasanjo showed at this time that he did not believe in short cuts. He instead relied on unwavering commitment and hard work to get him to his goal. He issued stern warning against the diversionary, though attractive, practices found in war situations and gave everything in him to the war. His single-mindedness was amply rewarded with the ultimate collapse of the rebellion and the surrender of the Biafran forces to him.

Perhaps the overarching personal attribute of Gen. Obasanjo, which holds the key that opens the door of accomplishments for him, is his humility. My first experience of Gen. Obasanjo's humility was when the latter was the Federal Commissioner (Minister) for Works and Housing in the dispensation of Gen. Yakubu Gowon. I met

Gen. Obasanjo, when I was carrying a deep prejudice and resentment against highly placed public officers. Based on my previous experience with some of them, I had written off all others, present and future, as arrogant, self-indulgent and insensitive. I was at the time an Assistant Secretary in the Federal Ministry of Works and Housing. When on the occasion in question, which unfortunately we cannot here go into in details, he observed my reluctance to come near him and we were to work together for the following two months, he left his seat on the high table, carried his food tray in his own hands and joined me at the obscure corner of the restaurant, where I sat. He did not stop there; he took my teacup and drank what was left therein. He then kept gazing at me warmly and with a show of camaraderie. I was stunned beyond what I can now describe because I had never seen such humility in any Nigerian occupying such a high public position. The outcome is a relationship between us that has hitherto subsisted.

Many people equate humility with diffidence. Humility is not diffidence; it is instead the ability to 'stoop to conquer'. Many people painfully prolong their problems because the place, where the solution to their problem is located does not befit them to visit. They are generally hampered by their age or office to show the deference required to get the solution to their problem. The agent of solution to a particular problem may also be reckoned too low on the social ladder to be found in the company of the 'big man', whereas the 'big man' is actually dying inside. He is dying inside, not because God has not heard his prayers but because his pride would not allow him to take possession of what He has provided.

It was humility that made Col. Obasanjo, on assuming command of Third Marine Commando Division, to acknowledge the achievements of his predecessor, all the officers and men of the Division and those, who had lost their lives in the war. He did not come with any presumption and neither did he boastfully suggest to them that he was coming with something new or superior. It was humility that enabled Col. Obasanjo to encourage the input of all his officers into his final operational plans. Not all of them were first class officers and neither were all their contributions flawless but allowing them to have their say in turn afforded him the opportunity to hear other perspectives to the problem on the ground and the various options available. These contributions enriched his decision making process and also gave the officers the sense of belonging that brushed up their self-worth and confidence. Finally, Col. Obasanjo was by his humility able to secure the commitment of his troops to the success of the final plan.

They now rightly saw it as the product of their collective contributions.

Finally, as indicated earlier, it was Gen. Obasanjo's humility that prepared the ground for the ultimate reconciliation that followed the cessation of belligerent hostilities. In his work on the Civil War "Nigeria and Biafra: My Story", Lt. Col. Efiong seems to take for granted the peaceful and friendly reunion of Col. Obasanjo with the Biafran military leaders at Amichi after the former's surrender broadcast. Reading his book in question, one finds Lt. Col. Efiong trying hard in a rather overbearing style, to present himself as a flawless participant in the entire event of the civil war. He totally suppressed the unexpectedly friendly attitude of Col. Obasanjo, when he met the former and his colleagues at Amichi.

This is understandable in view of Col. Efiong's situation. Labouring under a heavy load of self-guilt over his poor sense of judgement in joining the rebel cause, he wanted to rewrite history and so cover up his wilful error. However, notwithstanding his defensive posture in his work under reference, what poorer judgement could there be than pursuing a rebel cause as Lt. Col. Efiong did? In contrast to Lt. Col. Efiong's account is that of Col. Patrick Anwunah, quoted earlier. The story of the Amichi incident and the rebel surrender, even as told by Lt. Col. Efiong himself, only made Gen. Obasanjo loom larger in humility, God's weapon for the destruction of pride and its attendant evil.

Gen. Oluleye too, in his book Military Leadership in Nigeria: 1966–1979 derided the victorious performance of Obasanjo, as having been achieved at a high material cost and further that the latter presented it as if it was his own effort alone. These certainly must have emanated from an extraneous prejudice in the late General's mind and not from the facts of how the Division was administered by Obasanjo and the latter's presentation of his success.

In the first place, the prudence of Obasanjo as GOC, Third Marine Commando Division attracted the written commendation of Chief Obafemi Awolowo, the then Federal Commissioner for Finance. In the second place, Obasanjo's style of administration and his conduct of the affairs of Third Marine Commando Division, when he was in charge, as told by Obasanjo in his book, amply quoted in this work and as conveyed in my interviews with some officers and men of the Division at the time in question that are still alive, was characterised by inclusiveness, discipline and fairness. Obasanjo also in any discussion about the war, characteristically pays tribute to the officers and men of his command and to the Army Headquarters, for their invaluable roles in bringing about the success of the Division.

One cannot but just wonder then what actually informed Gen. Oluleye's disparaging remark about Obasanjo's victory. It is certainly not the facts of the events in the Third Marine Commando Division, when Obasanjo was the Commander of the Division. It is sadly, an unfair portrayal of the person and character of Obasanjo and of how he viewed his victory.

An Excellent Military

Head of State

Chapter Seven: Drafted Into Politico-Military Service

At the end of the war, Gen. Obasanjo returned to his parent unit, the Army Engineers, as the Inspector of Army Engineers, a role that he more or less combined with that of GOC 3Marine Commando Division. He led the Engineering Corps to construct the Oju Elegba–Moshalashi road in Surulere, Lagos. The standard was expectedly not perfect, largely because funds were not provided for the construction of the drainage that was needed to shield the road from erosion. It was however a trail blazing effort in social responsibility and in providing a constructive role for the army in peacetime. If this had been sustained, the Nigerian Army would have transformed to a peacetime development-oriented army. It would also have made unnecessary the demobilisation that followed the war and its attendant socio-economic implications that turned the exercise to a snare for the Yakubu Gowon administration. Brig. Obasanjo left the command of the Engineering Corps to attend a course at the Royal College of Defence Studies in London in 1974. At the Royal College of Defence Studies, his project, titled 'British Aid to Nigeria' was judged as one of the best projects produced on that course.

At the end of the course, Brig. Obasanjo returned to Nigeria to be appointed into Gen. Yakubu Gowon's cabinet as Commissioner (Minister) of Works and Housing. While he was yet the Commissioner of Works and Housing, there was another coup d'etat in the country. The coup swept away Gen. Gowon and his Government and brought a new dispensation under Brig. Murtala Muhammed, who became Head of the Federal Military Government and Commander-in-Chief of the Nigerian Armed Forces. Brig. Olusegun Obasanjo also became the Deputy as Chief of Staff, Supreme Headquarters and Brig. Yakubu Danjuma became Chief of Army Staff. There were other appointments including appointments into the Supreme Military Council, the Federal Executive Council, and the National Council of States.

The euphoria that accompanied the victorious end of the war had died and both the military and the populace were getting increasingly less comfortable with the unresolved issues thrown up by the war. There were three major issues: the overblown size of the Army, corruption and the return of the military to barracks. There were other secondary or ancillary issues but these three issues were so paramount that the failure of the Gowon administration to resolve them finally spelt its doom.

The first issue was that at the beginning of the civil war the total strength of the Nigerian Army stood at about 10,000 officers and men but by the end of the war, it had risen to well over 250,000. The obvious effect of this phenomenal numerical increase was that more than four-fifths of Defence budgetary allocation was eaten up by overheads. This was at the expense of training, acquisition of modern armament and equipment and the replacement of obsolete ones. It was unarguably not good for any nation.

The second was the issue of corruption that had pervaded the Government at both the Federal and State levels. The third was the non-withdrawal of the military from politics. There were two sub-issues involved in this. There was the feeling that if civilians were in charge; that is, in the shoes of Gowon at the centre and Ojukwu in the East, at the beginning of the crises and given the same circumstances, there would have been no war at all. This was because at a certain stage, the two leaders would have agreed to a peaceful dialogue and compromise. The second sub-issue was the nature of the withdrawal.

Demobilisation was not as easy as one might think, especially in the Nigerian situation at that time. At the end of the war, the problem of the Nigerian Army was not only the numerical strength of the Army, there were also problems related to the question of who were to be demobilised, by what method and how they were to be reintegrated into civilian life. These problems surfaced because the 1966 crises brought in their wake a resurgence of ethnic loyalties that made seemingly routine and innocuous issues practically intractable.

There were about 70,000 Yoruba recruited into the Army during the war. Many of them had some previous education and therefore might not be expected to find it difficult to get other jobs, if demobilised. This however could not be said of the ex-servicemen, who responded from all over the North to the call to service, when the war broke out. They fought gallantly and contributed in no small measure to the successes of 1 Division, where they were well represented. While they were retained in the army, training, promotion and recruitment could not be done because being veterans, they were generally too old for all that.

Notwithstanding, they deserved a good treatment as compensation for their patriotic participation in the war. They therefore could not be shoddily and carelessly discharged into the unemployment market. It was for this reason suggested in some quarters that they should be retained on the Army payroll or be handsomely compensated financially before sending them into retirement. The reason was that it would be difficult for them to find employment elsewhere, if demobilised because many of them had little education and they were too old for retraining in a new vocation.

There was also a third group made up of soldiers from the Middle Belt area of the country that at this time constituted the majority of the army. Drawn from an area with a long tradition of providing manpower for the military profession, they were unskilled and lacked adequate educational qualifications that could easily earn them employment outside the military. They too creditably acquitted themselves during the war and it would certainly require a programme of extensive retraining to give them any chance of finding civilian employment. The conclusion here was also that this category of soldiers should be retained.

All of these threw the Gowon government into some confusion because demobilisation also had inadvertently become a political issue. The Government therefore needed to carry out this important exercise without exposing itself to accusations of ethnic bias and provoking professional jealousy and discrimination. In addition, the government was afraid of accusation of ingratitude to those who fought to unite the country. These explain why Gen. Gowon suddenly decided against demobilisation by compulsory retirement and instead proffered voluntary retirement, which in effect meant that nobody retired.

This was also the time, when civil servants seemed to be having things their way. They had security of tenure and predictable career progression. They were also not exposed to any serious occupational hazards and they seemed at this time more advantageously positioned to benefit from the then ongoing Indigenisation Programme of the Federal Government. These developments made the average military officer, who was operating under conditions that were far from ideal, feel that he did not compare favourably with his counterpart in the civil service and in business. The poor accommodation and living standards of soldiers after the war, in addition to the failure of the military government to clarify its stand on the issue of demobilisation and other aspects of army reorganisation, also weakened the morale of the soldiers and provoked sharp, though subdued, criticisms from the military commanders.

Side by side with the issue of demobilisation were also the issues of return to civil rule and the withdrawal of the military to the barracks. The public debate that accompanied these issues proffered a number of options. The first was to have elections that would produce a government made up entirely of civilians. The second, championed by Dr. Nnamdi Azikiwe, was a diarchy; that is, a government made up of civilians and soldiers. The third was a presidential system that would retain Gen. Gowon as the President but with a civilian cabinet. The fourth was a continuation sine die of the existing military dispensation. Since there were no organised political parties, these options remained ill defined, abstract and generally fluid. Meanwhile, politicians were becoming restive and more vociferous in their demand that the country should return to civil rule as quickly as possible.

The Military Governors did not help matters as they, by their lifestyle and conduct of government business, brought a lot of discredit to the military government. Their poor performance attracted open criticism and consequent pressure on Gen. Gowon to change them. However, for reasons that are not quite explicable yet, but most probably out of fear that such a change would inevitably provoke a demand for changes in other areas, Gen Gowon refused to change the Governors. The demand for the redeployment of the State Governors was given extra strength in 1974 when allegations of corruption, backed by affidavits were brought against the Benue-Plateau State Governor, Police Commissioner Joseph Gomwalk and Mr. J. S. Tarka, who was a Commissioner (Minister) in Gen. Gowon's cabinet.

Somehow, while in respect of army reorganisation Gowon failed to take a definite and decisive stand, he also took a rather unwelcome stand in respect of the allegations against his Governor and Commissioner. He unilaterally absolved Gomwalk of any wrongdoing and allowed Tarka to quietly resign his position in the cabinet, while he kept his corrupt gains. This further fuelled the agitation for the withdrawal of soldiers to the barracks and a return to civil rule.

Gen. Gowon seemed to have by this time boxed himself into a corner with his indecision about the time of return to civil rule and on demobilisation. He probably intended to pursue the option of transmuting into an executive President in a civilian government but it met a stiff opposition within the army. It was in response to the welter of agitations for a return to civil rule that Gowon sought to buy time with his historic announcement of 1 October 1974. He said in this speech that the previously announced date of 1976 for a return to civilian rule was no longer realistic. Commentators have judged this move to be a very grave error. It was a bad reflection on any leader, and a military leader in particular, to renege on a voluntarily made promise.

It however appeared as if Gen. Gowon himself thought that he could substantially turn the situation around with some manoeuvres that he made thereafter. He reconstituted the Federal Executive Council to reduce the membership of civilians and correspondingly increase the military/police membership. Unfortunately, this accentuated the condemnation of the action by politicians. It in fact inspired a more vigorous call for an immediate return to civil rule. Besides, it gave bureaucrats more voice and prominence in the government to the displeasure of senior military officers.

In addition, Gen Gowon also chose to implement without any rational basis the aspect of the Udoji Public Service Review Panel Report that gave generous pay increases to civil servants and soldiers. This again, contrary to Gowon's expectation backfired, partly because the inflationary effect of such a jumbo pay rise was very unhealthy for the economy. Secondly, it opened the Pandora box of agitation from professional civil servants, who in spite of Udoji were still excluded from top administrative posts. Those in public corporations, the academia and the private sector were not left out of this drama as they too asked for a salary review that was comparable to the Udoji pay rise granted to their counterparts in the civil service. The outcome of what Gen. Gowon expected to warm him into the hearts of the people was that it brought him into disrepute, as he ultimately had to capitulate to a general wage increase based on Udoji. He also agreed to a greater measure of parity by professionals with the administrators.

The effect of the Udoji award spiralled to consume a considerable proportion of defence budget, bringing to the fore once again the urgency of a definite decision on demobilisation. Until the government gave demobilisation the attention it deserved, the appalling living condition of soldiers must be attended to, one way or the other. It was the only way to nip the discontent that was spreading through the army in the bud. The Government therefore embarked on a massive construction of barracks, which necessitated massive importation of cement that arrived in quantities that overstretched the facilities of the Nigerian Ports Authority. The result was an unprecedented port congestion that unavoidably heightened the already galloping inflation created by the Udoji awards.

Furthermore, General Gowon left intact the Supreme Military Council that had all the Military Governors as members. This did not go down well with the Divisional Commanders, who were senior in rank to most of the Military Governors. The failure to reassign the Military Governors clearly undermined the credibility of Gen. Gowon, who had promised in his speech of October 1974 that they would be reassigned. The Military Governors too, on their part, were not unaware of the clamour for their removal. They therefore slipped into extravagance and undisguised corruption that further fuelled the demand for their reassignment.

On the eve of 29 July 1975, Gen. Gowon stood as one who had failed woefully in his objectives. He had succeeded in dragging the army into disrepute by his failure to honour the date he voluntarily chose for a return to civilian rule. The military therefore became an object of so much derision that some soldiers kept their uniforms in the office because they were ashamed to be identified as soldiers. Apart from political failure, Gen. Gowon had also brought upon the country a wave of inflationary pressure, failure of facilities and severe shortages. All his efforts and manoeuvres to strengthen his position therefore merely worked to further weaken it and unite his opponents against him.

This brief account of the environment that gave birth to the coup d'etat of 29 July 1975, when Brig. Olusegun Obasanjo took his first steps towards a milito-political accomplishment is to provide a window, from where to take a glimpse of the mind of the Colonels, who overthrew the government of Gen. Yakubu Gowon. This is important because it is the raison d'etre for the forced change and therefore the barometer for measuring the success of the regime that supplanted that of Gen. Gowon. It could be rightly said that Gen. Gowon, whether he knew it or not, built on sand and invited the whirlwind.

The Colonels who carried out the coup of 29 July 1975 did not have to dig at all before finding an array of incontrovertible lapses, which their patriotic instinct invited them to come and redress. The most worrisome among these lapses was the credibility of the Army, which Gen. Gowon had impaired by his refusal to honour his own word to return the country to civil rule in 1976. It would appear that most of the other issues that the new regime came in to address followed from this one.

The 29 July 1975 coup installed Brig. Murtala Muhammed as the new Head of the Federal Military Government and Commander-in-Chief of the Armed Forces of Nigeria with Brig. Olusegun Obasanjo as Chief of Staff Supreme Headquarters and his Deputy. However, those who carried out the coup did not want to participate in the government ushered in by their coup because they wanted to show that they had no selfish motives. Gen. Obasanjo on the other hand, insisted that they must participate fully to avoid replicating in Nigeria the Neguib/Nasser Egyptian experience.

It did not take time to form a full-fledged government. The erstwhile GOC Third Division, Brig. Yakubu Danjuma became the Chief of Army Staff. The Supreme Military

Council was then reconstituted to exclude the State Governors but a new body, the National Council of States, made up of the Head of State, the Chief of Staff SHQ, the Service Chiefs, the Divisional Commanders and the State Military Governors, was also constituted. As for the composition of the Federal Executive Council, the new Government preferred a preponderance of military officers in the Council, while preference was given to technocrats and professionals in the appointment of civilian members into the Council.

With the conclusion of the inauguration of these three organs of Government, the administration swung into action. It turned its attention to the sensitive and pressing issues on which the previous administration failed to act. The controversial census figures were cancelled, the World Festival of Arts and Culture was postponed because of poor preparation and the scale was also pruned down. This was because the facilities being constructed for the event would certainly not be ready by the previously scheduled date for the Festival. More importantly, the cost of the event far outstripped the available budgetary provision. Panels were inaugurated to look at various national issues including the creation of more States and the continued role of Lagos as the Federal capital. The future of Interim Common Services Agency (ICSA) and the Eastern States Interim

Assets and Liability Agency (ESIALA) was also to be looked into.

The issue of corruption was speedily handled with a mass retirement of public officers on grounds of corruption, divided interest and declining productivity. Panels were set up to investigate the assets of allegedly corrupt public officers and those found guilty had their assets confiscated. The welfare of the troops was given top priority. All military detainees were released except two, who were notorious for sadistic acts during the war. The administration adopted a low profile, to discourage the ostentatious lifestyle of the ruling class. It also took steps, by personal example, to promote the use of goods made in Nigeria.

Within three months of its inception, the administration had effectively touched all facets of national life. By 1 October 1975, the new Government announced its five-stage programme of transition to civilian rule. The programme included the creation of new States, the inauguration of a Constitution Drafting Committee, the conduct of Local Government Elections, the inauguration of the Constituent Assembly, the lifting of the ban on political activities, the actual elections and the formal handing over to a democratically elected Government on 1 October 1979.

With these actions, the new administration of Murtala Muhammed succeeded in raising the almost dead morale of the people and regaining public confidence. Things were going so well that the violent disruption unleashed by a group of soldiers six months into the inception of the Murtala administration in what has since then come to be known as the Dimka coup, was greeted with widespread public condemnation and outrage. Later investigations revealed that one of the immediate causes of the Dimka coup of 13 February 1976 was the new configuration that emerged from the coup of the previous July.

The Dimka coup was on its own a significant event with implications far beyond the narrow confines of political interruption. Those details are however not part of this work. We will therefore not delve into them beyond the fact that though unsuccessful, the coup nonetheless produced the demise of Gen. Murtala Mohammed. After the death of Murtala Mohammed, the Supreme Military Council found a worthy successor in his Deputy, Gen. Olusegun Obasanjo.

Chapter Eight: Welcome History

The Nigerian public received the death of Gen. Murtala Muhammed with a genuine sense of loss and deep sorrow. The citizenry had, within the short period of his reign as the Head of the Federal Military Government, become used to seeing state duties discharged with dispatch and sincerity of purpose. Public trust and confidence in the leadership of the country had been restored and everybody was feeling an emerging new Nigeria characterised by public discipline and a promise of corporate progress.

The general public seemed by this time to have forgotten or forgiven Murtala's disastrous mistake that led to the Onitsha debacle and the consequent massacre of thousands of Nigerian troops by the rebel soldiers. Murtala had come to be identified with a new and ebullient spirit of national rebirth and patriotism. The death of Murtala was therefore a serious psychological setback for the nation. Unfortunately, the nation had also not completely put behind her the unfortunate consequences of the events of 1966 that accentuated ethnic loyalties within the body politic and anti-climaxed in a gruesome thirty-month-long civil war.

Moreover, the public was generally not familiar with the significance of hierarchy in the army. Hierarchy did not seem to play any significant role in the political configuration that emerged from the previous coup of July 1966. The January 1966 coup was different. Maj.-Gen. Aguiyi-Ironsi was the most senior Army Officer, and though he did not plan the coup, he emerged as the leader after the coup because of his seniority. The coup planners were even said to mark him down for elimination but he quickly seized the initiative and outwitted them to become the Head of State. In other words, if things had gone the way of the coup plotters, a Major or a Lieutenant Colonel would most likely have been Head of State. That would have been over and above a significant number of more senior officers. In the July 1966 counter-coup, the planners installed Lt. Col. Yakubu Gowon as Head of State over and above a significant number of more senior officers. Therefore, when Gen. Murtala Muhammed died, there was nothing to give the public any realistic expectation of Gen. Obasanjo becoming his successor.

Apart from Gen. Obasanjo's personal grief and disenchantment with a system that seemed helpless and unable to prevent the fate that befell a sincere and committed patriot like Murtala Muhammed, he was himself not at all expecting to succeed Murtala as Head of State.

However, the Supreme Military Council lost no time in deciding by consensus, and also ensuring, that Gen. Olusegun Obasanjo succeeded Gen. Murtala Mohammed as Head of State. Thus history again returned to the present.

When Gen. Obasanjo, then Col. Obasanjo, was appointed the GOC Third Marine Commando Division six years before he succeeded Murtala Mohammed as the Head of State, a widespread apprehension greeted his appointment. In a dispassionate comparison of Gen. Obasanjo with his predecessor in the command of Third Marine Commando, Ken Saro-Wiwa wrote:

"The man who took over the command of the Division (Third Marine Commando) was the very antithesis of Col. Adekunle. Where the latter was trim and sprightly, Col. Obasanjo was burly and seemingly slow; where Col. Adekunle gave you the impression that time was rushing past at the speed of light, Obasanjo was deliberate. Not for him the shouting, the tremors, the trepidation, the fear which the presence of the G.O.C. 3 Marine Commando Division was meant to engender. When you stood before Adekunle, you were made to feel that the distance between you and the grave was thread-thin and that you dared not have a slip of the tongue in your discussions with him. But standing before Obasanjo, you met a genial man who might break into a scowl and tell you off in a few words, or engage you in a long, pleasant debate." Ken Saro-Wiwa, op. cit. p.215.

Here again, Gen. Obasanjo formed a sharp contrast to his predecessor who, in the name of swift action, characteristically committed himself to actions that presented him as an impetuous, impulsive and rather erratic person. The Nigerian public with its love for excitement therefore greeted Gen. Obasanjo's succession to Gen. Murtala Muhammed as Head of State with widespread pessimism just as they did when he was appointed as GOC Third Marine Commando Division about six years earlier. It appeared as if the history of Nigeria assumed a dramatic irony with Gen. Obasanjo playing the lead role.

As GOC Third Marine Commando Division, he was faced with the unenviable task of reviving and motivating the Division that had at the time of his appointment virtually ceased to be a fighting force. This time around as the successor to Gen. Murtala Muhammed, he was faced with the daunting task of sustaining public morale, which was at its highest then. The public expected him to show no difference at all from the seemingly unmatchable standard and tempo of his predecessor, particularly in the execution of government policies and programmes. The taste of the pudding is however in the eating although Gen. Obasanjo was actually the engine house that powered the outward fiery and awe-inspiring visibility of Gen. Murtala Muhammed.

The Dimka coup was a painful distraction that brought with it some problems for which the administration was not prepared. The first of such problems was the threat of sectarian violence, particularly in the predominantly Muslim parts of the North. The failed coup was interpreted in these parts of the country as an attack against Muslims because the plotters were largely from the predominantly Christian parts of the North. Gen. Obasanjo quickly fell back on traditional rulers, religious leaders and community leaders all over the country and especially in the areas most threatened. They were charged with the task of giving assurance to their people that the coup was not an attack against Muslims. They were also expected to assure all the residents in their respective domains of their safety. In addition to the socio-religious leaders, members of the Federal Executive Council and the Supreme Military Council, as well as State Governors were also involved in this reassurance and damage control effort. Alongside this exercise was also the appointment of a Northern Muslim, Lt. Col. Shehu Yar'Adua, as the second-in-command to the Head of State, though he was junior in rank.

While this was going on, the Government began the process of bringing the coup plotters to justice by setting up a

Military Board that had the GOC 1 Division as the Chairman. After the conclusion of the preliminary investigations, a court martial that had another distinguished officer, Maj.-Gen. Emmanuel Abisoye, as Chairman, was set up to try those found prima facie guilty of participating in the coup. As soon as the court martial pronounced judgement over the accused persons, the Supreme Military Council (SMC) was convened to consider the verdict and as soon as the SMC gave its approval, the executions were carried out according to the law. The handling of the Dimka abortive coup was the first litmus test of the Obasanjo administration. The expeditious manner in which Gen. Obasanjo handled the matter contrasted sharply with the way Gen. Ironsi handled the equally failed coup of January 1966. It was a proof of Obasanjo's transparency and evidence that quickly dispelled any rumour or insinuation of a cover-up from high places.

Gen. Obasanjo did not stop at this. He sought enduring honour for the name and memory of the departed Head of State by ordering that the largest airport in the country, the Ikeja Airport, be renamed after him and his photograph displayed in all public buildings side-by-side with Gen. Obasanjo's own. This continued for one year, after which Gen. Obasanjo caused the image of the late Head of State to be imprinted on Nigeria's highest currency denomination at that time. These honours were in recognition of the contribution of Gen. Murtala Muhammed to national progress and good governance. They were also to prove beyond any doubt the innocence of Gen. Obasanjo in the sad event that led to his succeeding Gen. Murtala Muhammed.

This might sound simplistic and unduly patronising but it was the foundational step that could mar or make the Obasanjo military dispensation. The events that started in January 1966 and its consequences remained a painful reminder of how the Nigerian Army, by the sheer insensitivity of a group of very few officers, lost its sense of unity, camaraderie and brotherhood. Unfortunately the nation was dragged into it and the cost to individual family units and the nation in terms of human and material losses, as well as corporate retrogression, can never be fully compensated. By dealing expeditiously and judiciously with the failed Dimka coup, Gen. Obasanjo helped the nation to regain her bearing and quickly continue the march towards socio-political and economic development.

Furthermore, the coup also exposed how tenuous the nation's security was. The Special Branch of the Nigeria Police that was in charge of security felt a sense of failure and the Head, who was also the Inspector General of Police, offered to resign. Gen. Obasanjo however refused to accept his resignation because of his sincerity and commitment to the administration. Besides, the problem of national security at that time hung on the absence of a strong security apparatus. This was the problem that immediately faced Gen. Obasanjo.

He recalled Col. Abdullahi Mohammed, who was then the Governor of Benue-Plateau State but was before then the Staff Officer in charge of Intelligence at Army Headquarters. Col. Abdullahi was given the arduous task of planning and establishing what emerged as the National Security Organisation (NSO). The Organisation proved effective without being intrusive. Many years later under another military administration, the organisation, pioneered by Gen. Abdullahi Mohammed was rechristened State Security Service (SSS).

Lastly, there remained the threat that the composition of the Brigade of Guards constituted to the Obasanjo administration. While trying to identify the security-fragile areas of the Government, Gen. Obasanjo found that the officers and men of Plateau State origin, where a large number of the coup plotters came from, were preponderant in the composition of the Brigade of Guards. This was because the Angas, Gen. Gowon's tribe, who were numerically superior in the composition of the military personnel in the Brigade of Guards then, was located in Plateau State. This was a security problem in that such a biased concentration might unwittingly create an environment for disloyalty and ethnically motivated security breaches.

After a prolonged rumination about how to handle this problem, Gen. Obasanjo ordered a neutralisation of the Command. This meant that all the personnel of the Brigade were dispersed by posting them into other formations of the Nigerian Army throughout the country. A new Brigade of Guards was then formed with entirely new and mixed troops. With the problems caused directly by the failed coup fully attended to, Gen. Obasanjo turned his attention to the consolidation of the policy decisions hitherto taken.

The failed coup left its vicious stamp on all aspects of national life. The first was the sustenance of the low profile posture of the government under Gen. Murtala Mohammed. In the circumstance of the tragic and violent death of Gen. Murtala Mohammed, it seemed very difficult to sustain the low profile. There were all kinds of opinion offered by official advisers and the general public, such as that, which blamed the low profile posture of the administration for the murder of Gen. Muhammed. It was argued that extending the low profile posture to the security of the Head of State exposed him to wanton fatal attack.

Gen. Obasanjo soon realised that the low profile policy was becoming another type of war in the face of the seemingly plausible argument that low profile and security were mutually contradictory.

On the other hand, Gen. Obasanjo knew that low profile was a necessary frontal assault against the profligate and self-indulgent propensity of the Nigerian middle class; especially senior public officers. He realised that it was going to be a bloodless and non-dramatic revolution that needed more than legislation and official Circulars to sustain after Gen. Muhammad's death. The fact that the principle also needed to extend beyond Federal officialdom to the entire citizenry complicated matters for Gen. Obasanjo and his administration. He therefore, in his characteristic way decided to lead by example and live out every letter of the low profile policy, no matter the cost.

Gen. Obasanjo adopted the Peugeot 504 as his official vehicle, even when playing host to a foreign Head of State. He sold his personal car, a Jaguar, which he brought to Dodan Barracks and bought a Peugeot 504 instead. In addition, only locally produced food was served in the State House. Foreign wines were banned and Dee Bee wine, locally made from kola nut and palm wine were served. Apart from his military uniform, he wore only Nigerian dress. Let me briefly tell a story connected to this.

Maj. Gen. Joseph Garba, now resting with the Lord, was the Commissioner (Minister) of External Affairs. During one of his official trips abroad, he bought a pair of particularly trendy hand-woven Italian shoes for the C-In-C, Gen. Obasanjo. Maj. Gen. Garba was very happy and proud to have done that for his C-In-C. Then, there was shortly afterwards an event, the particularity of which I cannot now remember. The C-In-C came to that programme in his outmoded shoes. Gen. Garba was very angry and could not wait for the programme to end. Immediately the programme ended, he marched, not walked, to the C-In-C and wondered, why he would not stop embarrassing the nation with his ugly shoes. He said that he bought and gave him the shoes that he gave him so that he would stop embarrassing everybody with his boring shoes.

Gen. Garba was shocked stiff when he heard Gen. Obasanjo reply that in actual fact, he had given out the shoes to Capt. Ekpo Archibong, his ADC. Gen. Garba turned to me in a harmless rage. The smile that was trying to come out of my mouth retreated as I quickly pleaded that I was not Capt. Archibong. He then said: "yes, I know, but get him here right now." I did not have to go anywhere because Capt. Archibong was not far away. Gen. Garba ordered him immediately to produce the shoes there and then.

The C-In-C was just laughing all along and shortly after, Capt. Archibong came back with the shoes. Gen. Garba continued: "put the shoes down." Capt. Archibong did and Gen. Garba said: "Ekpo, where on earth have you ever seen a bloody Captain wearing this type of shoes?" Capt. Archibong then tried to explain that he did not ask for them and up till that moment, he did not even know the source of the shoes and had never put them on. Gen. Garba commandingly interrupted him: "shut up, you bloody Captain! Do you need to be told before you know that these are not for a bloody Captain's feet?" At the end of the comedy, Gen. Garba went away with the shoes with a promise that he would get a Captain's shoes for the ADC, when next he travelled abroad.

The shoes were unfortunately smaller in size than his feet. Gen. Garba therefore took them to the Chief of Staff, late Gen. Shehu Musa Yar'Adua, to see if the shoes fitted his feet. They fitted Gen. Yar'Adua's feet and Gen. Garba gave them to him, as a present but deliberately did not tell him the story behind the shoes. Gen. Yar'Adua gratefully accepted the shoes.

A few days later, Gen. Yar'Adua told the C-in-C of the beautiful gift of a pair of hand–woven shoes from Gen. Garba. Gen. Obasanjo burst into laughter and asked if Gen. Garba told him any story about the shoes. Then he told the story himself. Gen. Yar'Adua was not amused but he grudgingly received the shoes. We all laughed but the message to Gen. Garba and us, that is, Capt. Archibong and me was unmistakable. This story shows the depth of the sincerity of Gen. Obasanjo and his administration.

Gen. Obasanjo did not restrict low profile to his official bearing. He enrolled all his children in the Nigerian public school system and he spent his Leave, which was far between, in Nigeria. When he launched the Operation Feed the Nation, he carved out an area, about half of a plot of land in Dodan Barracks, where he carried out pilot farming. He managed this farm with his own bare hands and was only assisted by me, his Private Secretary. No official gardener or agriculturist or even a hired hand ever worked on the farm. He also did not, throughout his tenure, seek medical attention outside Nigeria, not even to take advantage of an official overseas trip. Without formally saying it, he also expected all the people holding positions in the administration to follow suit because he believed that it was the right thing to do at that time.

In furtherance of the low profile policy and in a bid to encourage local production at the same time, the Obasanjo administration imposed a ban on luxury items, such as lace materials, champagne and so on. When the Customs discovered them in any cargo, they were confiscated. Some of the confiscated goods were either burnt or given away as gifts. The ones sent to Dodan Barracks were taken to the office of the Staff Officer (Welfare), who in turn distributed them among the officers. I used to take my own share of drinks home for hospitality to the retinue of visitors that I used to have. I did not see the moral implication in this; I just considered it harmless.

However on one occasion and for the first time, lace materials were distributed. I did not have any lace in my wardrobe at the time and I liked the ones sent to me. I then gleefully carried them to Gen. Obasanjo to show him. I had never before then seen him so angry. He asked me if I did not see the self-contradiction and hypocrisy in confiscating those items from some Nigerians and giving the same to some other privileged Nigerians for their use. If Gen. Yar'adua, the Chief of Staff, had not promptly intervened, those of us involved would have lost our jobs. That was the end of that sort of impropriety in Dodan Barracks.

With regards to the economy, the Commissioner of Transport began to tackle the spiralling inflation that resulted from the port congestion by implementing some measures to combat port congestion. These measures included the procurement of new berthing facilities, finding facilities for emergency discharge of goods, initiating renegotiation with suppliers to recall their ships that were on the berthing queue or stop further deliveries, while efforts were intensified for the construction of permanent port facilities.

The approach of the government to the cement armada as it was notoriously known, was not altogether smooth sailing. The suppliers sued the Federal Military Government in foreign courts over the debts owed to the former and got judgement against the latter. Eventually, the Federal Military Government succumbed to negotiation as agreed by the suppliers but was still able to continue with its anti-inflation drive.

While the administration was tackling port congestion, it began at the same time to address the problem of inflation with the setting up of a Panel under Prof. Onitiri, a renowned economist. The Onitiri Panel submitted two Reports in which it recommended short, medium and long term, anti-inflationary measures. The first Report made recommendations on monetary and fiscal policies, price control, national goods supply and distribution, rent, housing, land, food production and marketing, as well as rail, road and water transportation. The recommendations were accepted and acted upon. Further studies were instituted, where it was found necessary. The recommendations on Land Use fell into this latter category.

The Obasanjo administration then proceeded to look at the 1972 Indigenisation Decree. This was to give practical expression to the administration's commitment to the development of a national economy generated and controlled by Nigerians. This was in contrast to an economy that put Nigerians at the periphery of global trade, serving only as middlemen and commissioned agents. The exercise was intended to achieve a three-stage control over a period, starting with ownership restructuring, then boardroom control and finally, management control. The failure of the 1972 Indigenisation Decree to achieve even the first of the three goals set for it, led Gen. Obasanjo to set up the Wole Adeosun Panel. The Panel was expected to identify the obstacles that frustrated the 1972 Indigenisation Decree and proffer ways to remove such obstacles.

The Panel worked fast and recommended some amendments to the 1972 Decree. These amendments were debated at the Federal Executive Council and accepted with amendments as the Government thought appropriate. The accepted recommendations of the Wole Adeosun Panel were implemented in the 1977 Nigerian Enterprises Promotion Decree. This Decree was significant for its novel idea of reserving for workers in public enterprises ten per cent equity participation. It was however, sadly, not implemented beyond the Obasanjo administration.

Perhaps the most celebrated economic policy of the Obasanjo administration was the Operation Feed the Nation that was inspired by the key role of agriculture in the nation's economy and the citizen's life. The programme aimed at involving the entire populace in sustained food production and ultimate food security through mass participation in agriculture. Agriculture had suffered prolonged neglect as a result of the civil war and the drastic reduction of farm labour by the population drift to urban areas.

The population drift was itself caused by our lopsided economic development policies that concentrated infrastructural development in the cities. Rural dwellers were on the other hand, condemned into a primitive life that offered nothing but hardship and economic stagnation. The general lack of interest in agriculture, heightened by the availability of oil and the concomitant oil money mentality, made the Obasanjo administration involve not only the three tiers of government but also traditional rulers, community leaders and the media in the implementation of this agricultural policy. Gen. Obasanjo himself set the example with a small farm at Dodan Barracks, his official residence, which as said earlier, he personally managed.

The Obasanjo administration also introduced the Agricultural Credit Guarantee Scheme that encouraged Commercial Banks to give agricultural loan facilities to farmers at preferential rates of two to three per cent below the prime-lending rate. In order to make the Commercial Banks more willing to cooperate, such loan was guaranteed with seventy-five per cent repayment by the Central Bank. The Government then made it mandatory for Commercial and Merchant Banks to reserve a certain percentage of their loan portfolio to agricultural and agro-allied enterprises.

The administration further introduced subsidy on agricultural inputs, such as fertiliser. Gen. Obasanjo's speech at the launching of Operation Feed the Nation revealed the tremendous determination of his administration to take the nation to the level of self-sufficiency in agricultural production. He said:

"In addition to what the State Governments have already ordered for this cropping season, the Federal Government will make available to all the State Governments 50,000 tons of fertilizers for distribution to farmers.

From now on, farmers will pay a uniform price for each type of fertilizer they buy irrespective of where they live. These prices are heavily subsidised by the Federal Military Government. Similarly, arrangements have been made to multiply large quantities of improved seeds so that in the next few years all farmers in this country can plant the high-yielding seeds available from our research institutes. Fishing nets and simple implements such as hoes and cutlasses, produced from local foundries will also be available whilst large quantities of pesticides are kept in readiness to prevent pests from frustrating our efforts." Fed. Ministry of Information, A March of Progress: Collected Speeches of H. E. Lt. Gen. Olusegun Obasanjo, p. 42.

The administration intended the Land Use Decree among other things, to encourage agriculture, while it also established grains storage facilities all over the country to promote grains production. The Government further introduced nationwide Agricultural Development Projects (ADP) for a well-planned, well-organised and harmonised development of the rural areas. The administration encouraged the River Basin Authorities to collaborate with State and Local Governments in assisting local farmers at subsidised rates to clear and prepare their land for planting. The State and Local Governments were later to be reimbursed for such assistance to the farmers.

In collaboration with the World Bank, the administration also established the Agricultural and Rural Management Training Institute in Ilorin, to train farmers in general farm management. With rice fast becoming the staple food of

Nigerians and the popular interest shown by Nigerian farmers in poultry production, the Obasanjo administration took a very bold step to encourage local rice and poultry farmers to increase their production. The farmers too responded with great enthusiasm and by the end of the Obasanjo military administration, the nation had attained self-sufficiency in both rice and poultry production.

This was the catalyst for the upsurge in agricultural activities that the country witnessed during the immediate post-Obasanjo military era. Unfortunately however, this was not sustained. President Shehu Shagari, for reasons certainly contrary to sound economic judgement, opened the floodgate of unrestricted importation of rice, chicken, maize, and so on. Expectedly, the policy somersault ridiculed the efforts of the farmers and dampened the growing enthusiasm. The unavoidable outcome was stunted local production and the ultimate death of those promising agricultural sub-sectors.

There was no sector of the economy that the Obasanjo administration did not touch with a view to making every sector efficient and productive for the betterment of the living condition of the people. The successes achieved vary from one sector to the other, largely because of the limited time and manpower resources available to the administration. The economy, particularly manufacturing and agriculture, however took inspiring and significant leap forward during the regime. Although the administration could not help resorting to external borrowing, the borrowed money was spent on the development of infrastructures. Some of these infrastructures, such as ports, roads, airports and power, have not been replaced or improved upon since then. They are still serving the nation till today.

The most important social policies of the Obasanjo military administration, instituted side-by-side with the expansion of tertiary education and referral Teaching Hospitals, were the Universal Primary Education (UPE) and the Primary Health Care (PHC) schemes. However, while the UPE was an expansion of, and an improvement on, the pioneering Free Primary Education scheme instituted by Chief Obafemi Awolowo in the old Western Region, the UPE has unfortunately not received adequate attention and improvement from succeeding administrations after the Obasanjo military administration. This explains why the scheme has failed to meet the demand of the rapidly increasing Nigerian population effectively.

On the international plain, the Gen. Murtala Muhammad-led Nigerian military government had appointed a Study Panel under the chairmanship of Prof. Adebayo Adedeji. The Panel examined the entire Nigerian foreign policy and made appropriate recommendations. Prof. Adedeji Panel's Report recommended that Africa should be the centrepiece of the administration's foreign policy. This recommendation was adopted but the administration preferred to use the concentric circles approach in the implementation of the recommendation. It gave our immediate neighbours priority attention in the Government's foreign policy consideration. The next level after that was the question of political independence for all the countries of Africa, which took a large part of the foreign policy initiatives of the Government.

After the demise of Gen. Murtala Muhammed, Gen. Obasanjo, as Head of State began a shuttle diplomacy to our neighbouring countries. This was borne out of the fact of the beneficial or negative role that a neighbour could play in matters that affect another neighbour. The invasion of Uganda by Israel in the latter's historic raid on Entebbe and the role of our neighbours during the civil war had taught the administration a lesson on the strategic advantage of maintaining cordial relations with neighbours. This led to working visits to the Republic of Benin, the Republic of Cameroun and the Republic of Togo. Gen. Obasanjo's shuttle diplomacy was not restricted to the West African sub-region. He also visited the frontline States of

Tanzania, Mozambique, Zambia and Zaire. He had visited Angola as Chief of Staff, Supreme Headquarters.

The situation in Angola presented an auspicious opportunity for Nigeria to translate from a docile African country to a fiery lion, capable of leading the rest of Africa into a new era of dynamism and respect. By 1975, when Gen. Murtala Muhammed became the Head of State, the OAU took a neutral stand on the Angola question. This was expressed in the Nigerian government's advocacy of a government of national unity in Angola. There was nothing wrong in this if it was left at that. It however became untenable and unacceptable, when both the United States of America and apartheid South Africa started working together in support of the United Front for the Total Liberation of Angola (UNITA) led by Savimbi.

The new military administration of Gen. Murtala Muhammed quickly recognised the contradiction in anti-apartheid Nigeria working, consciously or unconsciously, in the interest of apartheid South Africa or failing to give active support to the progressive movements in Angola and Mozambique. This was the first warning to the new Nigerian Military Government that the position of the OAU for peace through the installation of a Government of national unity needed to be re-examined.

The cooperation of the USA and apartheid South Africa with UNITA against the MPLA unmasked the desperation of UNITA to rule Angola at all costs, even at the expense of African interest. The new administration felt that the fact that UNITA decidedly aligned with apartheid South Africa, for whatever reason, should disqualify it from participation in the government of any African country. It was in this circumstance that Nigeria made a complete u-turn and swung her support totally behind the MPLA.

While Nigeria was still carrying out subtle diplomacy among neighbouring African countries to drum support for the installation of a government of national unity, South Africa was moving its troops to attack Angola. To worsen the situation, the then President of the United States of America sent a note through his Ambassador in Lagos, virtually instructing the Government of Nigeria on how to handle the Angolan issue. The note from President Ford was seen by Nigeria as an unwarranted interference in Nigeria's affairs and it was treated as such. These two events sold MPLA completely to Nigeria. When Gen. Murtala Muhammed declared the support of Nigeria for the MPLA in his speech titled Africa Has Come of Age to the OAU Extra-Ordinary Summit of 11 January 1976, it took the whole world by storm and instantly shot Nigeria to global diplomatic prominence.

The recognition of the MPLA in Angola was in total disregard of American pressure over the issue. This expectedly drew world attention to the emerging weight of Nigeria in international politics particularly, where African interest was directly involved. The rising stature of Nigeria became unstoppable as America found that there was no Soviet influence in all the steps being taken by Nigeria. Under Gen. Obasanjo also, Nigeria acted in every situation transparently in line with her conviction as to what was in Nigeria's national interest. The other consideration was the total liberation of Africa from all forms of colonialism, neo-colonialism and political servitude.

The refusal of the Obasanjo administration to accede to the request of the then American Secretary of State, Henry Kissinger to visit Nigeria was based entirely on the contradiction of receiving the architect of American policy that lacked any sensitivity to Africa. However, with the election of Jimmy Carter as President of the United States of America, there was a positive official policy change towards Africa by the government of the United States. Not only did President Carter send emissaries to Lagos, such as Andrew Young, a civil rights protégé of Martin Luther King Jnr., he also paid a visit to Nigeria, the first American President to do so.

Gen. Obasanjo too did not fail to take good advantage of this change. He visited the United States of America, a visit that coincided with the 32nd session of the United Nations General Assembly. In his address to the Assembly, Gen. Obasanjo drove home Nigeria's stand on apartheid, African decolonisation, African representation on the Security Council and other issues. It was yet another feather to the glowing cap of Nigeria.

The foreign policy of the Obasanjo administration with Africa as its centrepiece was generally dynamic, powerful and uplifting. This explains why Nigeria, in spite of not having geographical proximity, became a member of the Frontline States. It was an honour based on the political, diplomatic and material commitment of the Obasanjo administration to the liberation struggle. Nigeria made the independence of Angola irreversible. Nigeria worked in concert with the Frontline States, the governments of the United States of America and the United Kingdom to prepare the ground for the independence of Zimbabwe, the independence of Namibia and the end of apartheid regime in South Africa. Nigeria's Foreign Minster, Brig. Joseph Garba, Cyrus Vance and Andrew Young, both of the United States of America under President Jimmy Carter and David Owen of the United Kingdom under Prime Minister Jim Callaghan, were at the vanguard of this struggle.

Gen Obasanjo, in the course of projecting the new Nigeria's foreign policy visited Romania and Poland and also played host to World Leaders like Seyi Kountche of Niger Republic, Leopold Senghor of Senegal, Houphouet Boigny of Cote d'Ivoire, Sekou Toure of Guinea, Julius Nyerere of Tanzania, Helmut Schmidt of the Federal Republic of Germany, Jablonski of Poland and Ceausescu of Romania. Gen. Obasanjo met all the World Leaders, whose power, influence, diplomatic leverage and their countries' economic activities bore relevance to the decolonisation and total liberation of Africa and the peace, security and economic progress of Nigeria.

Gen. Obasanjo took drastic actions against any nation that stubbornly continued to sabotage African efforts to achieve the death of apartheid and the total decolonisation of Africa. When the British Government under Mrs. Margaret Thatcher was uncooperative over the implementation of the United Nations Resolution 435, the Obasanjo administration nationalised Barclays Bank and British interest in British Petroleum. He then rechristened it African Petroleum. Gen. Obasanjo went further to move Nigeria's Foreign Reserve from pound sterling to dollar account. When Mrs. Thatcher expressed a desire to pay an official visit to Nigeria after the Commonwealth Summit in Zimbabwe, she was advised that such visit was inauspicious. These actions expectedly jolted the Mrs. Thatcher-led British government and prompted Britain's change of her official position to the Zimbabwean question.

In all his radical policy decisions, Gen. Obasanjo's transparency, commitment, integrity and demeanour were above board. This attracted to him so much global respect and honour that he was brought into the picture of any policy initiative about Africa by the great powers before the conclusion and implementation of such policy. With this new global influence and power, Nigeria became a genuine partner with the world powers on issues affecting Africa.

Gen. Obasanjo attended the OAU Summit meeting in Monrovia, Liberia in 1979. The meeting was climaxed by a unanimous motion of commendation in his honour, passed by the African Leaders present at that meeting. The award, which is an Attestation of Commendation, reads as follows:

"Vote of Congratulation and Appreciation Extended to General Olusegun Obasanjo, Head of State and Commander-in-Chief of the Armed Forces of the Federal Republic of Nigeria.

The Assembly of Heads of State and Government of the Organisation of African Unity meeting in its Sixteenth Ordinary Session in Monrovia, Liberia from 17-20 July 1979.

Considering the exceptional qualities of statesmanship of General Olusegun Obasanjo, Head of State and Commander-in-Chief of the Armed Forces of the Federal Republic of Nigeria.

Considering the services he rendered to Africa.

Noting with high appreciation his immense contribution to the cause of Liberation of African Continent and towards peace in Africa as well as in the world.

Having heard with emotion, the speech delivered at the opening ceremony of the Sixteenth OAU Assembly in which he announced his imminent handing over of powers.

Considering that throughout the years of his office as the Head of the Federal Republic of Nigeria, President Obasanjo never ceased deploying sustained and permanent effort so that Africans could solve their own problems themselves and so that Africa asserts itself in all its entity and authenticity in the world.

Considering finally the far-sighted vision, a special quality of President Obasanjo whose dedication, sense of responsibility and strong commitment are well known and appreciated by all;

1. *Address its warm thanks to President Olusegun Obasanjo, worthy and brilliant son of Africa.*

2. *Commends President Obasanjo for all achievements as Head of the Nigerian State, not for his own country but for the entire African Continent.*

3. *Assures him of the unanimous appreciation of his colleagues and the participants of the Sixteenth OAU Assembly."*

The success of Gen. Obasanjo on the international arena was not at the expense of domestic issues. These were the burning issues that prompted the political change, which ushered his predecessor and him to the saddle of government. The major reason for the overthrow of Gowon was the reneging on his promise to hand over power in 1976. There was something in African leaders at the time that made them characteristically unwilling to relinquish power once installed, whether by the barrel of the gun or by the ballot box. The problem of succession therefore remained the Achilles heel of African political leaders. It was the test that every African leader had failed woefully. When Gowon announced the indefinite postponement of his hand-over date, he was just behaving true to type. The question then was whether Gen. Olusegun Obasanjo of Nigeria, who was enjoying considerable national and international acclaim, would also fail the test.

Before Gen. Murtala Muhammed died, he had announced a political programme that consisted of certain critical issues that must be dealt with before handing over power. These issues included Creation of States, the location of the Federal capital, Local Government Reform, Census, the Constitution and the process of actual elections. Before his untimely death in the failed Dimka coup, Gen. Murtala Muhammed had inaugurated the Irikefe Panel on the Creation of States, the Aguda Panel on the Federal capital and the Constitution Drafting Committee.

All the panels submitted their Reports and decisions were taken on them. It then became the lot of his successor, Gen. Obasanjo, to implement all the decisions. The Irikefe Panel recommended nineteen States, which was discussed and approved with minor amendments at a joint meeting of the National Council of States and the Supreme Military Council. The amendments included leaving Cross River State as one State instead of splitting it into two. The second was carving out the present Ogun State instead of merging it with Lagos State as one State. The third was carving out of Ife and Ilesha from Ondo State to form part of Oyo State. Obasanjo faithfully implemented the decisions.

After the creation of States, the Obasanjo administration also implemented the recommendations of the Aguda Panel on the Federal Capital, which had been accepted by the Government without any amendment. The administration thereafter turned its attention to Local Government reform. The Reform was subjected to wide discussions by all kinds of interest groups, ranging from State Governments through traditional rulers to politicians and administrators.

The Reform recognised Local Governments throughout the country as the third tier of Government and gave them the same functions. They were to receive their allocations direct from the Federal Government and not through the State Governments. Traditional rulers were also allowed to play advisory and traditional roles. The thrust of the Reform was the empowerment of Local Governments to serve as effective instruments of development at the grassroots level and bringing the government close to the people.

The promulgation of the Local Government Reform into law was followed by Local Government elections, which were contested on non-political party lines. The elections went smoothly throughout the whole country. The elected Chairmen of the Councils became the Chief Executives of their Councils and they were assisted by Councillors charged with responsibility for specific services such as Health, Education, Works, and so on. Thus the Chairmen and the portfolio Councillors constituted the Executive Arm of the Councils while the whole Council constituted the Legislature. The Judiciary was made up of Customary or Area Courts and Magistrate Courts.

The Administration limited its action on the Census to the basic steps that would make Census exercise less political and therefore less contentious. The administration to this end, attempted to strengthen the databases from which census figures are generated by first, a Decree that made the Registration of Births and Deaths mandatory. The Universal Primary Education Scheme that kept reliable statistics of children of school age followed. Last, the administration introduced the National Identity Card Scheme. It reasoned that these three approaches would make future census exercises less political and the figures more reliable. It left the Census issue at that and deliberately did not attempt any actual headcount because its tenure was too short for a thorough census.

The Constitution Drafting Committee submitted its Report within one year of its inauguration. The Draft Constitution was submitted to the Constituent Assembly made up of members elected by the Local Governments and a few government nominees. While the Constituent Assembly was busy with its work, the Electoral Commission was inaugurated. This, more than any other action, convinced many cynics that Gen. Obasanjo was actually determined to succeed, where General Gowon and many other African leaders failed.

The Supreme Military Council carried out a careful and exhaustive deliberation of the Report of the Constituent Assembly and approved it with a total of seventeen amendments. The amendments were made to strengthen the Constitution for good governance and national development after the military Government would have handed over power to a democratically elected administration. On Wednesday 20/9/1978, Gen. Obasanjo held a State reception in honour and appreciation of members of the Constituent Assembly. On the following day, 21/9/1978, the ban on political activities was lifted and the State of Emergency that had been in force since 1966 was also lifted.

The implementation of Gen. Obasanjo's political programme was not entirely smooth sailing. It also had its hiccup. The inclusion of a Federal Sharia Court of Appeal in the draft Constitution was a contentious issue, not only among the delegates to the Constituent Assembly but also within the Supreme Military Council. Since the division was along religious lines, Gen. Obasanjo resorted to an informal consultation with Sharia scholars; among them was Dr. Abubakar of Bauchi. Dr. Abubakar was not only an erudite Islamic scholar, he had also served as Chairman of the Area Court Review Panel and was at one time or the other the teacher of many incumbent Grand Khadis and other Islamic scholars around.

Dr. Abubakar, in his meeting with Gen. Obasanjo, categorically stated that there was no need for a Federal Sharia Court of Appeal and that he would not recommend it. Armed with this well-informed opinion, Gen. Obasanjo moved to douse the tension the Sharia was generating in the Constituent Assembly. He led the entire members of the Supreme Military Council to address the Constituent Assembly. He warned them against allowing any sectarian issue to deteriorate and stall the transition programme that was actually going smoothly. Happily they heeded the warning and the work of the Assembly continued unhindered. Eventually, Chief Simeon Adebo played a critical role in resolving the Sharia question in the Constituent Assembly. This was another instance of Obasanjo's unusual approach to military dictatorship. Under his administration, there was regular nation-wide and broad-based consultation on all national issues.

The actual elections also presented another problem. The Constitution provided that to be declared winner in the Presidential elections, a candidate must have 25 per cent of the votes cast in 2/3 of the States of the Federation. The intention was to ensure that a Presidential aspirant actually had a spread of political support far beyond his ethnic boundaries to qualify to be the President of a multi-ethnic nation like Nigeria. However, with nineteen States, the question arose as to what constitutes 2/3 of nineteen? The interpretation of 2/3 of nineteen States therefore became another big problem at the end of the Presidential elections. Unfortunately, nobody was prepared for that sort of problem because it was not envisaged by the Constitution.

Finding the right answer to this question engendered a politico-legal imbroglio, which some politicians were ready to exploit for unmerited electoral advantage. Pressures mounted from various quarters as to what practical interpretation should be given to '2/3 of the nineteen States' of the Federation. Gen. Obasanjo courageously resisted the pressures from various quarters to amend the relevant provision of the electoral law at that time, when the elections had been held. He instead insisted that it was the duty of the Federal Electoral Commission (FEDECO) to interpret and apply existing electoral laws. The Federal Electoral Commission eventually adopted the mathematical solution provided by a politician, not the Government, to the problem. This did not go down well with the political parties that were not favoured by the interpretation adopted by FEDECO. One of the aggrieved parties, the UPN then decided to go to court for adjudication. The party lost in the court and the transition programme was brought to a peaceful and successful end.

The civil war, by its nature did not pose any problem for Gen. Obasanjo because his success was in line with popular wish for the war to come to an end. His success as Head of State on the other hand encouraged appeals to him from within and outside Nigeria to stay on as a military Head of State or as a military-turned-civilian Head of State. His colleagues in the Organisation of African Unity, notably President Kenneth Kaunda of Zambia, President Houphouet Boigny of Liberia, President Leopold Senghor of Senegal, President Siad Barre of Somalia and many more, made such appeal to Gen. Obasanjo. He however in spite of the powerful pressures from these African Statesmen, stuck to the word jointly decided by him and his predecessor to hand over power on the date they jointly agreed to do so. He thus as a military Head of State repeated his success story of the Nigerian civil war by faithfully and voluntarily handing over power in spite of pressures to the contrary from within and outside Nigeria.

Figure 9 - Chief of Staff Supreme Headquarters

Chapter Nine: Transferable Principles Of Success

The hard analyst may see the military accomplishment of Gen. Obasanjo as the natural outcome of his military training. He however became Nigeria's military Head of State by the providential act of God. He did not anticipate the events that brought him into office and so did not formally train for it. In any case, there is no school, where practical politics is taught. The nearest thing to it is the study of Political Science, an academic discipline concerned with political institutions and political processes. Gen. Obasanjo did not have any formal training even in this subject. Besides, when the opportunity came for him to occupy the exalted position of Head of State, he attempted to spurn it. He had to be persuaded and even subtly blackmailed into accepting it. He learnt the art of governance in office as Head of State.

Apart from not having a relevant professional training for the art of governance, the Nigerian political milieu also harbours a peculiarity that makes heading the government a particularly trying experience. The country is multi-ethnic with three preponderant ethnic groups. This leaves the remaining groups that together constitute a majority of the population, distributed across the entire nation in numerous smaller ethnic groups, as minorities. Secondly, Nigeria is multi-religious but with two dominant faiths, Christianity and Islam. This also leaves other faiths and religious cults, operating unnoticed but exercising effective control over their members, even when such control is prejudicial to official and civilised rule of conduct. Thirdly, Nigeria has an elite middle class that forms about five percent of the total population. However, by virtue of its education, official position and wealth, this small fraction of the population consumes directly and indirectly a disproportionately much larger percentage of the nation's resources. This class also has the advantage of moulding and directing public opinion through the media and the rumour mill, expectedly along its selfish interests.

Three issues that were not terribly dissimilar in the instance in question further compounded the situation sketched earlier. The first is that Gen. Obasanjo was not part of the group that brought about the military Government he was called to lead after the demise of Gen. Muhammed. One might therefore ipso facto still wonder, if it was not too risky to accept the offer. The second was that the events that led to the Nigerian civil war had sadly further entrenched the divisive factors of ethnicity and religion among the polity. This made it appear as if the decision of Gen. Obasanjo to accept the offer to succeed Gen. Murtala was very foolish because majority of the officers, who planned and executed the July 1975 coup were from the North. The Yoruba therefore still saw the new administration as a Northern government with Obasanjo only as a stooge or an instrument in the hand of Northerners against the Yoruba.

The third was the populist effect of the unconventional disruption of the system through Gen. Murtala's sacking of hitherto 'untouchables' and the prompt attention given to state matters. Gen. Murtala Mohammed thus cut the image of an example of what a leader and leadership should be in a country that was in a hurry for development, like Nigeria. This did not only heighten public expectation, the public also personalised the administration's activities and saw the sudden death of Gen. Murtala Muhammed as the end of the unfolding socio-political revolution in the country. There were therefore those, who felt that Gen. Obasanjo might not be able to sustain the pace and standard set by his predecessor.

There were also those, who wanted to see another Gen. Murtala Muhammed; with the same face, the same voice and demeanour in Gen. Obasanjo but unfortunately, that was not possible. Such people therefore lost all interest in the latter and whatever he might eventually come up with.

There was in addition another strand of opinion held particularly by those, to whom the policies and actions of the Gen. Murtala Muhammed's dispensation were not favourable. This group hoped that Gen. Obasanjo would reverse or review the decisions and actions of his predecessor. All these socio-political undercurrents made Gen. Obasanjo's new role less enviable. It also did not encourage the general public to expect any good performance from him.

Within the first three months of the administration, Brig. Joseph Garba was obviously disturbed by the crescendo of complaints by the populace that Obasanjo was slack, slow and unexciting. He then came to Gen. Obasanjo to discuss this wrong public perception and attempt to identify anything that the administration had done wrong so that they might be redressed. Gen. Obasanjo too was not unaware of the complaints and unfavourable remarks. He thanked Garba but confidently told him that he had not done anything wrong and would therefore not allow himself to be stampeded. Three months later, that negative perception changed.

The invitation to Brig. Obasanjo by the leaders of the July 1975 coup to join the government that emerged from it as Chief of Staff, Supreme Headquarters was on a personal merit. The average Nigerian is susceptible to various competing, and sometimes conflicting, loyalties that might make him sometimes less objective. However, when a group of Nigerians with a common goal seriously get together to solve a problem among them, they always look dispassionately for those among them with the track record to work out the desired solution. This is true in families, professional groups, business organisations, social groups, etc. The military is also not different from other organisations in looking for the best people among itself to solve a problem.

The officers know among them those that are good, bad, corrupt, honest, lazy, hardworking and so on. They know who among them are capable of carrying out certain tasks successfully and those, who are not capable. The other ranks also know their officers inside out. In fact, the general saying in the military is that junior officers are better to write senior officers' Reports. The junior officers, who led the coup of 1975, knew Obasanjo's ability and happily, he lived up to their expectation and to national expectation also.

The first principle of accomplishment to be considered in this part of our study is therefore TRACK RECORD. The track record of Gen. Obasanjo was in fact impeccable. He excelled in all the courses he attended. He performed with unadulterated professionalism all the tasks that were assigned to him in the Congo, Cameroun and here at home. Nobody could intimidate him. He led the Third Marine Commando Division to victory over the rebels and received the Instrument of Surrender from the rebel leadership. He was known to be disciplined, loyal, honest, objective, broad-minded, hard working, detribalised, committed to the unity of the country and imbued with transparent integrity. He had also never been involved in any coup plot. In fact, during the July 1966 crisis, late Gen. Hassan Usman Katsina is quoted to have said prophetically:

"We must do everything to protect Obasanjo from harm. Nigeria will need him in future." Mrs. Oluremi Obasanjo: Bitter-Sweet: My Life with Obasanjo". Surulere, Lagos, Diamond Publications Limited, 2009, p. 42.

It is then no wonder, when a group of army officers saddled themselves with the responsibility of delivering the nation from a drift to chaos and disintegration, Brig. Obasanjo was one of the three people they judged to be capable of achieving this.

Many people fail to experience a breakthrough in their chosen field because they lack the track record that could shoot them into a position of higher responsibility. They may have innate talents, appropriate training and exposure but these cannot on their own promote a person. The Bible says unequivocally that the gift of a man would make a way for him. This however does not refer to dormant gifts but to active gifts that are characteristically exercised and tested. Some people are afraid of higher responsibility because they don't want anything that would expose their weaknesses. In the case of some others, it is the problem of low esteem. Both attitudes rob such people of the opportunity to build a track record, without which they cannot be trusted for a higher responsibility.

The truth is that there has to be a venture in order to be a gain. Without making an attempt to do something, one cannot succeed in, or be marked out for, that thing. While there are many reasons, why a man may fail to build a good track record, the point being made here is that everybody starts to climb the ladder of life from a base. Movement upwards on the ladder depends upon whether the climber can be trusted to hold out on a higher pedestal. This is so because a step is taken from a firm footing on a lower rung to a higher rung of the ladder. This is how experience and track record are built.

It is however sadly ironic that our leadership recruitment method has been turned upside-down by a polity that sees everything in terms of money. They regard merit and other virtues as worth little or nothing. The nation is finding it increasingly more difficult to achieve good governance because of the personal quality of some leaders. A member of the Senate, who is a retired Police Officer once alleged that many serving senators were crooks that he had investigated, while he was in the Police Force. Besides, we have some State Governors whose track records range from being commercial bus (danfo) drivers to being crooks and yet they became Governors.

Another former Governor, who is presently standing trial in England over allegations of fraud and money laundering, was in an open court of proper jurisdiction identified as an ex-convict and yet he retained his position as Governor. However, for as long as we relegate track record in our leadership recruitment system, so long will it be impossible for us as a nation to achieve greatness. There must be a scrupulous and open examination of the background and track record of all those who aspire to leadership positions in this country, from the ward to the national level. Any blot on the profile of anyone should lead to immediate disqualification.

However, thanks go to God for making us living witnesses of the unpleasant consequences of our corporate error in allowing those without any track record to lead us. We are also living witnesses of the beautiful consequences of the divine accident that allowed a person like Gen. Olusegun Obasanjo with an excellent track record to lead us. The difference I believe is clear. The same thing applies to individuals. Those who are desirous of success must begin to build a very good track record from the earliest days of their lives.

The second principle is COMMITMENT. From the moment Gen. Obasanjo agreed to serve under Gen. Murtala Muhammed, in spite of the fact that he was senior to the latter in enlisting in the army, he committed himself totally to the job. This commitment did not only subsist throughout the life of the administration, it actually increased as far as he could stretch it. He did not hold anything back in that he demonstrated transparent selflessness. He did not seek any private advantage as he subordinated every other interest to the good success of his administration.

He employed formal and informal channels to seek and acquire appropriate knowledge on issues that he needed to know something about. Examples were the Saturday meetings he held with people from different callings and others representing various interests; including the radical left, traditional rulers, religious leaders, businessmen, academicians, professionals and other opinion leaders. The meetings were meant to generate well-informed opinions for the enrichment of policy decisions and promotion of public understanding of official plans.

While he believed that perfection is an exclusive divine attribute, he was nonetheless meticulous in what he did and he strove to achieve flawless conclusions. He did not take any undue advantage and neither did he allow anybody to take undue advantage of him or his administration. Character failure on the part of some individuals, whom he had to work with, did not discourage him. He always took precautionary measures to frustrate perspectives and plans, from any quarters, which might be inimical to the success of his administration. He was also noted for dispensing justice within the limits of the law, without fear or favour.

When some people in the Constituent Assembly were going to derail the administration's transition programme over the Sharia, his commitment drove him to seek accurate information about the Sharia from outside the Assembly. When he had received the information he needed, he confronted the Assembly. That action saved the transition programme.

Moreover, his commitment to the total liberation of Africa was demonstrated in radical, as well as daring, official decisions that ultimately earned him and our country great respect in the comity of nations. Gen. Obasanjo did not see his occupying the highest office in the land at this time as the summum bonum but as another opportunity for a continuing track record. It was no wonder that another military government that came about five years after the Obasanjo administration christened itself "an off-shoot of the Murtala-Obasanjo regime."

The sacrifice that commitment demands may sometimes be difficult in our cultural setting with its extended family orientation. This however is where Gen. Obasanjo characteristically demonstrates an impressive strength of character. Let me illustrate this with a story. A cousin of Gen. Obasanjo was at this time a member of staff of Pilkington Glass, Apapa. That cousin missed his promotion and he went threatening that he would deal with the company by reporting the management to his 'brother', the Head of State; that is, Gen. Obasanjo. When the threats filtered into the ears of the management, they carried out their own discreet investigation. They found out that the man had on his face the type of tribal marks that were on the face of the Head of State. This was suggestive of tribal affinity.

The management of Pilkington Glass therefore quickly reversed their earlier position about the man and promoted him. They also paid him arrears of about eleven months. Later, this man visited Dodan Barracks and gleefully narrated the story of his exploit to the Head of State. Gen. Obasanjo was not happy about it at all. He therefore directed that Pilkington Glass should be informed that their employee in question used his name improperly. He further directed that the man should be reverted and the salaries and allowances he had collected as a result of the unmerited promotion should be recovered from him. The company complied.

This story is typical of Gen. Obasanjo's commitment and openness in his personal conduct and in the conduct of State affairs. As seen in this story, Gen. Obasanjo was so committed that he did not allow the sentiment of affinity to compromise him. Mr. Carpenter, who was the Secretary to the North-Western State Government at that time, in an interview, attributed the success of Gen. Obasanjo to his deliberate policy of surrounding himself with competent Nigerians, instead of doing so with ethnic Yoruba loyalists or Yoruba 'cabal'.

Many people are today operating at a level that is far below their God-ordained capacity, while some others are wallowing in outright failure because they are not committed to their calling or to anything for that matter. Some are looking for an easy way out or a quick fix, not what they can commit themselves to for lasting prosperity. Such people change vocation and occupation in the face of the slightest difficulty. They become rolling stones and they naturally gather no moss. Commitment leads to perseverance, which in turn affords deeper knowledge and promotes experience, resourcefulness and creativity. These four are the bringers of breakthroughs.

Lack of commitment is the reason for superficiality, which makes nothing but a mediocre of a person in his or her calling. A prevalent trend that works against commitment in our environment is the get-rich-quick mind-set. Many people are looking for what will turn them into multi-millionaires overnight but nature rarely works that way. Every step we take in life is like a seed that has a gestation period before it begins to produce fruits. A committed person will give everything to an enterprise in his hand and patiently grow it to success.

The third principle is HARD WORK. Gen. Obasanjo worked very hard as demonstrated by the spirited attempt of his administration to improve all aspects of the nation's life in spite of the limited time it had. Besides, those that had worked with him also testify of his robust capacity for hard work. He initiated policies that made the system serve the citizens better and also made State institutions bring out their best. He searched the whole spectrum of the Nigerian society to bring out bright and reputable individuals for their contribution to the national development efforts. He visited all the Local Government areas in the country. He made numerous foreign trips to foster Nigerian national interest and enlist global action for the total decolonisation of Africa and the economic liberation of the black race.

Records show that he read all his Council memoranda and he was as a result always in control of deliberations during Council meetings. This did not make him a dictator as he deferred to other opinions, when necessary. He was always the first to arrive in the office and the last to leave there at the close of the day. He daily left his office as if he was not coming back there again. When historians write detailed history of the period between 1975-1979, Gen. Obasanjo's name will be printed in gold for his hard work, which enabled his regime to accomplish so much within so short a time.

There is no alternative to hard work in any quest for success. In all endeavours, time always moves faster than the speed required to reach one's predetermined goal. Sometimes one would wish that the anointing of Joshua came upon one, to prolong the day for more daily work. In order to rise above the average and stay on top, one must work hard.

"The heights by great men reached and kept

Were not attained by sudden flight,

But they, while their companions slept

Were toiling upward in the night." - H. W. Longfellow, The Ladder of St. Augustine.

Many people resort to unnatural methods, such as the use of drugs to be able to work more because hard work is the key to success. Unfortunately it is an anti-social and deadly method that can cut short the life of the user. One of the trappings of high office or any leadership position is the delusion that the whole nation or group is at one's command to do one's bidding. The day that a leader begins to entertain such delusion is the beginning of his downfall because corporate success is determined by the quality of the leadership.

In the case in point, everybody in the higher bureaucracy knew that Gen. Obasanjo did not only read his memoranda, he also highlighted, marked, underlined and asterisked sections that were germane or were of particular interest. Therefore, no Commissioner, as Ministers were known then, brought an ill prepared memorandum to Council and got away with it. Similarly, nobody could hide any private agenda in a memorandum and expect that it would not be detected. Gen. Obasanjo would discover it because he would have read everything line by line, no matter how voluminous.

His hard work kept both the Commissioners and Permanent Secretaries always on their toes. He discovered every genuine and deliberate mistake in their submissions. He knew at any given time what should be going on in every

Ministry or Department. We have heard in this country leaders, who lay the blame for the lapses and failures of their administrations on their advisers. Gen. Obasanjo was not one of such public officers because he knew and participated in every policy decision, to which he gave assent. When therefore he gave assent to any official policy or action, it was because he believed in it.

The degeneration of the nation into corporate ease is demonstrated by the almost total reliance of the governments of the Federation on oil revenue. Solid minerals and agriculture are not popular means of wealth creation because they require hard work to extract and grow. The so called civil society groups that are crying about poverty in the nation never encourage the people to work hard on other God-given resources. Is it any wonder then that increasingly more people live below the poverty line?

In many States of the Federation now, more than 75 per cent of able-bodied young men live on commercial motorcycle (okada) because it brings in enough income for daily subsistence. Besides, not less than 85 percent of the budgets of most States of the Federation are financed directly from Federal allocation. This is a very unhealthy trend. Until we go back and appropriate the age-old virtue of hard work and industry into our body politic, individual deprivation and collective poverty will not cease.

The fourth principle is TRANSPARENCY. Our Lord Jesus Christ enjoined us to remain in the light. What this means in practical terms is a call to transparency. Gen. Obasanjo conducted the affairs of government with maximum transparency when he was in government. He never held any secret meetings with any ethnic or socio-cultural group about anything. He did not harbour any hidden agenda. When tell tales came to feed him with any information about anybody, he called the person concerned and challenged the talebearer to repeat what he said earlier in the presence of the person reported on. He was therefore never a part of any messy or underhand transaction. His friends at any given time were those, who had something beneficial to offer towards the successful implementation of his administration's programmes and policies. It is no wonder then that he enjoyed a tremendous amount of confidence among his colleagues.

Transparency is a personal resource for the good management of the affairs of one's life in that a transparent person is predictable. He does not harbour ulterior motives that can be misunderstood and he therefore cannot be lured into any scandal or be distracted. Transparency is an effective shield against intrigues, false accusations and unprofitable distractions.

The fifth principle is INTEGRITY. Perhaps the area where the public most expected Gen. Obasanjo to fail was in his integrity with regards to the policy decisions of his predecessor; particularly the political programme. Gen. Obasanjo however proved the cynics wrong, when he fulfilled the promises of his administration. He ensured a faithful implementation of all the policies that his predecessor began, including the political programme, which he saw to its expected end. No stage or aspect of it suffered any hitch; let alone postponement for even one day.

In this regard, the personal character of Gen. Obasanjo was fully stretched as various people within and outside the military, as well as within and outside the government, put pressure on him to postpone the hand over date. He stoutly resisted all the pressures and faithfully handed over as promised by his predecessor. Equally praiseworthy was his conduct of the transition programme, including the elections. Although the UPN contested the result of the Presidential election, this was clearly provided for in the electoral law that gave room for any aggrieved person or party to seek relief through the courts.

The integrity of Gen. Obasanjo in the conduct of the affairs of the State, when he was the military Head of State, was not in any doubt. Not only did he not try to build any house, he also stopped the building that he had started to put up near the University of Ibadan. He took this decision because he chose to be above board, even when it was at the cost of his personal welfare and legitimate aspiration. His integrity in office, more than anything else, gave him the global approval and respect that he has continued to enjoy since then.

There is no place, where integrity counts in life as much as in business and inter-personal relationships. Some people fail to find help, when they need help because of the doubts that hang over their integrity. Integrity is the basis of a successful business relationship with Financial Institutions and other business groups. Besides, when a manufacturer advertises a product, the amount of response from the public is determined by the degree of confidence the public has in the company. Many of our politicians too become unpopular with the electorate because their integrity has been impaired by their failure to fulfil their campaign promises. We are social animals living inter-dependent lives. Integrity is the key that unlocks the help needed from others for good success in our private endeavours.

The sixth principle is HUMILITY. One of the characteristics of coups d'etat is the upset that they bring into existing hierarchical configuration within the military. This, more than any other thing, is the reason for the instability of military regimes. Military officers guard their ranks jealously. Therefore, when a relatively junior officer is thrown up to a higher rank or higher responsibility as a result of a coup or reorganisation, all the officers who hold higher ranks would be swept away into retirement. When Gen. Danjuma was, as a result of the July 1975 coup, appointed the Chief of Army Staff and promoted to the rank of Lieutenant General, the discontent of many officers, who felt superseded was so deep that it was cited as the principal reason for the failed Dimka coup.

When also as a result of the death of Gen. Murtala Muhammed Col. Shehu Yar'Adua was appointed Chief of Staff, Supreme Headquarters, and promoted to the rank of Major General, there were passive protests from some officers of higher rank. Some of them who needed to pass their files through the Chief of Staff, Supreme Headquarters to the Head of State, chose instead to do so through the Chief of Army Staff, whose seniority they accepted. It was therefore a mark of great humility for Brig. Obasanjo to accept to serve under Brig. Murtala Muhammed who was junior to him in enlisting in the Army. In Gen. Obasanjo's own words:

"As if apologising, they pointed out that real politik would necessitate making the offer of Head of State to Brig. Murtala Mohammed, this I realised was in deference to my seniority to him in enlisting in the Army. I quickly cut in to say that I was prepared to serve as Second-in-Command if that entailed shouldering real responsibilities and not sinecure job of allocating quarters to civil servants." Olusegun Obasanjo: Not My Will, Ibadan, University Press Limited, 1990, p. 12.

The humility of Gen. Obasanjo is proverbial. His estranged wife, Mrs. Oluremi Obasanjo, still recalls a relevant incident thus:

"He was a very humble man. During one of his visits to our house, he saw my mother carrying some heavy load on her head as she returned from the market. He rushed to her, took the load from her, and carried it on his head into our house. My mother was touched. Here was a senior military officer, a car owner, humbling himself performing a chore he could easily have ordered someone else to do." Mrs. Oluremi Obasanjo: Bitter-Sweet: My Life with Obasanjo" Surulere, Lagos, Diamond Publications Limited, 2009, pp. 22-23.

Gen. Obasanjo did not acquire his humility in office. It is his innate attribute that has helped him to win many life's skirmishes. We see in his wife's account that his humility, more than any other attribute, won her for him. Mr. Kelechi Anosike certainly gets it wrong when he describes Gen. Obasanjo as 'a master of intrigues' in his book Olusegun Obasanjo: The Man, The Message, The Movement published by Kelechi Anosike, Abuja, 2006. This assertion merely shows that many of his friends do not really know him. The problem with many of Obasanjo's opponents is that they allow themselves to be deceived by his dough exterior and uncanny humility. They therefore throw careless challenges at him and because they are ill prepared, they end up being floored.

On the other hand, Gen. Obasanjo does not take any step just because he woke up from a particular side of his bed. He sees every issue beyond the present and therefore spends a lot of time before such issue comes to a head. He examines it from various perspectives and assesses it in the light of all conceivable scenarios and eventualities. He is always well prepared before launching himself into any action. Be that as it may.

Gen. Obasanjo's humility stood him in a good stead in this new role, where he had to work first, in a subordinate position with Gen. Murtala Mohammed and later, with

Gen. Danjuma and Maj. Gen. Shehu Yar'Adua, practically as colleagues of almost equal rank. As Head of State, he did not relate with his immediate Assistants patronisingly or in an air of superiority. Instead, he related with them cheerfully and with transparent openness. This in turn earned him their respect, support and cooperation. Without this attribute, he most probably would not have recorded more than minimal success; notwithstanding the best of intentions.

The Bible has said it all: "Pride goes before destruction." There are times when it becomes expedient to put aside all airs and walk towards our predetermined goal in humility, practically stooping low, or even very low. In this way, one is able to mobilise all available hands on to deck for the achievement of one's goal. When we walk in the path of humility, success is better assured because it attracts love, protection and enrichment and at the same time diverts negative publicity.

The seventh principle is KNOWLEDGE. Gen. Obasanjo is a lover of knowledge, largely because knowledge gives the confidence and assurance that one is doing the right thing in the right way. He therefore consciously sought information from far and wide about any issue. He had a large number of friends scattered across all walks of life, from whom he sought information about anything. His pool of friends cut across traditional boundaries of gender, religion, academic, socio-economic position and ethnicity.

When his administration was taking steps to combat inflation, he was in the habit of calling my wife to go as far as Ifo, a village in Ogun State, whose market is noted for all types of consumable agricultural products. Her assignment was to check the prices of commodities such as vegetables, yam, rice, beans, and so on all the way from Lagos to Ifo and sometimes beyond. This sort of channel, in addition to official channels of information such as government ministries, departments and agencies, constituted his resource base for the regular supply of accurate and unbiased information about any issue.

Gen. Obasanjo was therefore at any particular time more knowledgeable and better informed than any other single Nigerian, about any issue bearing on governance. This was why, in spite of not being a Muslim, he could handle the Sharia issue in the Constituent Assembly rightly in a way that removed its threat to the success of the whole transition programme. His decisions and policy initiatives were never grounded on impulses, rumours or emotions but on accurate and up-to-date facts and figures. Many of us are guided to our decisions by what works for somebody else or by our emotions or subjective perception of what we intend to do. Inexorable failures are then blamed on innocent and extraneous factors.

An enterprise founded on knowledge has a much higher chance of succeeding than that built on the impulse of the moment. A highly respected citizen of this country was a few years ago appointed as Minister of Power and Steel. The emotion-laden and often jejune analyses of our uninformed media on the problem of power in the nation carried him away to announce to the public that he would solve the problem of power within six months. This was even before he had looked at the problem at all. He ended up messing himself up because by the time he was reassigned to another Ministry, after he had spent over one year in Power and Steel, he had not succeeded in scratching the problem on the surface. His reassignment to another Ministry was indeed a timely face-saving intervention for him.

When late President Umaru Yar'Adua assumed office as President, one of his earliest public pronouncements was that he would increase power generation to 6,000MW within his first year in office. To actualise this, he promised to declare a State of Emergency in the power sector, apparently without any knowledge or understanding of the constitutional requirements for, and the implications of, the declaration of a state of emergency. In any case, by the time he died, about two and half years after the Presidential promise, there had been nothing like a state of emergency and power generation was less than 1,500MW. Both the Minister referred to earlier and our dear late President acted sincerely but without knowledge and the consequence was, inescapable failure.

These examples underscore the importance and the power of knowledge in our endeavours. Those, who seek success in their endeavours must give high priority to acquiring enough relevant knowledge through training and information gathering. Lack of knowledge would lead to trial and error, slow progress, wastage of scarce resources and stunted success or outright failure.

An Excellent Farmer

Figure 10 - Criss-crossing his farm on a bicycle

Chapter Ten: The Poverty of Success

When Gen. Olusegun Obasanjo handed over the reins of government to the democratically elected government of Alhaji Shehu Shagari in 1979, he was just about forty-three years old. Within the first half of a normal lifetime, he had behind him notable accomplishments in two radically different disciplines that conferred on him a socio-political stature that was unmistakably and irresistibly great. Apart from the actual accomplishments, the manner with which he earned them made him no less than a colossus. His earned recognition spread across the entire globe, from Abeokuta his home place to Europe, through America and to the farthest parts of the world.

On the day he handed over the reins of government, he returned to Abeokuta in a motorcade escorted by two helicopters of the Nigerian Air Force. A mammoth crowd led by His Royal Majesty Olowu of Owu met him at a point about twelve kilometres from Abeokuta. Owu is one of the five kingdoms that constitute Abeokuta and the Olowu is the king of the Owu kingdom. Gen. Obasanjo happened to belong to the Owu clan of Abeokuta. He was mobbed by the jubilant crowd singing and dancing to traditional drums usually beaten to honour victorious sons of Owu.

The crowd got increasingly bigger as the convoy proceeded to the palace of His Royal Majesty, Alake of Abeokuta. A white charger was brought for him to ride to the Alake's palace. It was a particularly colourful occasion charged with deep emotion of joy and transparent affection towards him. The joyous occasion ended with a big civic reception and a Church service. It was a glorious homecoming that made everyone associated with Gen. Obasanjo proud. He described his feelings about that day thus:

"The crowd and their reaction were overwhelmingly heartening. I had a mixed feeling of pride, satisfaction and accomplishment." Olusegun Obasanjo, op. cit. p.207.

The feeling he had was natural for a truly successful person. His accomplishment so far was indisputable. However, his success is also paradoxically the problem, in that such a huge success needs to be seen for what it is. It is a means to an end and not an end in itself. The immediate challenge for Gen. Obasanjo was how he would manage such a huge success at such a young age. Would he retire into unproductive self-glorification or a private life of self-indulgent ease? What more did he need to aspire to?

Managing success is ordinarily a very difficult thing to do because of the nature of success. It can intoxicate and lead to a permissively unproductive lifestyle. This is compounded in our cultural setting, where success has a peculiar anti-climactic connotation. When Lech Walesa of Poland ceased to be President of his country, he returned to the Gdansk shipyard. It would in our cultural setting take an unnatural courage, but one regarded by the public as utter shamelessness or a curse, for anybody in a circumstance similar to that of Lech Walesa, to even contemplate, let alone, dare such a descent.

Success, particularly the sort of success that had come Gen. Obasanjo's way, had socio-economic implications. His place on the social ladder had advanced to the very top and for that reason, what he chose to do, where he chose to go to and the manner of doing all these must also be carefully considered. The only tolerable thing for him to do was to join the league of local chiefs and try to become a mandarin peddling influence at official circles on behalf of fellow chiefs. The success of Gen. Obasanjo also ordinarily precluded him from certain vocations that were considered to be inappropriate for someone of the social stature he had attained. On his part, he said, "I cannot go around government offices asking for contracts or supplies." Gen. Obasanjo therefore returned home after the tumultuous reception to ponder on what to do next. Notwithstanding the fact that he owned a few investments, he had no doubt in his mind that whatever he chose to do, he had to start from the very beginning. It was not an easy task but he had four reference points from which to begin his consideration.

The first was that apart from being just in the prime of youth, Gen. Obasanjo is by nature very restless. It was therefore absolutely impossible that he would retire into a life of unproductive ease. He must find something worthwhile and really engaging to channel his robust energy into. The second reference point was the lesson that he learnt from the crises that bedevilled the nation, particularly the army, in 1966. The third was the political factor in the career advancement to senior positions in all the public services of the Federation, including the Army. The fourth was what he learnt from ruling, and managing the affairs of, this country for three and half years. In this circumstance, whatever he decided to do could not be an accident or just an impulsive action like his enlisting in the Nigerian Army.

The failed coup d'etat of January 1966 began a lingering tragedy for the officers of the Nigerian Army, who joined the army before then. Lt. Col. C. O. Ojukwu, who later led the Biafra rebellion, described the period before the coup in his Random Thoughts, p. 21, quoted by Maj.-Gen. J. N. Garba in the latter's "Revolution in Nigeria: Another View", pp.54-55:

"I do not know whether you understand really how we live in the army. An officer is a brother to the next officer. When you are moving around, as soon as you arrive in the garrison, you automatically go to the officers' mess and there you eat and drink with everybody. If you spend the night there, you have to share a bed with any officer, but if the officer is married, he will leave the bed for his wife and you two will sleep on the mat. This is how the army functions. You eat together, live together and act together. One man's friend is the other officer's friend. We were almost the same."

Lt. Col. Ojukwu continued in the same work to describe in a brief but tragic detail how the 'paradise' he described above in the Nigerian Army was mutilated and destroyed by the coup of 1966:

"That evening people ate together, and went out together and then suddenly, at the appointed time, the same people with whom you ate and drank invited you outside and there machine gun was opened up."

The confusion and disorientation that gripped the surviving members of the officer corps as a result of the crisis cannot be fully captured in any writing. It was particularly devastating for them because as described by Lt. Col. Ojukwu, the crisis almost destroyed the soul of the Nigerian Army. They had not quite put this sad incident behind, when like a volcano, the retaliatory coup of July the same year erupted with malignant ferocity against Ibo Officers. Within a few days, what started as a violent expression of internal discontent within the army rapidly snowballed into an indiscriminate assault against the Ibos, within and outside the army. The anti-climax was the consequent attempted fragmentation of the country into regional ethnic groups with everybody, including men of the Armed Forces, abandoning their places of abode and running for safety back to their region of origin. This incident, from all practical purposes killed the fantasy of any Nigerian to regard anywhere outside his native place his home.

Gen. Obasanjo was not shielded from this ill wind. His escape with his life from the hands of the rampaging Northern soldiers in July 1966 was providential. His wife, Mrs. Oluremi Obasanjo narrowly escaped a fatal attack in Kaduna by a mob that mistook her for an Ibo girl, when she was shopping in the market. Gen. Obasanjo, who built his first house in Kaduna, had to escape with his wife through the help of Major Hassan Usman Katsina, who gave specific prophetic instructions that nothing must happen to Obasanjo because the country might one day need him. In the circumstance, whatever plans the latter might have made about retirement must be realigned to the current realities. Accordingly, Gen. Obasanjo started from that time to look at his hometown as the only place, where he could hope to spend his life in retirement. There, farming seemed to be the only thing he could do, especially if he retired at a fairly senior rank.

This was the time when the idea of farming as a second career first entered into his mind but it remained dormant for another decade and half. He however began to take steps that would facilitate the realisation of this tentative decision if and when it became necessary. To this end, he bought his first farmland at a place called Alomaja, near Ibadan in 1967 and in 1968, he bought another at a place called Owiwi, near Abeokuta. After the war, he attempted to buy another farmland at Igboora but the Igbole community in Igboora, from whom he wanted to buy the land had a tradition of giving free farmland to a successful warrior, who so wished. With his victory in the civil war that had at that time just ended, Gen. Obasanjo qualified for this concession and was accordingly given free what he had proposed to buy. All he then paid for the Igboora farmland were kola nuts, bitter kola and a few bottles of schnapps. With the traditional presents received from him, the land was properly conveyed to him. This explains his sentimental attachment to that farm. Gen. Obasanjo naturally plans big and so he went ahead to purchase another piece of land at Lanlate. It was many years later, when he had firmly decided on farming as a second career that he purchased the Ota farmland, which eventually became the most popular. The Ota farm became so popular because it was the first to be put into use in order to take advantage of the huge Lagos market.

When Gen. Obasanjo attained the rank of Brigadier-General, he felt that political considerations might stall his career advancement beyond that rank. He reasoned that if promotion were based solely on merit, there were most probably five Brigadiers that would advance to the rank of Major General. If three of the five Brigadiers came from the same political zone, it would be unrealistic then for him to expect to be promoted. He then sought the permission of the then Chief of Staff (Army), Major General Hassan Usman Katsina to register a Company that he might eventually need. The latter granted the permission for Brig. Obasanjo to register a Company that he named 'Temperance Enterprises Limited'. It also remained dormant for as long he was in the Service.

Gen. Obasanjo left the seat of power with a wealth of experience in administration and management, as well as a huge exposure to the dynamics of national economic development. He had been persuaded, while in office that agriculture held the ultimate solution to the socio-economic problems of Nigeria and indeed of Africa. This is because it assured food security, it is a vibrant foreign exchange earner and it is a sustainable source of raw materials for industrialisation. In addition, agriculture is the largest employer of labour. It is the only enterprise that could keep the majority of the citizens productively engaged. When he had examined all these references, he chose to go into agriculture. He based his decision on a number of parameters that were in furtherance of his avowed desire to remain relevant in our national socio-economic development efforts.

Gen. Obasano's interest and belief in agriculture as a catalyst of national economic development were clearly shown in the Operation Feed the Nation (OFN), a major policy initiative of his administration. Apart from reviving and popularising agriculture, which was virtually dying as a result of prolonged neglect, the OFN was also intended to bring dignity into farming and provide an infrastructural base for agricultural entrepreneurship. It is on record that within its short span of life, the Obasanjo administration turned around the dwindling state of agriculture and kept it on its way of becoming a popular vocation even among the elites. More importantly, the nation became self-sufficient in poultry production and was almost self-sufficient in rice production.

What the Obasanjo administration achieved in the agricultural sub-sector of the economy was a great success that further encouraged his tenuously held preference for farming in retirement. He saw the period of retirement as an opportunity to practically demonstrate and propagate in a private and individual capacity, the benefits of agriculture. Going into farming would also provide unassailable proof of his sincerity about his official policies, particularly agriculture. Besides, it would also bring the huge potential of agriculture for national economic development into the open for all to see. In addition, his going into farming would certainly attract into farming the enlightened attention and accumulated economic resources of wealthy middle class entrepreneurs and corporate organisations.

Figure 11 - In the Chicken Coop

Chapter Eleven: Laying The Foundation

The Bible laments through the mouth of David, the man after God's heart that if the foundation is destroyed, there is nothing that the righteous can do. This declaration underscores the importance of a good foundation in every human life and endeavour. We are familiar with foundations more in relation to buildings than any other activity but the truth is that everything on earth rests on a foundation. Therefore, if we want our actions to produce the expected good results, we must strive to build them on a strong foundation. It is only a strong foundation that can keep our vision alive and shield our endeavours from errors and slow progress or total lack of progress. A weak foundation or the absence of a foundation will lead to the destruction of lofty goals and ideals. Just as it is in buildings, the strength of any foundation is determined by the kind of materials used to build it.

The foundation that is dug deep into the ground and made of cement, sand and gravels, reinforced with iron, will certainly be able to carry a heavier superstructure than the one that is made of only sand and cement. Similarly in an enterprise, continuing prosperity depends largely upon the quality of the preparation given to it. The materials of a strong enterprise foundation are: land, money, trained and skilled personnel and basic infrastructures such as water, electricity and roads. There are also psychological requirements, such as commitment, self-discipline, resourcefulness and so on. The foundation for farming is not in any way different.

In farming, land is the most basic requirement. Unfortunately however, it is also in the southern part of Nigeria, the resource that is most difficult to acquire because of the traditional Land Tenure System that subsists in that part of the country. Land is seen to a large extent in southern Nigeria as a trading commodity instead of a resource for productive activity. The Land Use Decree of 1979 promulgated by the Obasanjo administration was intended to correct this fundamental clog. Unfortunately, successive governments have been at pains to enforce the Act. The result is the uncontrollable stranglehold on land by traditional landowners known as omo onile and their legal backers and land speculators at the expense of productive exploitation.

Although there are institutional arrangements for financial assistance to intending entrepreneurs, the Banks and Credit Organisations, which provide the loans and credit facilities do not give more than a fraction of what is required, and at an interest rate that suffocates the businesses. The point must also be made that the Banks and Credit Organisations do not offer financial assistance just for the asking. Their intervention in any enterprise is regulated by the nation's agro-industrial and monetary policies that are not often easily understood by intending borrowers. In addition are the Banks' internal measures to safeguard their own investment in the business for which they lend money. While this is the universal practice, it makes business development rather difficult in our underdeveloped environment, where overheads are unavoidably spread far beyond the sustainable limit of available funds. This partly explains why the average Nigerian businessman prefers to be a supplier, middleman, commissioned agent or a general trader.

The Nigerian business environment is further marred by our public infrastructures that have not significantly developed beyond the rudimentary level. The effort of the Obasanjo administration to improve power generation, which produced the Shiroro and Jebba hydro-electric projects when he was a military Head of State, was undermined by the acute shortage of middle level manpower and the imbalance in the supply and demand of electricity. There was also the problem of deliberate sabotage through illegal connection and destruction of national electricity installations. All these and organisational mismanagement within the electric power agency made the provision of electricity consistently inadequate at this time.

The three tiers of government share the responsibility for the provision of water and road but most of the roads that feed the main highways were constructed and maintained by the Local Government. Until the Local Government Reform of the Obasanjo administration in 1976, funding was a serious problem for Local Governments. This lack of funds made it impossible for Local Governments to have the quantity and the quality of the manpower they required for effective discharge of their statutory functions. The 1976 reform that made Local Governments financially independent of the State Governments expanded the capacity of the former to hire the quantity and the quality of the manpower they needed. Unfortunately, this did not immediately start to attract qualified and experienced people, especially professionals because in our society, the word 'local' culturally connotes 'backward', 'primitive', 'unenlightened' and 'uncultured'. They would prefer to work for the State or Federal Government or for the big companies in the city than for the Local Government.

This meant that every enterprise had to quickly assume the role of a Municipal Government, providing its own water, power and road. In the circumstance, every productive business enterprise was bedevilled with challenges that made it more likely to die within the first few years of its inception. Perhaps it was for these reasons that some people felt that Gen. Obasanjo was just using farming as a ploy to deceive the public. They not only believed that it would fail, they also believed that Gen. Obasanjo himself knew that poultry farming had no chance of succeeding under the Nigerian milieu described above. These challenges were further accentuated in the case of Gen. Obasanjo by the fact that there were very few trained and experienced poultry farming graduates around at this time. The few that were available were largely Extension Services staff of the Ministry of Agriculture. They were too few to be of any remarkable assistance to the practising commercial farmer, who therefore unavoidably had to rely largely on unskilled personnel.

We have gone into these details to give a good picture of the milieu in which Gen. Obasanjo was going to operate, when his mind was finally made up about poultry farming. As for land, he had acquired enough land as mentioned earlier but he now decided to use the one in Ota because of its favourable location and proximity to the huge Lagos market. Apart from Ota fast becoming an industrial city, Lagos, the seat of the Federal Government and the commercial capital of the nation at that time was also within easy reach from Ota.

His second step was to proceed to the Institute of Agricultural Research and Training at Moor Plantation Ibadan under Prof. Ajibola Taylor for a period of six weeks, to acquire an elementary knowledge of poultry farming. This was consistent with his usual practice of acquiring enough basic knowledge of anything he plans to do. This is part of his strength, which gives him an edge and a better promise of success in whatever he lays his hand on. 'Knowledge' they say 'is power'. Gen. Obasanjo sees knowledge beyond power; it is also success.

The third step was to take a loan. By this time, there was the Agricultural Credit Loans Scheme guaranteed by the Central Bank of Nigeria. The maximum amount that could be loaned to a single enterprise under this scheme was pegged at N1,000,000.00. Gen. Obasanjo took advantage of this scheme and with his gratuity and another overdraft facility of N250,000.00, he started off with a total of N1,500,000.00, which at that time amounted to about $3million or N450 million by today's rate of exchange. He spent the money on land clearing and land preparation, borehole and overhead tank, roads and tracks within the farm, electricity generating sets, warehouse and storehouses, feed mill, poultry houses and equipment for 20,000 layers and 50,000 broilers. He imported almost all the equipment and the day-old chicks.

As soon as the Letter of Credit was opened for the importation of the various items of equipment, NAL Merchant Bank, the Bank from which the credit was secured, demanded a comprehensive insurance of the Letter of Credit. Gen. Obasanjo did this with Niger Insurance Company. The ship was immediately loaded and set sail from Rotterdam to Nigeria for a period of five days. Two days into the voyage, the ship capsized and sank. It was a shock to Gen. Obasanjo, who without delay personally reported the incident to Niger Insurance Company.

The management of the Insurance Company was thrown into a paroxysm of shock and disbelief, as they were tempted to believe that it was either a deliberate act of sabotage or an outright lie. Then the company speedily set in motion its Accident Investigation machinery for verification and confirmation of the accident. When they had thoroughly investigated and confirmed that the ship truly sank, the Insurance Company paid what was due. Gen. Obasanjo however had to put up with a delay of about three months before continuing with the project. It was a frightening baptism of fire for him and his staff. It however also prepared them for future storms, trials and troubles.

Figure 12 - Posing with his statue on his farm

Figure 13 - A lesson in self-reliance and leadership. Gen. Obasanjo, working on his "Operation Feed the Nation" farm assisted by his Private Secretary, the author

Chapter Twelve: Becoming An Excellent Farmer

Contrary to the forecast of failure by some people, Gen. Obasanjo went into his new career, full of confidence and hope that he was going to break new grounds of success in poultry farming. He therefore subordinated every other interest to the farm. He told his wife, Mrs. Stella Obasanjo:

"Give me three years to face this farming with undivided commitment and devotion. If I see no sign of success after three years, I will come back to the drawing board."

His first problem however was adjusting to dealing with his civilian staff, whose orientation was different from what he knew in the barracks. He however from his personal experience came to the conclusion that the success of any team with a mission depended to a very large extent on the welfare and discipline of team members, working together for the success of the mission.

As for staff welfare, he ensured prompt payment of salaries and also provided modest facilities such as decent accommodation, canteen and traditional games that enlivened the staff. In addition, he made their work less boring by incorporating cultural entertainment during lunch break into the farm schedule. As for discipline, he adopted the military style. A normal workday began at 7 am. with a staff parade and the bell was used to announce the time to change from one activity to the other.

Gen. Obasanjo attempted to institute a high standard of discipline among the staff. As one, who believes in leading by example, nobody was exempt from the rules of the Farm. There were therefore no sacred cows when justice had to be dispensed. There is a story of the time his first child, now Sen. Iyabo Obasanjo-Bello, was undergoing her industrial attachment as a Veterinary Medicine student on his father's farm. One day, Iyabo reported late for duty and she was locked out at the gate along with other latecomers. They all lost that day's wage and Iyabo in addition received a sharp reprimand the following day.

At its inception, the farm had a staff made up of Gen. Obasanjo, Charles Igbodo, two tractor drivers, his driver, Baba Ota who happened to be one of the omo onile and the farm guard. Dr. Soleye, his friend, occasionally accompanied him to the farm. After the clearing of the land and proper farm work began, more workers were recruited. They were mostly Ghanaians, who fled from the national economic downturn in their country and migrated to Nigeria to seek greener pasture. As the work increased, so also did the workforce on the farm increased with attendant personnel problems.

In spite of his personal vigilance, some members of the staff still engaged in pilfering and outright stealing. The first person designated as farm manager was a Nigerian who initially warmed himself into Gen. Obasanjo's heart by his seeming industry and deceptive innocence. He however could not hide his true character for too long, as he was soon found to be involved in the disappearance of Two Hundred Thousand Naira from the coffers of the farm. He took an ill advantage of the trust that Gen. Obasanjo had in him to steal the money. Only part of the money was recovered from him but he was immediately sacked and on the day he was dismissed, he was found with stolen chicken and eggs.

Gen. Obasanjo also at this time had speaking engagements that frequently took him outside Nigeria. Although the period of absence on such occasions was short, he however always sought the assistance of his friend, Dr. Soleye to oversee the running of the farm during his absence. Then on one occasion, the farm received a new stock of day-old chicks and Dr. Soleye instructed the farm manager to apply the normal insecticide around the pens that housed the chicks to prevent red ants from attacking them. Unfortunately, the farm manager either forgot to carry out Dr. Soleye's instruction or he thought that it was not necessary because he did not yet feel the need for it. He failed to carry out Dr. Soleye's instructions. After Dr. Soleye had left the farm, it rained. The rain usually calls out foraging red ants and on this occasion, they sprang out into the pen of the chickens. The bite of the ants decimated the chickens. They died in thousands. More than three thousand chickens died overnight. Dr. Soleye was expectedly disturbed because he ought to have ensured that his instruction was carried out before leaving the farm for Abeokuta the previous night.

Gen. Obasanjo easily loses his temper in arguments, when the other side insists on a glaringly untenable position. One would therefore expect a nerve-wrecking rage over the loss of so many chickens by the sheer carelessness of the farm manager. Dr. Soleye found it difficult to report the incident to his friend when he returned from his trip the following morning because he actually expected such rage from him. However, when Dr. Soleye reported the incident to him, the reaction of Gen. Obasanjo stunned him.

While Gen. Obasanjo felt sad over it, he did not dwell on the disappointment. He remarked that it was one of the challenges commonly experienced in business. It must however not be allowed to discourage one because according to him, 'what cannot break you cannot make you.' He then immediately moved to do other things that would contain the continuing loss and prevent such from happening again. Dr. Soleye remarked that he was baffled but also convinced by the incident that Gen. Obasanjo was going to be very successful in poultry farming because his unexpected reaction to the big loss showed rare commitment.

Apart from losses occurring from staff carelessness and misbehaviour, there were incidents of deliberate sabotage by stealing and pilfering. Sometimes eggs were pilfered and sometimes, chickens were strangled and made to look as if they died naturally. Whenever such happened, Gen. Obasanjo gave the dead chicken to the attendant in charge of the cage where it occurred. He soon discovered that dead chickens daily littered the farm. The attendants too were always happy to have the dead chickens. Then it occurred to him that it might after all be the deliberate handwork of the attendants. He then stopped giving such dead chickens to the attendants and instead, ordered any chicken found dead to be buried after pouring kerosene or disinfectant or petrol on it. He checked where such chicken was buried everyday until it finally decayed and was of no use to anybody. Then the incidence of chickens dying without any discernible cause gradually reduced.

Mr. Agbaje was employed from Liberia to work on the farm. He displayed a good knowledge of poultry management and he was so hardworking that Gen. Obasanjo dared to trust him. It is probably one of Gen. Obasanjo's weaknesses that he easily trusts people. However, when that trust is betrayed, he moves to the other extreme, where it becomes extremely difficult, if not impossible, to regain his trust. When Mr. Agbaje was sure that he had warmed himself into Gen. Obasanjo's heart, he started to divert chickens to a farm he jointly owned with one of his friends. He had done it several times before he was eventually caught. He was dismissed after as much as possible from what he had stolen was recovered from him. He felt so ashamed that he returned to Liberia, where he came from. He later joined the army of Charles Taylor, where he died an untimely death.

There was also an Accountant who went to lodge the proceeds from the day's sales in the bank. On his way back, he stopped over in his house and sought the assistance of his wife to lacerate his back with a knife. His wife too cooperated but she was doing it so hard that the man started to groan and his groans attracted the attention of the people in the adjoining flat. They did not know what was happening but they unmistakably heard his groans accompanied with complaints from the man that his wife was pressing the knife too deep.

When he finished what he considered a perfectly credible alibi, he reported officially that armed robbers stole the money he took to the bank from him. Gen. Obasanjo then asked him how he could part with so much money without any struggle that would most likely leave him somehow injured. He quickly rolled up his shirt to show the self-inflicted wounds there but before any comment was made, one of the next-door neighbours of the Accountant came to the scene and asked from the latter questions that let the cat out of the bag. Gen. Obasanjo recovered the stolen money in full and dispensed with his services.

Apart from members of staff, who pilfered products and equipment to make quick money, there were also those who stole products for their pots. Gen. Obasanjo dealt with this by ensuring that members of staff, who wanted to have the products of the farm in their pots must buy such products. They must in addition show their Receipt with the purchased product to the staff at the gate before they were allowed to take the products out.

A group of Ghanaian workers invaded the processing department one night. They removed the motors of all the processing machines there. They not only succeeded in removing the motors, they also carried them out of the farm to Alaba market where they sold them off. As part of the efforts to unmask the perpetrators, Gen. Obasanjo followed a hunch to Alaba market. He detailed Mr. Charles Igbodo to carry out a covert search for the stolen items in the market.

It did not take Charles too long to discover the motors already on sale at Alaba market.

He then tricked the traders who bought the motors from the dishonest Ghanaians into coming with him to Ota. There, the Alaba traders were shown the machines and their identification numbers to convince them that they had bought stolen goods. Once they saw the machines and they realised that the game was up, they confessed that some Ghanaian workers from the farm sold the motors to them. They then begged for forgiveness. All the motors were recovered. The workers who stole them were also identified and appropriately disciplined. The buyer, from that day became a friend and an informant for the farm.

The problem of pilfering and stealing persisted and Gen. Obasanjo dealt with it firmly. He knew that his presence on the farm often made a difference in that his close supervision of the activities of his staff helped to reduce malpractices. Besides, suspicious losses were recovered from those responsible; that is, those whose mistakes, carelessness or connivance directly or indirectly caused such losses. In addition, guilty individuals were sanctioned and any weakness in the system was promptly addressed in order to prevent a future occurrence.

Apart from imposing sanctions on pilferers and saboteurs, Gen. Obasanjo regularly carried out all night patrols and did guard duties with some members of his staff, particularly Charles Igbodo, a barrack boy, to discourage night robbers. The Bible describes the heart of man as deceitful and desperately wicked. Gen. Obasanjo had ample experience of this trait of man on his farm with the criminal ingenuity displayed by some members of his staff. They sometimes colluded with outsiders to steal and pilfer farm products and equipment. In spite of his close supervision and commitment, he succeeded only in reducing the incidence of sabotage and pilfering. He could not totally prevent it.

On nights that he mounted patrols, the internal saboteurs would sing and sporadically shout a particular slogan, aparo j'ako; that is, the bush fowl is walking through the farm. It took a long time before Gen. Obasanjo knew what the shout and the song actually meant. They were actually a coded warning from the internal saboteurs to their colleagues and external perpetrators against attempting any nefarious activities that night. Night guards too were not left out, as they were experts in throwing items over the fence, to be retrieved from behind the fence after the close of work. The most ingenuous of such night guards was a 65 years old man, who often sneaked into the poultry house. He would steal egg, slightly break them, bury them in hot ash and take them out when it was safe for sale.

Gen. Obasanjo found that whenever he was on night patrol, there would be no serious incident but once he was not, there would be reports of stealing and losses. When he decided to use women as poultry attendants, there was a noticeable reduction in the level of malpractices although it did not take too long for eggs to start finding their ways into ladies' head ties and corsets. Speaking about this experience on his farm, Gen. Obasanjo remarked that there were good boys and good girls as well as bad boys and bad girls.

Internal sabotage was not the only problem that confronted Gen. Obasanjo on his farm. The fact of being a former Head of State did not shield him from the overzealousness of some officials, who just wanted to prove a point. Obasanjo Farms once placed order for day-old chickens from Belgium. The chickens were to be received early in the morning so that they would be conveyed to their pens in good time before sunrise. If they were conveyed after sunrise, they would be exposed to stress from the heat of the sun and the result would be decimation of the chickens. The staff of Obasanjo Farms were on this occasion at the airport as early as 04.00 hours to take delivery of the consignment at 05.00 hours. As the chickens were being driven out of the airport after proper delivery, the Customs stopped the consignment for inspection.

This was not the first time that the Farm would import day-old chickens and all documentation was in this instance as always, correct. After the inspection, the Customs officials, for reasons best known to them, delayed the consignment until well after mid-day before asking the vehicle to go without offering any reason for the delay. By the time they gave permission for the vehicle to go, all the chickens, 100,000 in all, had died. There was no provision for legal redress against culpable government officials for any damage caused by them in the course of their legitimate duties. Thus Gen. Obasanjo lost about $75,000.00 but in his characteristic manner, he bore his loss silently. He refused to make any fuss about it and neither did he make any official report. When he took recourse to the Insurance Company, the company refused to pay on the grounds that the chicks arrived at the airport in good condition. He also on his part refused to be discouraged.

Furthermore, Gen. Obasanjo found that anytime he travelled, he would spend the first two weeks after his return, trying to correct the wrongs committed by his staff, while he was away. His trips abroad were necessary and some of them were speaking engagements that provided him the funds for family and social commitments. If he did not have such additional sources of income, he would unavoidably be dipping his hand into the proceeds from the farm. This made his overseas commitments part of the strategy for the development of the farm. Whenever he was in Nigeria, he spent most of his time on the farm and he did this with incredible vigour. According to Mr. D. W. Atsu, the Managing Director of Obasanjo Farms:

"In the early days of growing the farms, he could get up early at Abeokuta, reach Igboora Farm at 5.00am, proceed to Lanlate (both in Oyo State), make a detour to Aiyetoro, and reach Ota Farm before 10.00 am."

He also had to deal with the problem of inadequate finance by resorting to almost interminable loans from different Banks. The banks had no problem offering their assistance; not only because of his erstwhile position as the Head of State of Nigeria but more, because of his integrity and the prospect of the farm. The banks were impressed by what he was doing. They examined his proposals and physically inspected the farm several times. They were satisfied that the project and the way Gen. Obasanjo was managing it, justified their collaboration. The farm thus became indebted to NAL Merchant Bank, UBA, First Bank, Afribank and Union Bank.

In spite of a well-calculated projection, things did not always go as planned. Gen. Obasanjo fell behind schedule in the repayment of his loans. There was also along the line the Government's Structural Adjustment Programme and the Banks soon forgot that he was a former Head of State. In his anxiety to be a good debtor to his banks, First Bank, UBA, Union Bank and NAL Merchant Bank, Gen. Obasanjo invited all of them together for a meeting to work out modalities for restructuring his loans and strengthening the operations of his farms. This turned out to be a strategic error that was very inimical to the farms as the banks ganged up against him. Instead of granting a lifeline for the farms, the banks were collectively tightening the noose. With some funds generated from a trading business, Gen. Obasanjo managed to break the rank of the creditors and thus set him and the farms free from their shylock-grip.

They eventually agreed to write-off part of the accrued interest to enable him continue repaying without stalling the farms' operations. He also embarked on some trading in agricultural products and agriculture-related equipment and it helped. Apart from continuing business relationship with the Banks in question since then, others such as Access Bank, GTB, Wema, Unity and Zenith have joined the group of the business partners of Obasanjo Farms. This taught him a general lesson that one should at all costs prevent one's creditors from ganging up against one; otherwise, it could spell doom for one's business. This experience stood him in a good stead when, later in life as the elected President of Nigeria, he had to negotiate debt relief for the country. It was an almost impossible task but which he undertook successfully.

The challenges of Gen. Obasanjo in farming were not limited to personnel and funding. He also had to deal with the natives, more popularly known as omo onile; that is, the traditional landowners. Long after Gen. Obasanjo had perfected the transaction on the Ota farmland, the landowners came demanding money. At first, Gen. Obasanjo felt that they were a bunch of hungry people, who needed little money to spend on immediate needs. He reasoned that when the farm matured and its commercial activities reached full bloom, these so-called landowners would become involved as part of the beneficiaries of the farm's economic activities. Much as he hated giving or receiving free money, he gave some money to the agitators for social events such as marriage, burial and naming ceremonies. However, when the so-called landowners persisted in their demand, he called their bluff and reported to the traditional ruler, who quickly called them to order but not until they had made a great nuisance of themselves.

From the beginning, Gen. Obasanjo had a clear vision of taking his farm to the level of a conglomerate. In order to achieve this, he made up his mind right from the first day of business on the farm about the way he would run the farm. He decided to adopt a backward integration approach and plough back all profits into the farm. He also decided that every activity; that is, all transactions, interactions and relationships that related to the farm were to be carried out purely and absolutely on the basis of business. The implication of this was that nobody; including him, would take anything out of the farm without paying the appropriate market price. When he started to have table birds and turkeys, he fully paid from his pocket for every gift of chicken or turkey he gave to his visitors or friends during festivals. Thanks go to God for his pension and the income he earned, though irregularly, from his speaking engagements abroad, as well as yet some income from his property investments within Nigeria. These extra sources enabled him to dedicate every income coming from the farm to the growth and expansion of the farm.

Backward integration in business is not a new approach to growth but many entrepreneurs avoid it because they lack the capacity to manage and carry it through. Backward integration is a steady step towards self-sustenance, self-sufficiency and diversification in production. Gen. Obasanjo started with the importation of day-old chicks. He then added the importation of fertilised eggs for the production of day-old chicks and gradually moved to hatching and breeding. Today, Obasanjo Farm produces its own fertilised eggs, day-old chicks, broilers and layers. His farms together now produce about 1.8 million broilers and 1.2 million layers. The farms produce everything, without any exception, required in a poultry farm; ranging from research in foundation stock, grand parent stock and parent stock, through egg trays and poultry feeds, to bags and product packaging materials. His success in backward integration encouraged him to integrate forward and diversify his agricultural business.

Gen. Obasanjo has established Parent Stock Poultry Breeder Farm at Igboora, the Lanlate Grand Parent Stock Poultry Breeder Farm, the Great Grand Parent Poultry Breeders and Pure Line Poultry Breeders Farms. Obasanjo Farms has a strong Research and Development Department that has succeeded in producing Africa's first world-class Pure-line Poultry Breeder Farm. It has the capacity for the supply of Grand Parent Stock poultry breeder chickens for the entire African continent. The Research and Development Department of Obasanjo Farms has also, in conjunction with Marshall Breeders of India, produced the first Nigerian broiler, named Obamarshall. In addition, the Research and Development Department offers consultancy services to needy farmers all over the country.

As Gen. Obasanjo gathered experience in his poultry-farming career, he learnt the importance of packaging and presentation of farm products for the market, whether for local or international market. Gen. Obasanjo believes that a particular knowledge has value only when it is applied for the improved living standard of the people. He therefore embarked on the production of packaging materials to further enhance the presentation of his farm products. The success of the Farm in backward and forward integration has greatly helped to realise and sustain the focus of Obasanjo Farms to achieve quality, quantity and variety in production.

It is remarkable that Obasanjo Farm, which started as a modest holding at Ota with a staff comprising him, his driver, Charles Igbodo, two truck drivers, and occasionally, his friend Dr. Ona Soleye, now spreads beyond Ota to other parts of the country including Zaria, Kaduna, Calabar, Igboora, Jos, Owiwi, Mambilla, Lanlate, Delta State, etc. with a total of about 7,000 workers on its payroll.

The activities of Obasanjo Farms also include, in addition to poultry, turkey, piggery, fish farming, ostrich and emu farming, commercial production of Beijing ducks, grass cutter, palm oil, mushroom, cocoyam, plantain, banana, vegetables, cassava, gaari, animal feed, floating pellets for fish and livestock, egg tray, maize, chicken box, packaging materials and hybrid seeds.

It has further planted three million teak trees, which now offer training opportunity to Wildlife and Forestry students. It has also hosted academic groups from the International Forestry Association. Internationally, Gen. Obasanjo is now venturing into West, Central and East Africa, to encourage accelerated transnational efforts for the achievement of food security and food-for-all in Africa.

Perhaps the most important benefit of Gen. Obasanjo's venture into farming is the attraction to farming of notable Nigerians such as the late M. K. O. Abiola, Brig.-Gen. S. O. Ogbemudia, Adm. M. Nyako, Gen. Abdul Salami Abubakar, Gen. T. Y. Danjuma, Air Vice Marshall Shekarau, and many corporate bodies such as Guinness, UAC, SCOA, Afprint and so on. Before venturing into politics and becoming the Governor of his State, Adm. Murtala Nyako was the President of the All Farmers' Association of Nigeria, (AFAN). Now, for the reason of Gen. Obasanjo going into farming and making such a great success of it, agriculture has regained its pride of place in the national economy. More people are going into different areas of agriculture and agro-allied ventures, which gives a good prospect of the attainability of food security in Nigeria in the shortest time possible.

The success and the spread of Obasanjo Farms in, and outside, Nigeria is an eloquent testimony of his uncommon qualities and ability to achieve great success in whatever he makes up his mind to do.

Chapter Thirteen: Transferable Principles Of Success

Gen. Obasanjo enlisted in the army without previously giving it any deep thought. On the other hand, he gave farming a deep thought before going into it. In spite of his preparation, his early experiences on the farm left him in no doubt that he needed more than material and financial preparation to be a successful farmer. However, being a well-endowed man and one with the basic training and adequate experience for a reasonable level of success in any endeavour, he saw those challenges together as an impetus to press forward.

The foundational principle upon which Gen. Obasanjo's achievement in his farming career rests is COURAGE. Courage in this instance is the ability to act upon one's conviction, regardless of danger or disapproval. The first man, Adam, needed a helper, whom God provided in the form of Eve, his wife. Thus God created man a social being, which also implies that more hands than just one man's hands are needed for the realisation, or otherwise, of a person's dreams or ideas. An idea usually passes through a process in the mind of the person, who conceives the idea before it becomes an established idea or a decision, to be implemented or pursued. This is the stage when an idea becomes a cause, a project or a programme.

Part of the process of an idea becoming a decision is when the idea is subjected to an enlarged perception in the form of inputs from sources such as spouse, friends and people, who have recognisable knowledge by formal training or by practical experience in the matter in question. Those who offer inputs into an idea bearing on business, do so from different perspectives, which range from the socio-economic, through the psychological, to the environmental perspectives. This usually leads to the review, reassessment, or even outright cancellation of an idea. The purpose is to ensure adequate preparation, reduce the margin of error during implementation and so increase one's chances of success, when the idea is finally implemented. Many ideas and dreams are however killed by the unhelpful inputs received at their conceptual stages.

The two sources from which a person can receive inputs to his idea are the formal and the informal sources. The formal source is made up of the professionals, who have formal training in the relevant discipline. This source is less harmful because its inputs are largely based on verifiable data and calculable projections. On the other hand, the informal source is more susceptible to errors because it is more often than not, based on subjective judgement, hearsay, poorly observed and isolated incidents, sentiments, emotions and prejudices, as well as unverified assumptions. In spite of the usually spurious bases, upon which some informal inputs stand, they are by far more effective. This is most probably because we dabble into a particular business not entirely for economic reasons. We also do so for the reason of self-esteem.

A person could advise his spouse against a particular business venture not on its commercial merit but because it is psychologically incongruous or because it is susceptible to indecent exposure. A venture could also be dismissed on account of a reason as nebulous as 'oh, it is not befitting' or 'at your age? No' or 'Not again; I can count on my fingertips so many people, who have done that business and failed'. Therefore, to succeed in a business, one needs more than a good or well-reasoned idea. One needs the idea, the commitment, the appropriate knowledge, the understanding, as well as well-grounded inputs and solid pieces of advice from both formal and informal sources.

Gen. Obasanjo was never in want of advice or inputs from both formal and informal sources. Late Chief Simeon Adebo, a distinguished, widely respected and actually successful technocrat was the first to advise Gen. Obasanjo against farming because of its concomitant problems and risks. In the Yoruba context, this was enough to condemn the latter's farming idea into permanent rest.

Chief Adebo was older, seasoned, highly experienced and indeed, much more experienced, widely respected and deeply loved by Gen. Obasanjo himself. Within the Yoruba cultural milieu, it is ordinarily difficult to set aside the advice of an elderly person. However, when that person has the age, stature, endowment, accomplishment and genuine love that Chief Adebo had, the advice is, from all intents and purposes, a command that must be obeyed by all means.

Gen. Obasanjo displayed an uncommon courage to set aside the advice of Chief Adebo and proceed with farming. While Gen. Obasanjo was polite and sufficiently respectful not to say outright 'no' to Chief Adebo, he did not say 'yes' either. He only said that he would give it a trial and if it did not work, he would abandon it. It is interesting that five years later, when Chief Adebo saw the tremendous progress made by Gen. Obasanjo on the farm, he praised him for sticking to his decision to be a farmer. He was also humble enough to say: "you were right and I was wrong." Where are the species of Simeon Adebo in our country? Are they now endangered or even extinct?

Architect Arc. Lai Balogun, a close friend of Gen. Obasanjo and also a successful architect, one day visited Gen.

Obasanjo on the farm. He expressed disgust and personal embarrassment brought upon his friends such as him, by Gen. Obasanjo's choice of farming as a second career after occupying the State House. The visitor wondered why Gen. Obasanjo preferred the uncertainty and hardship associated with farming to the ease and big commercial reward realisable from available alternatives. He then came up with a well-articulated proposal, supported with graphic and architectural drawings to turn the farmland to a venture that would effortlessly begin to yield hundreds of millions of naira within a very short space of time.

Gen. Obasanjo listened to him carefully and replied him with a thought-provoking lecture on social responsibility. He asked his friend how many people would be employed by his plan. He had no answer to that question as Gen. Obasanjo went further to tell his friend that he was more interested in the creation of jobs and in adding value to the environment, than in making money. The visitor left dissatisfied, still wondering, what could make a sane person prefer the hardship of farming to effortless enrichment.

Another friend, Chief Asabia, advised Gen. Obasanjo to use the profit from the farm for something else instead of ploughing it back into the farm. Had Gen. Obasanjo taken this advice; the benefits that we see today in the business would never have happened. There were many more pieces of advice from various quarters aimed at turning Gen. Obasanjo away from farming. The bases of such pieces of advice ranged from farming not being a befitting vocation for a former Head of State, to the attendant risk involved in farming. Gen Obasanjo however set aside all such advice and courageously carried on with his farming. The courage of Gen. Obasanjo can be fully appreciated if the various pieces of advice he received are viewed from the psychology of advice.

It takes a special grace of God and rare humility for a person offering advice on any issue to do so dispassionately. Advisers easily assume a superiority of wisdom, perception and understanding or even omniscience on the issue in point. They therefore see their advice as having the precision of an oracle that would be foolhardy to ignore. It is also intricately connected to the self-esteem of the person giving the advice. When a piece of advice is ignored, the adviser, more often than not, subconsciously feels hurt. He takes offence because it is an affront on his self-esteem. He then wrongly paints the person who rejects his advice as obstinate, self-conceited, self-opinionated and so on. He also begins passively to wish the latter failure in the pursuit in point because it is the only thing that can redeem his self-esteem. The failure of the pursuit would provide the consolatory opportunity for him to say 'did I not tell you?'

Many promising ideas and lofty ambitions are truncated out of the fear of 'what people would say'. In the case of Gen. Obasanjo, he tactfully turned down the pieces of advice that were contrary to his vision. He was also not intimidated by the possibility of a deluge of revulsion of feelings against him by his advisers. He just did what he had to do and stuck to it. He surrendered to time to confirm him in the hard choice he had made. Gen. Obasanjo's initial courage, which he has also hitherto sustained, is the critical key that enabled him to take his agricultural enterprise to the height it occupies today. It is by any standard a conglomerate now. It is a real business.

Let us all, whether in public office or in private position, exercise courage for success. Jesus Christ spoke about Christians who are neither hot nor cold and he warned that he would not regard them as belonging to Him. This is a warning to Christians, who lack the courage to profess their faith, most probably for fear of persecution. These are Christians who stand for nothing and are known for nothing. Their life is not driven by conviction or vision but by 'just-in-case mindset'. They do not know that there is an element of risk in every action, even in eating. While eating, a small morsel of food may miss its track from the gullet and go into the trachea. Such accident causes coughing and a lot of pain and discomfort that can bring about grave complications if not swiftly attended to. We must however still eat to keep alive, in spite of the risk. Although danger and risks abound, courage is the essential quality that we need for the take-off and the advance in human endeavour.

The second principle is COMMITMENT. The thread that runs through our brief account of Obasanjo Farms so far is commitment. His commitment is eloquently expressed in the catalogue of daunting problems that he encountered all the way and how he managed them all without giving up. They were problems that practically and continually challenged the progress of the farms. The losses that were attributable to internal sabotage, collusion and mischievous overzealousness of government officials were more than enough to ruin the farms and force him out of it but Gen. Obasanjo persisted without wavering.

It is commitment that sustains interest and vision in the face of difficulties. It is impossible to achieve anything worthwhile without commitment to that thing because problems are bound to come. Commitment engenders persistence and persistence gives the experience, competence and creativity that would eventually perfect our efforts and take us to the predetermined goal. Gen. Obasanjo has the capacity to focus on one issue at a time and shut out any distraction; regardless of the seeming attraction.

Commitment starts from the motivation for going into an enterprise. Sadly in Nigeria today, money and other extraneous rewards are the motivation for the choice of business vocation, career and even academic discipline. There are those who are looking for what would yield quick and fat money and others, who just want to prove a point by what they are seen to be doing. These are like the people in the Biblical parable, who built their houses on sand. When the storm and the flood came, the houses collapsed due to the absence of a good foundation. If the interest of Gen. Obasanjo in farming were defined by money, the first loss he sustained would have made him abandon that vocation. He however carried on in the face of drawbacks and eventually, he won. In the stormy weather and vicissitudes of life, it is unalloyed commitment that keeps one going, when everything else seems to be saying the contrary.

The third principle is SELF-DISCIPLINE. Our cultural setting with its extended family system and the derived principle of being one's brother's keeper is basically good but it is in practice, unfriendly to business growth. In our locale, the social and domestic responsibility of an average middle class entrepreneur is invariably far beyond his earned income. It takes a lot of discipline to be in control of the pressure that emanates from the needs of family members and keep one's spending within one's earned income. This contrasts sharply to what obtains in post-industrial economies, where a father cannot just for the reason of being the father, expect a free lunch from his daughter's restaurant. On the other hand, a father here would claim as a right, daily free lunch in his daughter's restaurant. He would even sometimes go in there with his friends and still insist on free lunch for him and his party.

Although the idea of doing business with borrowed money is not strange to us but in spending, many of us hardly draw a line between capital, which is borrowed money, and profit. In addition, the individual's perception of his social status dictates how he responds to the economic demands that pile up on him. In the case of Gen. Obasanjo, who was at this time a former Head of State, everybody around him most probably believed that he held in his hand the key of solution to all problems. He was therefore daily inundated with all kinds of requests for money and other favours that tasked his time, his financial resources and his goodwill.

It never crossed the mind of those seeking favours that nothing is free on earth. Somebody or something somewhere, pays for every favour that one receives. Every money spent from the farm comes from the sale of the products of the farm. It is from the sales that loans are paid and growth is engineered by ploughing back the money realised to the business. The chicken or egg given out free ordinarily as hospitality to an august visitor would to some extent set the general attitude of the staff to farm products. The supervisor that watches an indiscriminate hand dipping by the proprietor into the proceeds from the farm, would soon develop a conscience that does not restrain him from freely dipping his own hands in like manner into the coffers of the farm.

Gen. Obasanjo stoutly resisted all temptation to run the farm unprofessionally. He refused to be an absentee farmer, and he ensured that he paid fully for whatever he took from the farm for any purpose. He did not give himself to any ostentatious living. In fact, he disappointed many people, who expected to see his working environment as a former Head of State to be exactly like what obtained in the State House. They were disappointed to see a sharp contrast, an ordinary farmer's office. Gen. Obasanjo's office, for the first ten years, had neither carpet nor air condition and his dress and bearing while on the farm made many people, who visited the farm mistake him for one of the chicken attendants.

He joined his labourers to off-load maize and other products into the warehouse. He ensured that there was no wastage of any kind and he kept himself strictly within the limits of best business practices. It is remarkable that the farmhouse, where he later transferred his office to also had nothing to suggest to any observer the Olympian height of a military commander and Head of State that he was coming from. There was not any kind of embellishment or decoration. His office was just a room sparsely furnished with a table and two hard wood visitor's chairs.

Many businesses are ruined because of the personal indiscipline of the proprietors. He once told me the story of a man in Abeokuta who, encouraged by what Gen. Obasanjo was doing, also went into poultry farming with a bank loan. As soon as he started to produce eggs and a reasonable income was coming from the sale of eggs, he went to his cashier every Saturday to withdraw money for weekend parties. The business folded up within five years.

In contrast, Gen. Obasanjo denied himself of all luxuries and the vestiges of the paraphernalia of a former Head of State, to nurture his farm. Expectedly, the result is a great success story. Let those, who are not doing well in their business examine themselves. They should learn modesty in their lifestyle and restraint in the use of their resources. In farming and other endeavours, there can be no success without sacrifice and self-discipline.

The story is told of the mid-eighties, when the Nigerian economy was experiencing a recession and the workers in Obasanjo Farms volunteered to reduce their salaries in order to avoid what looked like imminent retrenchment. They reasoned that since, as they all knew, the man (Gen. Obasanjo) had not diverted the proceeds from the farm to something else but ploughed everything back into the farm, they also should be ready to voluntarily make any necessary sacrifice in the interest of the farm. They were very happy to make the sacrifice and not too long from then, the farm emerged stronger from the national economic crisis.

The fourth principle is KNOWLEDGE. The quest of Gen. Obasanjo for knowledge is insatiable, particularly in respect of any undertaking he ventures into at any given time. We have seen it standing him in a good stead in his roles discussed earlier. He believes that knowledge is the foundation of any human undertaking. When a man fumbles in his enterprise, it is most probably because he lacks knowledge.

When Gen. Obasanjo decided on farming, he enrolled for a six-week course at the Institute of Agricultural Research and Training at Moor Plantation, Ibadan. The course was designed to expose participants to all aspects of arable crop and animal farming, including mechanical operation, storage and processing. This was to complement his preparation for his farming career. When he wanted to diversify into aquaculture, he proceeded to the University of Oklahoma for the relevant training. The courses turned out to be invaluable and irreplaceable.

Many people dabble into vocations and businesses, without the basic knowledge or the desire for it. The result is invariably a poor start that is characterised by trial and error that in turn engenders speedy failure or very slow progress. The acquisition of knowledge on the other hand, leads to the building of competences and confidence that assure success in any business venture. The decision of a former Head of State to return to school to seek formal preparatory knowledge for a second career, is a loud counsel to all of us, who are entering, or hoping to enter, a new career.

The fifth principle is HUMILITY. We have talked earlier about the proverbial humility of Gen. Obasanjo. It is no wonder that even in his second career, it remains one of the pillars of his success. It was humility that made him succumb to a formal agricultural training at Ibadan in spite of being a former Head of State. It was humility that made him 'relegate' himself to the humble lifestyle of a proper farmer. He was not ashamed that he dressed like a farmer. He was not ashamed that in matters relating to the conduct of his agricultural business, he was not accorded the proper recognition that he deserved as a former Head of State.

He was not ashamed to expose himself to all the vagaries of farm life. He was neither ashamed nor intimidated by media ridicule over his looks and bearing, while on the farm nor was he ashamed to work with labourers as a porter. He ate with his workers and performed guard duties with them. These are areas, where many have led their business enterprises to failure. In the case of Gen. Obasanjo, his humility and lack of pretence helped him to accept and practise the discipline required to grow a farming business. That made it possible for him to successfully wade through the turbulent waters of our business environment and take his business to an enviable height.

The sixth principle is LEADERSHIP. A significant part of military officer training is on leadership. On this important subject Gen. Obasanjo had this to say in an interview:

"There are many attributes that people bandy around but I regard eight as most essential. They are knowledge, vision, integrity, passion, courage, team management, discipline, communication and fear of God. Other attributes or qualities either emanate from or are variants of these eight essential imperatives. An organisation must be cohesive, motivated, focussed, confident, forward looking with a sense of mission and shared value. There must be an organisational culture and ethos."

Gen. Obasanjo, the proprietor, chairman and chief executive of Obasanjo Farms has and practises the right mix of the above principles in the management of the Farms. This, coupled with divine health and mental alertness, easily explains the phenomenal success of Obasanjo Farms. Today, Obasanjo Farms is the largest poultry farm in Africa and it is still growing and expanding.

Accomplished Democratically Elected President

Chapter Fourteen: A Divine Visitation

There is a beautiful story in the Biblical book of Luke as follows. Jesus Christ looked around Him and burst into tears. His disciples wondered what could move Him to tears. When they eventually asked Him, He told them that Jerusalem would, not too long from then, be destroyed and no amount of fasting and prayer could change the impending catastrophe. The disciples were further bewildered because they had believed that prayer and fasting could remit sins. Jesus Christ then told them that the coming calamity of Jerusalem was inexorable because the children of Israel spurned 'the visitation of God', that is, the providential opportunity to prevent the calamity. This prophecy of Jesus Christ was actually fulfilled in AD 70, about seventy years after the prophecy.

Christians, since then to this day, have learnt to watch out for the visitation of God in their lives to respond to it appropriately. However, while nobody in His right mind would spurn a God-sent opportunity, it just happens that the 'visitation of God' does not always manifest in a way that everybody would recognise it. Sometimes, it may be cloaked in pain or in a pleasant experience or even in an extraordinarily commonplace incident. Since we never pray for pain, we most often do all we can to avoid pain, even when God intends it to be the door that would lead us to our breakthrough. On the other hand, if it is a pleasant experience, we most often enjoy the good contained therein and ignore the underlying divine message. If it is a commonplace event, we also most often disregard it as one of those things because we are always looking for the stupendous and the dramatic. We therefore need a discerning spirit to recognise and understand God's strategic moves in our lives and in our time and know the expected response.

Job is another notable character in the Bible, whose story starts with a prologue that explains the impending terrible suffering that awaited him. We, who read the story today, are like an audience seated in a theatre to watch a drama. We have the privilege, which Job did not have, to preview the drama from the prologue. We therefore know that Job was not in any way causally responsible for the deluge of suffering that satan was about to unleash upon him.

When Job began to experience satan's victimisation, he naturally saw it as an undeserved suffering because he did not watch the prologue. He was therefore at great pains to accept the sufferings coming upon him. Had he known what we know now; that is, had he known that he was only being called to confirm God's excellent assessment of him, the story would have ended much earlier than it did. Job would have even taunted satan to send more afflictions and his uninformed friends too would not have had the opportunity of their unprofitable pontificating.

The practical application of these biblical stories is the unseen hand of God that works in our situations and our own corresponding natural tendency to rise up in absolute ignorance against what God is doing. Our God remains the same yesterday, today and forever! He sometimes takes us through a very difficult terrain to settle us down in the end at His predetermined happy goal.

Gen. Obasanjo too began his own journey through such difficult terrain, when he woke up one morning far away in Copenhagen, Denmark to the beginning of a visitation of God. However, like most mortals in similar situation, he did not immediately know it. He however got it right by sheer 'blunder'. On the morning in question, Gen. Obasanjo woke up to privileged information that he was on the death list of Gen. Sanni Abacha, the worst ruler that Nigeria has ever produced. He was therefore advised to stay away and avoid going back to Nigeria.

He was amused because he never imagined that Abacha would do such a thing, when he had not committed any offence either against the State or against the person of Abacha. He rejected the offer of a political asylum from a friendly country, the USA and defiantly went ahead with his plan to return home but a day earlier, by cancelling a scheduled visit to France. Needless to say, he thus exposed himself to the deadly fangs of Abacha.

He had gone to Copenhagen in Denmark as a UNDP ambassador for a United Nations conference. Though a successful warrior earlier in life, he had by this time long retired from the art of war. He had become used to peace and non-violence and the benefits of living in peace and harmony with everybody that came his way. He was not foolhardy but as if he watched the Heavenly Executive Council meeting of the Most High, he refused to stay back in Copenhagen, Denmark. He committed himself into the hand of God and walked like a man into the waiting hands of death wearing the body of Abacha.

Then, right at the airport on his arrival in Nigeria, was the ordeal that started, like an executive joke, with the seizure of his passport. What followed a day later was an arrest under the most ridiculous pretext that he was being invited by the Assistant Inspector General of Police (AIG) to advise the AIG. What followed again was an accusation that he was plotting a coup against Abacha. His detention, which was also punctuated with humiliating interrogation sessions, ended in a kangaroo trial. The outcome was a sentence, first to life imprisonment and then, after series of high profile interventions and pleas from different parts of the globe the sentence was commuted to fifteen years imprisonment.

Abacha actually intended to eliminate Gen. Obasanjo in prison. He was therefore marked down for the worst kind of inhuman treatment that was preceded by a spell of total isolation. The condition in Nigerian prisons is among the most primitive in the world but apart from that, to descend from the position of former Head of State to that of prisoner and for no legal or moral reason, was sufficiently devastating. Why would God allow this?

There was a Heavenly Executive Council meeting of the Trinity but Obasanjo was not present at that meeting and so could not answer the question 'why?'. What if he died in the incarceration? Only a person present at the Heavenly meeting too could answer that question. Obasanjo was not there and no mortal was there. Thus Gen. Obasanjo found himself face to face with a divine visitation; not in the way that it came to Abraham but in the manner that it came to Job.

The incarceration of Gen. Obasanjo along with some other illustrious Nigerians sent an ominous signal to a disoriented national populace and a bewildered world. Appeals to Abacha mounted from the international community on behalf of the convicted so called coup plotters; particularly Gen. Obasanjo and his former Deputy,

Shehu Yar'Adua but Abacha was not moved. Appeals also came from the UN Secretary General, Helmut Schmidt of Germany, former US President Jimmy Carter, Andrew Young and various American organisations, including the Carter Centre, the Council of Foreign Relations, the Carnegie Commission, International Peace Academy and many others. South African President, Nelson Mandela sent Archbishop Desmond Tutu to appeal to Abacha while Pope John Paul, Germany, the USA, Canada, the United Kingdom, Brazil, India, the Organisation of African Unity, Presidents Museveni of Uganda and Mugabe of Zimbabwe sent delegations to Abacha. Australia, and Mexico also appealed to Abacha for clemency. In all, Abacha received over 70 letters of appeal, including a handwritten one from Mrs. Benazir Bhutto, the then Prime Minister of Pakistan, but all to no avail except the token commutation of the sentences to twenty-five years imprisonment for Yar'Adua and fifteen years for Obasanjo.

Then, the nation woke up one morning to the news of the death of Maj.-Gen. Shehu Yar'Adua in Abakaliki prison. About the same time, Chief Alfred Rewane was assassinated, Kudirat Abiola, the wife of the incarcerated M.K.O. Abiola, was also murdered in broad daylight and nobody was in doubt that the death and murders all came by the hands of Abacha's killer squad. Mr. Alex Ibru narrowly escaped death in a way that pointed to the members of the same Abacha killer squad as the perpetrators. It then became clear that the commutation of sentences of Obasanjo and the other convicted phantom coup plotters was mere window dressing. In the light of the bizarre circumstances surrounding the death of Yar'Adua and the incidences of assassination and attempted assassination of various political activists and outspoken individuals, it was very clear that Abacha had not given up his original plan to physically eliminate his perceived enemies; among whom Obasanjo was the chief.

There was widespread fear for the safety of Gen. Obasanjo's life. He too was, more than anybody else, aware of the danger to his life. He committed his life into God's hand and most probably by God's direct leading, stayed away from food from the prison, to avoid poisoning. He cooked his own food, which he initially purchased with his own money. He refused to accept medical examination or treatment from official prison doctors or doctors from Abuja and insisted on a doctor from the General Hospital. As if by divine arrangement, the doctor that came from the General Hospital turned out to be a young man from Oke-Ogun in Oyo State, who was more interested in building an unblemished medical career than in any other thing.

Dr. Olusegun Ajuwon took up the management of Gen. Obasanjo's health in a very professional manner. This could work only for some time and from all indications, Abacha was not relenting. When a doctor was sent from Abuja to Yola prison to poison Obasanjo by injection under the pretext of taking his blood sample, Dr. Ajuwon was there with his own needle and syringe to take blood sample without allowing the Abuja doctor to touch Obasanjo. Happily, God preserved the life of Gen. Obasanjo. Hitherto had the machinations of Abacha to eliminate Obsanjo failed, and all of a sudden, Abacha died in his sleep.

The death of Abacha produced a new military government headed by Gen. Abdulsalami Abubakar, who tried to dismantle the evil machinery that Abacha had installed. He reversed some of the evils that the latter had perpetrated in so far as such evils were reversible. He released all political prisoners, including Gen. Obasanjo and other convicts of the phantom coup. Within a short while, Abdulsalami Abubakar set in motion a transition programme that turned out to be credible, as it culminated in the installation of a democratically elected government.

Figure 14 - Obasanjo, a Civilian President

Chapter Fifteen: Obasanjo Again

One night in 1979, when the handover of the reins of government to civilians was well in view, two strange middle-aged men knocked the door of my house at about 12 mid-night. I opened the door and I knew by their dress that they were members of the Celestial Church of Christ. They claimed to be emissaries with a very important message for the Head of State, Gen. Obasanjo. When I told them that it was impossible to see the Head of State at that hour, they persuaded me to follow them to the person, who sent them. I went with them against my wife's advice.

They led me to the Headquarters of the Celestial Church of Christ at Makoko, Yaba to see their supreme boss, Rev. Oschoffa. There, the man of God told me:

"There will in future be in the country some trouble that will involve Gen. Obasanjo and after the trouble, they will beg him to be Head of State again."

He then bade me good night. When I was already in a safe distance from the place, I started laughing alone in my car. Nothing, I thought at the time, could be more preposterous because I knew Gen. Obasanjo's mind about the political office he held at that time. When I told him later in the morning what happened the previous night, he not only laughed but also remarked:

"You, and the person who told you that, are both sick."

Both of us forgot everything about it almost instantly.

In all the build-up to the imprisonment of Gen. Obasanjo, up till his release, neither of us remembered the incident narrated above; let alone draw a linkage. The thing that was paramount in his heart after his release was his welfare. Then he thought of his family and all those within and outside Nigeria that had joined in the call for his release from prison. Lastly, he thought about his farm, into which he had put so much effort and resources. There were many things in these areas yearning for his attention and all of them required ample time and resources. The countries and the organisations that cried for his release from Abacha's prison spread across the entire globe. The appropriate thing to do was to visit them all, thank them and appeal to them to sustain their interest in the peace, stability and progress of Nigeria.

Beyond this, his thoughts about Nigeria were of pity and prayerful wish that God would help her. He did not read any prophetic meaning to the dream he had in prison, where he found himself in a palace. He did not see it more than a figment of his wild imagination as he said to himself: "I am not from a royal family, so what am I doing in a palace?" Gen. Obasanjo therefore did not see, let alone covet and prepare, for any role in party politics, the acceptable machinery throughout the world today for political change.

Much as he knew that Nigeria needed change, he did not foresee any role for himself in bringing about such change. He appraised the state of his farm and began arrangements for a thank-you-tour to the countries, organisations and individuals that stood by him during his dark days. Unknown to him however, the decision taken by the Heavenly Executive Council about him at the beginning of his travails in the hand of Abacha was different from his private calculations. He did not know that the time was then ripe for God to plainly interpret to him His visitation that spanned the previous three and half years, which was accurately predicted by Rev. Oschoffa about two decades earlier.

Sanni Abacha became Nigeria's military Head of State as part of the unfortunate consequences of the annulment of 12 June 1993 Presidential elections, a grave and indelible error of the Babangida administration. By the time Gen. Obasanjo was released from prison, Chief M. K. O. Abiola, who was acclaimed to have won 12 June 1993 elections, was still in State detention. This was under the pretext that he dared to declare himself the President on the basis of the released results of the annulled 12 June elections. Abdulsalami Abubakar, who succeeded Abacha as the military Head of State was desperately looking for ways to resolve the political logjam created by the annulment and the consequent incarceration of Chief Abiola. While Adulsalami was busy looking for the way out, Chief Abiola suddenly died in detention.

Abdulsalami, fearing the unhealthy insinuation and interpretation that a significant section of the public, particularly the Yoruba, might give to the sudden death of Abiola, ordered an autopsy by Canadian experts, in which Chief Abiola's personal physician was to participate. Notwithstanding the effort of Abdulsalami to prove that there was no official foul play in Chief Abiola's death, it was widely perceived by the Yoruba to be a conspiracy between the military and the Northern political class. The North that had actually had far more opportunities than any other group to rule the country was now seen as decidedly unwilling to allow other groups, especially the Yoruba, to occupy that exalted position. The Southern political elite too had responded by coalescing into an underground political opposition group named National Democratic Coalition (NADECO).

This group used its resources and leverages to chorus, popularise and aggravate, within and outside the country, widespread disaffection against the Interim National Government led by Ernest Shonekan and the government of Abacha that supplanted it. On his part, Abacha countered with spates of detention and assassinations. This was an ominous development for the country because it painted an unmistakable picture of a nation on the fast lane to political anarchy and ultimate disintegration.

The only way out then was to use the opportunity created by the death of Abacha to develop a political programme that would correct the anti-Yoruba perception widely and tenaciously held among the Yoruba. When taken from the unwarranted annulment of the 1993 elections that would have produced a Yoruba President for the first time, to the morbidly anti-Yoruba stance of the Abacha regime, one can see how this perception was fast becoming a political ideology and a rational basis for another internal belligerent confrontation.

This anti-Yoruba politics was so glaring that even the North, hitherto seen as unwilling to allow other tribes outside the Hausa-Fulani to be President, also adopted this perception. The North then not only became conciliatory but the Northern political leadership also in the interest of the peace and unity of the nation actively called for the emergence of a Southerner, particularly, a Yoruba as the civilian President. There could be no better opportunity to make this happen than the political programme being put together by Abdulsalami Abubakar. Achieving this consensus was only one hurdle; the other was that it must go through the democratic process. In other words, the southerner or the Yoruba candidate must be the choice of a political party and he must go through the process of elections.

Furthermore, the military had ruled the country for an uninterrupted period of fifteen years that witnessed a cumulative culpable mismanagement of the affairs of the nation. If the transition being considered at this stage inadvertently produced a government that did not harbour sympathy for the military, it might provoke the military into a defensive reaction in the form of yet another coup. If that was allowed to happen, it would certainly spell doom for the growth of democracy and most probably turn the country to a praetorian State. This was a genuine fear because the Nigerian military had tasted political power without due accountability for so long that it might be difficult to contain them in the barracks. Any little incident could serve as a pretext for the military to seize power again. That was not all.

In addition to a government sympathetic to the military, there was also a desperate need for a government that would correct the ills of the past and set the nation on the path of political rebirth, social reorientation and economic revitalisation. Therefore, it was not just any Southerner or Yoruba that was desired to lead the country at that stage but one, who had a proven track record of industry, courage, probity and commitment to the unity of Nigeria.

Moreover, Nigeria had become a shadow of herself in the comity of nations. The government of Abacha, by its reckless and desperate dictatorship, had alienated the international community and Nigeria had become a pariah State. The only active link that Nigeria had with the rest of the civilised world was its oil. In fact, Nelson Mandela at one time advocated the boycott of Nigeria's oil. With the death of Abacha, Nigeria needed a new leader that would restore the dignity and respect that Nigeria used to have among the nations of the world. The track record of moral integrity, detribalised outlook, probity and international respect, as well as global admiration for Gen. Obasanjo fitted him perfectly into this laid out mould. The problem here again was that nobody was sure if he would be interested.

On his part, Gen. Obasanjo needed time to put behind him the horrifying and dehumanising experience of the previous over three years, renew his presence in his business ventures and continue his private local and international roles, as it was before his imprisonment. Party politics was not one of the areas, where he expected any role during this period of his life. He had also forgotten completely Rev. Oschoffa's 1979 prophecy. However, opinions soon started to filter around that he could yet offer quite a lot to his fatherland, which he had contributed so much to build and about which he was still very passionate.

Such suggestive voices did not pass by Gen. Obasanjo unheard but he never stretched his hearing to the point of thinking that he could ever seek elective office. He jokingly told a friend, who was trying to talk him into it that he had reached the highest peak in the ladder of achievement and had also descended to the lowest level of adversity and so did not see anything again between the two extremes worthy of his pursuit. Former President Babangida was one of those, who paid him congratulatory visit, when he was released from prison. Just at the point that Gen. Babangida opened the door of his car to go away at the end of the visit, he turned to his host and briskly hinted that the country might still need him. It did not go beyond that.

Not long after, his friend and senior contemporary at the Baptist Boys High School, Abeokuta, now Late Mr. S. M. Afolabi and Mrs. Titi Ajanaku, paid him a visit and spoke along the line that his country needed him. From this moment, the appeal became more direct and took the form of a deliberate invitation to Gen. Obasanjo to come into politics. They all expressed belief that he was the only one at the time, who could lead the country out of its lingering and debilitating state of failure. Mr. Martins Kuye soon joined, when he led a delegation called the New Era to invite Gen. Obasanjo into politics for the same reason. Then came Alhaji Lawal Kaita and Alhaji Atiku Abubakar, leading a delegation that was so far the largest to Ota farm, also to invite Gen. Obasanjo into politics to salvage Nigeria from obvious socio-economic decadence and precipitous political drift.

To crown it all, friends of Nigeria abroad, who were genuinely concerned about her, such as former President of the United States of America, Jimmy Carter, Andrew Young, the President of South Africa, Nelson Mandela, Bishop Desmond Tutu and more, also approached Gen. Obasanjo and tried to convince him to accept to run for the office of the President of Nigeria. He knew the gravity of the Nigerian situation and being very passionate about Nigeria, he just could not dismiss all the pleas. He therefore started prayerfully to ponder and consider the pleas.

He was, while this was going on, reading his Bible one day as he had become used to doing from his prison days. He found himself reading the story of Mordecai and Esther in the book of Esther. He was stirred by the question posed to Esther by Mordecai:

"...and who knoweth whether thou art come to the kingdom for such a time as this?"

This passage gave him a strong illumination as he now remembered where he was coming from. He remembered that he was, along with late Gen. Shehu Yar'Adua and Late Chief M. K. O. Abiola marked down by Abacha for elimination in prison. He knew that he did not escape death, while the other two died because of any superior personal merit on his part; it was entirely God's doing. He then threw the same question that Mordecai asked Esther to himself:

"Who knows if God spared my life just for a time like this?"

This was when he started to give positive consideration to the pleas.

The prolonged prodding and persuasion that stirred Gen. Obasanjo into accepting to join party politics and contest the Presidential elections did not for that reason make his road to the office of President easy. He first asked himself whether he would do a good job if he got elected. He was absolutely sure that he would do a very good job. Then he considered the possibility of failure at the polls and how he would manage it if it actually so happened. This he easily dismissed as he recalled his failed bid for the position of Secretary General of the United Nations. Besides, he said to himself that he had served time in prison and nothing else could be worse than that. Since he was released from prison, he had started to put it behind. Gen. Obasanjo therefore concluded that the fear of failure should not be allowed to undermine the purpose of God upon one's life. Thus, he did not allow the fear of failure to discourage him.

The next challenge he had to contend with was the Yoruba. Politics among the Yoruba at this time was still carried out under the shadow of the Late Chief Obafemi Awolowo who, while alive, deservedly had an overwhelming number of followers among the Yoruba elite and masses. This popular following of Chief Awolowo, which he actually worked for, was also boosted by the rumour popular among the Yoruba in the pre-1966 ethnic politics of Nigeria. The rumour was that the goal of a Federal dispensation headed by an Hausa-Fulani was to enslave the Yoruba and that it was Awolowo, who made this impossible. Once this mind-set was firmly created in the Yoruba populace, it became impossible to have other channels of leadership recruitment among the Yoruba. Late Chief S. L. Akintola, who favoured cooperation with the Tafawa Balewa-led Federal Government, was branded a traitor and a villain. Up till today, Akintola is remembered among some Yoruba as a traitor, who attempted to sell the Yoruba, his people, to the Hausa.

Chief Awolowo's later followers would just not let go of this absurdity because it was the only thing that could sustain their political leadership of the Yoruba. It was the only guaranteed passport to electoral success among the Yoruba. They therefore consciously created around Chief Awolowo's name a neo-mystical aura, which they used cheaply for a consistent political hold on the Yoruba. Chief Awolowo therefore continued even in death to be the nous controlling Yoruba politics and the pivot around which political activities among the Yoruba revolved.

The picture of Chief Awolowo as the one, who stood against the enslavement of the Yoruba by the Hausa-Fulani, his excellent performance as Premier of Western Nigeria, his reliance on radical young university intellectuals and his hard work, all combined to promote the belief among the Yoruba that he was the most competent person to rule Nigeria. While they might be free to think so and even right in thinking so, democracy is unfortunately not defined by competence but by numbers. In fact, one of the academic objections to the concept of democracy is the low quality of leaders it sometimes throws up. Leadership recruitment in a democracy is by election not by innate or acquired competence. In spite of the acclaimed performance of Winston Churchill in World War II, he lost the 1945 General Elections that followed the war. It is however not out of place to warn at the same time that a people, who lack a leadership recruitment system that produces the best among them as leaders, must also brace up for oppression and persistent underdevelopment, which are inexorable consequences of poor leadership.

In 1979, Chief Awolowo contested the Presidential elections but lost, trailing behind Shehu Shagari, who won the elections. However, Chief Awolowo and his supporters argued in part that the Federal Electoral Commission (FEDECO) should not have accepted the mathematical interpretation of the required 122/3 of nineteen States of the Federation volunteered by Chief Richard Akinjide. This interpretation made recourse to Electoral College unnecessary; whereas, Chief Awolowo and his supporters nurtured high hopes that the Electoral College would certainly turn the table in favour of Chief Awolowo. When FEDECO declared Shehu Shagari the winner on the basis of the interpretation of 122/3 by Chief Akinjide, Chief Awolowo went to court but the Supreme Court dismissed his application and upheld the election of Shehu Shagari.

Most unfortunately, the supporters of Chief Awolowo not only rejected the verdict of the Supreme Court, they also held Gen. Obasanjo personally responsible for Chief Awolowo's electoral failure and dubbed Gen. Obasanjo an enemy of Chief Awolowo. In the circumstance briefly described above, an enemy of Chief Awolowo was automatically an enemy of the entire Yoruba people.

The surviving supporters of Chief Awolowo are very influential and powerful. This is largely because they belong, by virtue of their education, to the articulate section of the society and also hold the commanding height of the economy and the media. They therefore have connections across the numerous classes of the Yoruba society. These easily give them an edge as public opinion moulders. Armed with these advantages, they saw Gen. Obasanjo's candidature in the presidential race at this time, as an opportunity to have it back on him. As soon as they learnt that he was a likely candidate in the presidential elections, they too rolled out in full force their machinery of hate against him.

Gen. Obasanjo was not caught unawares; in fact, he would have been very surprised if this group of people did otherwise. He ignored them and faced the opposition within his party, which was more critical. He had contesting the Party's nomination with him, political heavy weights; such as Dr. Alex Ekwueme, a former Vice President of Nigeria, when Alhaji Shehu Shagari was President. He was also a founding member of the Peoples Democratic Party and a man of no mean means. Also contesting against Obasanjo was Alhaji Abubakar Rimi, a former Governor of

Kano State and a neo-radical politician of the Late Aminu Kano political extraction. He was also a founding member of the Peoples Democratic Party. He was only at the eleventh hour persuaded to withdraw from the primaries by Chief Solomon Lar, the Chairman of the Peoples Democratic Party (PDP) then. Gen. Obasanjo, who had no political structure merely adopted the PDP and all its political machinery. In his characteristic manner, he threw himself into the challenge and emerged the winner of the Party ticket at the Party primaries conducted in Jos in 1998.

With this success, there was no turning back again. He assembled a team made up of the young, the middle aged and the elderly, who had something to offer. Among his team were seasoned politicians, academicians, experienced former civil servants and intelligent and vibrant young men that were full of energy and creativity. He then went round to mend fences with all the members of his party, who felt aggrieved as a result of his victory at the primaries. This was a novelty in Nigerian politics, where until Gen. Obasanjo came in, it was a winner-takes-all approach. The reconciliatory steps taken by Gen. Obasanjo assuaged the disappointment of a good number of those who felt unhappy. It provided hope of inclusion in the imminent Obasanjo dispensation.

Once he became the party flag bearer, he went into action. The impression created by some people that Gen. Obasanjo's 1999 electoral victory was due to the might of retired Army Generals could only be false because his campaigns were not carried out at night or in any kind of secrecy. He was seen by everybody, including the media that accorded due publicity to the campaigns, criss-crossing the entire country, meeting various interest groups and individuals and addressing rallies everywhere he visited. In addition, Gen. Obasanjo's party, the PDP was undoubtedly at that time the most electorally promising party of all the registered political parties in that it was a coalition of three dynamic and popular national political movements.

The first was the conservative movement represented by the likes of Dr. Alex Ekwueme, Alhaji Lawal Kaita, Chief Sunday Awoniyi and others. The second group was made up of the so-called progressives of the Second Republic, such as Alhaji Abubakar Rimi, Prof. Jerry Gana, Amb. Fidelis Tapgun, Dr. Iyorcha Ayu, Chief Jim Nwobodo, Chief Solomon Lar and others. The third was made up of the political group of Late Maj.-Gen. Shehu Yar'Adua, which had in it maverick politicians such as Alhaji Atiku Abubakar, Late Dr. Chuba Okadigbo, Chief Tony Anenih, Late Chief Sunday Afolabi, Amb. Yahaya Kwande, Senator Jibril Martins-Kuye, Dr. Segun Agagu, Alhaji Adamu

Ciroma and such others. The three movements together had a large political followership that spread across the entire country.

When the elections finally came, Gen. Obasanjo failed to secure winning votes in Yoruba land but he had an overall victory. The result of the election in Yoruba land did not come as a surprise to anybody in view of the sustained campaign of calumny against Obasanjo by the propaganda machinery of the Alliance for Democracy. The Alliance for Democracy was defeated in the elections. It won only six out of the thirty-six States of the Federation and all in the predominantly Yoruba Southwest zone. APP won nine States, while PDP won twenty-one States.

Notwithstanding their hostility to Gen. Obasanjo, the Afenifere arranged a meeting with him after he had won the Presidential elections. Gen. Obasanjo attended the meeting in the hope that it might offer an opportunity for a healthy rapprochement between them to bring all hands on deck in the task of nation building. He was however shocked stiff, when the agenda turned out to be what was in the Presidency for the Yoruba. This was tantamount to sharing the nation at night by a group of Yoruba leaders. Gen. Obasanjo felt disappointed but fortunately, the meeting was aborted before any discussion started because Chief Olu Falae was not present. The Afenifere however did not ask for another meeting with him throughout his two-term tenure as President of the Federal Republic of Nigeria.

In any case, it is Obasanjo again! Within one year, God in His mercy and sovereign wisdom led Gen. Obasanjo from the doldrums of the prison to the warmth and vibrancy of the State House, the highest office in the land. There he would direct the affairs of this great nation, as her elected President for the following eight years of two four-year terms. How great is our God!

The Nigerian Constitution provides for a four-year tenure for an elected Nigerian President but he can seek re-election at the end of the four years for another and final four-year tenure. Chief Obasanjo took advantage of this constitutional provision to seek re-election at the end of the first four years. He based his desire for re-election on the opportunity that would be created for consolidation and improvement on the gains of the previous four years. The achievements of Chief Obasanjo were so much that many people expected his re-nomination by his party for the second four-year term to be a matter of course. It however turned out to be another tug-of-war as opposition arose, one after the other, to challenge his re-nomination.

The Arewa Consultative Forum came up with an imaginary Agreement signed by Chief Obasanjo earlier in 1998 to hold office for only one four-year term and bow out for somebody else from the North. This occupied the pages of Nigerian newspapers for a considerable length of time until, at the appropriate time, Obasanjo made public a draft Agreement actually drawn for all Southern aspirants by some Northern elements. The proposal was for a Southern President, who would be just a figurehead while the Vice President, who would be from the North, would be the de facto executive President. Expectedly, Obasanjo refused to sign such an Agreement.

When the truth about the imaginary Agreement was finally known, it pulled the carpet off the feet of those expecting to use it against the re-nomination of Chief Obasanjo. The clamour about the fictitious Agreement portrayed the North as a greedy, hegemonic bloc bent on perpetuating a Northern political domination of the country. This Northern ploy therefore, rather than obstruct the re-nomination of Chief Obasanjo for a second term, enhanced its chances.

The failure of this ploy however did not quite silence his opponents, who made many more spirited efforts to thwart his re-nomination. A group joined the fray with a strong clamour for an Igbo presidency after the first four-year term of Obasanjo presidency. This did not go far as the North would, at that time, rather retain Obasanjo as President of Nigeria than have an Igbo President. This was part of the undying, silent under-current of Nigerian politics that had its roots in the Nigerian civil war. When this ploy also failed, the House of Representatives, under the leadership of Umar Ghali Na'Abbah, a man who hated Chief Obasanjo for his courageous and frequent criticism of the profligacy of the National Assembly, came up with a call on Chief Obasanjo to resign or face impeachment on grounds of nebulous and ill articulated constitutional offences.

Chief Obasanjo initially called it a joke because there was no cause for it. The oddity of the impeachment move by the House of Representatives was borne out, not only by Obasanjo's consistent good performance but also by the fact that the champions of the impeachment cause were members of the ruling Peoples' Democratic Party, the President's party. It was part of a spirited effort by the enemies of Obasanjo to edge him out before the expiration of his first term, apparently to offer his Deputy a fast track ascent to the Presidency.

Their first step towards achieving this fast track approach was the orchestrated campaign for the adoption of the Mandela model of one term, notwithstanding the difference between the Mandela and Obasanjo situations. The truth however is that Mandela chose one term in consideration of his age. By the time he completed his first term in office, he would be over 80 years old. The enemies of Obasanjo seemed to have a number of well-designed options to achieve their aim. Immediately after the failure of the Mandela model, Ghali Na'Abba, the then Speaker of the House of Representatives was cued to begin impeachment process against Obasanjo in the House of Representatives. This again failed woefully.

These clandestine anti-Obasanjo political manoeuvres were carried into the primaries of 2003. In an interview on the eve of the primaries, Atiku Abubakar, the Vive-President told the BBC that he was not yet sure for whom he would vote. In the meantime, he had entered into an understanding with Dr. Alex Ekwueme to vote for him in the primaries and avail him also of the votes of the Governors supposedly supporting him. The reward for Atiku was that he would run with Dr. Ekwueme but the latter would spend two and half years of his term in office and then hand over to the former, Alhaji Atiku. It is interesting that in spite of the enormous efforts of the enemies of Obasanjo to frustrate his renomination, they ended up unwittingly enhancing his chances.

Chief Obasanjo responded to the unfavourable build-up to the 2003 PDP primaries with brilliant manoeuvres and political ebullience. He also did not take anything for granted as he launched into the campaign with all his energy. He moved from one camp of delegates from one geo-political zone to the other, starting from NICON NOGA Hotel Assembly of South-West delegates and ending at the Protea Hotel Assembly of North-West delegates. The primary election was transparently conducted at the Eagle Square, Abuja under the close watch of the contenders, Dr. Alex Ekwueme, Alhaji Abubakar Rimi, Chief Barnabas Gemade and the incumbent President, Chief Olusegun Obasanjo. The outcome was a resounding victory for Obasanjo.

After winning the nomination of his party, he again made strenuous efforts to reconcile with those, who were aggrieved. He retained Alhaji Abubakar as his running mate and invited the others to join him in the ongoing rebuilding of the nation through the PDP. With the PDP house put in order, and the achievements of the previous years speaking eloquently and clearly for him, Chief Obasanjo began a nation-wide campaign that ended with 73 presidential rallies across the entire country. The Obasanjo campaigns constituted a feat that was not equalled by all the other political parties put together. The result was also an unequalled success in the actual elections. Chief Obasanjo won majority votes in 32 of the 36 States of the Federation and polled over 24 million votes nationwide, beating his rival candidate of the ANPP by almost 100 per cent margin.

Chapter Sixteen: Obasanjo The Elected President, 1999 - 2007

The country presented on 1 October 1999 to Gen. Obasanjo to rule for four years in the first instance was a world apart from, what as a military Head of State he handed over on 1 October 1979 to Alhaji Shehu Shagari, who won the preceding Presidential elections then. Nigeria was in 1999 very far from anything near the country of the citizens' dream. She had lost her leadership position as an emerging political and socio-economic giant of Africa. She had instead become notorious for persistent leadership failure and bad governance.

These ills manifested in official corruption, collapsed infrastructures, insecurity of life and property and frequent shortage of essential commodities; such as oil, notwithstanding that Nigeria was the world's sixth largest producer of oil. Nigeria had in addition become a pariah state, dealt with peripherally, as she took the back seat in the comity of nations. The ship of the nation was gradually sinking, while the polity, adrift under a purposeless military leadership, reeled in a paroxysm of despair and cynicism.

The election of Chief Obasanjo was therefore for him not an occasion for flamboyant rejoicing. It was instead an occasion for renewal and reactivation of all the goodwill he had and could still muster for the benefit of Nigeria. His election restored hope and confidence in the minds of the friends of Nigeria and the entire international community. In the circumstance of Nigeria, Gen. Obasanjo did not wait to be sworn in before he took off on a goodwill visit to the friends of Nigeria. In Africa, he visited Ghana, Niger, Cameroon, Republic of Benin, Togo, Ivory Coast, Egypt, Kenya, Tanzania and Mozambique. In the African countries that he visited, he told his audience, most probably for the purpose of emphasis, that a new democratic dispensation would soon be installed in Nigeria and henceforth, Nigeria would play her expected role and occupy her rightful position in the comity of nations.

In Europe, he visited the United Kingdom, France, Germany and Italy. In the Americas, he visited the United States of America, Brazil, Cuba and Venezuela. In Asia, he visited India and China. Chief Olusegun Obasanjo told his hosts that current realities made it necessary for the advanced countries of the world to work together in an atmosphere of cooperation and mutual respect for global peace, stability and prosperity. He then said that this goal would be difficult to achieve if African countries were left with the huge debts they were carrying. He argued to convince his hosts that the developed countries of the world should not expect to be shielded from the spill over of any problem caused in Africa by extreme poverty and a crippling debt burden. He further urged his hosts in Europe to move away from the conservative paternalistic approach to Euro-African relations and embrace a new era of constructive engagement, genuine partnership, fair and equitable distribution of resources and division of labour, as well as joint participation in the global decision-making process.

On 29 May 1999, Chief Olusegun Obasanjo was sworn in as the first democratically elected President of Nigeria, the most populous African country, after a fifteen-year-long period of military rule. In his Inaugural Speech, Chief Obasanjo said among other things:

"Nigeria is wonderfully endowed by the Almighty with human and other resources. It does no credit either to us or the entire black race if we fail in managing our resources for quick improvement in the quality of life of our people. Instead of progress and development, which we are entitled to expect from those who govern us, we experienced in the last decade and a half and particularly in the last regime but one, persistent deterioration in the quality of our governance, leading to instability and weakening of all public institutions. Good men were shunned and kept away from government while those who

should be kept away were drawn near. Relations between men and women who had been friends for many decades and between communities that had lived together in peace for many generations became very bitter because of the actions or inaction of government. The citizens developed distrust in government, as promises made for the improvement of the conditions of the people were not kept and all statements by the government were viewed with cynicism.

"Government officials became progressively indifferent to propriety of conduct and showed little commitment to promoting the general welfare of the people and the public good. Government and all its agencies became thoroughly corrupt and reckless. Members of the public had to bribe their way through in Ministries and Parastatals to get attention and one government agency had to bribe another to obtain the release of their statutory allocation of funds.

"The impact of official corruption is so rampant and has earned Nigeria a very bad image at home and abroad. Besides, it has distorted and retrogressed development.

"Our infrastructure – NEPA, NITEL, Roads, Railways, Education, Housing and other social services – were allowed to decay and collapse. Our country has thus been through one of its darkest periods.

"All these have brought the nation to a state of chaos and despair. This is the challenge before us."

He concluded this part of the address by saying:

"On my part, I will give the forthright, purposeful, committed, honest and transparent leadership that the situation demands."

Chief Obasanjo, in this Inaugural speech, mentioned all the ills plaguing the Nigerian society at this time and promised to take steps, including making institutional arrangements, to combat them effectively. Such ills include corruption, which topped the list, restoration of confidence in Government, crime, political reconciliation, the Niger Delta problem and maintaining harmony among the three tiers of government. The speech also listed some priority areas that could not be denied due attention any longer. The priority areas included the problem of the oil producing areas, corruption, poor service delivery, agriculture and food security, the debt burden, poverty alleviation and many more. The President was not in any illusion about the unavoidable painful concomitants of the reform measures that had to be taken in order to turn the nation around.

The implementation of the Obasanjo's Reforms expectedly drew a bitter wedge between him and the Labour Unions, which incessantly called out their members on strike in protest against one policy reform or the other. This quite undermined the speed with which the reforms were intended to translate into tangible socio-economic benefits for the people. However, he remained undaunted and forged ahead as speedily as the system allowed.

The first step taken by the new President was to cooperate with his party, the Peoples Democratic Party for the assemblage of a good team. Although his personal input in this was minimal, he insisted on an inclusive cabinet. Chief Obasanjo believed that everybody and every segment of the society had been wounded by the misrule of the recent past and all capable hands, irrespective of political affiliation, should be invited to take part in the gigantic task of rebuilding the nation. In addition, he intended inclusiveness to heal old wounds and usher in an era of healthy and progressive politics. He therefore appointed into his government offspring of bitter political enemies, some of his own political opponents as well as the children of some of his known bitter opponents. Although he won well over sixty per cent of the votes cast in the Presidential elections, he brought into his government members of the Alliance for Democracy (AD) and the APP that lost in that election.

He recognised that the adulteration of the military with political power made the military a kind of sword of Damocles hanging over the nation's democratic rebirth.

The citizenry was also quite apprehensive that the addiction of the military to political power might prompt them again, on the flimsiest pretext, to seize power and so destroy the present hopes of democratic development. Then came Obasanjo with his masterstroke of the compulsory retirement of all military officers that had ever held political office. It was a very courageous political decision and a particularly effective guarantee against future coups, as it broke the backbone of intending praetors.

Then, the new President set up the Independent Corrupt Practices Commission (ICPC) as well as the Economic and Financial Crimes Commission (EFCC) to combat official corruption and all manners of economic and financial crimes. Strangely however, in spite of the public disapproval of corruption in our national life and its negative effects on socio-economic development, the Bills on the EFCC and the ICPC had a very cold reception in the National Assembly. The Bills were delayed unnecessarily and considerably whittled down, under the pretext of defending personal liberty. The Bills also did not, for inexplicable reasons, receive deserving support from the media and that made the National Assembly get away with their distortion of the provisions of the Bills.

Notwithstanding the legislative distortion of the Bills, President Obasanjo got the right people to implement the provisions of the Acts in the persons of Justice Akanbi for the ICPC and Nuhu Ribadu for the EFCC. The support that he gave to these two organs made possible the courageous arrests and trials of some hitherto untouchable public officers, such as the then Inspector General of Police, Ministers, Permanent Secretaries, Chief Executive Officers of parastatals, Directors and some members of the National Assembly.

In addition, large sums of money were recovered into the national treasury from convicted corrupt officials. It is on record that the Obasanjo administration recovered over $1.25 billion, £100 million sterling and N50 billion cash from the late Abacha's family alone. By the time Obasanjo left office, the Lawyer/Agent of the Federal Government reported an outstanding $1.0 billion yet to be recovered. It was expected that the succeeding regime of Umaru Yar'Adua would recover it. I however could not at the time of writing this book ascertain, whether or not, the money was eventually recovered by the Umaru Yar'Adua administration.

In order to further strengthen the anti-corruption policy of the administration, Obasanjo established the Budget Monitoring and Price Intelligence Unit. The Due Process Mechanism operated by this Unit was able to save for the Federal Government a total of over 160 billion naira between 1999 and 2006. He set up Anti-corruption and Transparency units in Federal Government Ministries and Agencies. In addition, President Obasanjo seized every opportunity he had to denounce corruption and to urge members of the public to act against corrupt practices by refusing to offer or conceal, bribes for any service.

President Obasanjo then turned his attention to the public service and the quality of service delivery by public servants and public institutions. The Nigerian public service was at the inception of the Obasanjo administration bedevilled by corruption, poor work ethics, wastage, low morale, low productivity, inefficiency, individual laxity and general indiscipline. It was clear that the type of civil service we had at this time could not deliver the desired quality of service to the people. Government Ministries, Departments and Agencies needed an orientation of selflessness, discipline, efficiency, hard work and a good understanding of the contractual relationship between the Government, which is the service provider and the public, which is made up of the consumers. This relationship demands from the civil/public servants adequate, affordable, and good quality service delivered at the right time in an efficient and courteous manner.

In order to achieve this level of service delivery in our public service, President Obasanjo in 2005 launched the

SERVICOM to implement and supervise a new orientation that would produce an enhanced quality of service delivery by Government Ministries, Departments and Agencies. When he launched this body in 2005, President Obasanjo described its goal thus:

"Henceforth, the large interest of the society must be the focus of government officials, rather than the current position where the officials deliberately create bottlenecks to force citizens to part with money for services."

The direct outcome of this was the setting up of a Service Delivery Unit (SDU) in every Ministry, Department and Agency to monitor the trend and quality of service delivery. As a corollary, every Ministry, Department and Agency was instructed to draw up a Mission Statement and Service Delivery Charter to provide guidance as to what is expected from each one. This was a novelty that was meant to, and could, positively change our civil/public service and if sustained, make it an agent of abundant life. Besides, with the Economic and Financial Crimes Commission, the Independent Corrupt Practices Commission, the Due Process Mechanism and the equally new Public Procurement Policy, working together effectively, a wind of change silently began to blow over our societal landscape for the attainment of public service effectiveness, probity and accountability.

Shortly after the inception of the new administration, all the communal ill feelings bottled up during the fifteen-year-span of military rule broke out in spates of sectarian and inter-community clashes across the entire country. In the north, there were violent clashes in Jos between the indigenous and the so-called settler communities. There were also violent clashes in Kano and Kaduna. In the east, there was a widespread violent abuse of discontent perpetrated by restive youths in the Niger Delta region and between the Umuleri and Aguleri communities. In the west, there was a protracted bloody clash between Ile-Ife and Modakeke. These clashes, put together were as destructive as they were diversionary. The Obasanjo administration employed civilised methods of conflict resolution, ranging from persuasion, through minimum force, to appropriate socio-political reforms, to contain the violence.

In the case of the Niger Delta, the intervention of Chief Obasanjo started during his campaign tour of that part of the country before he was elected President. In January 1998, he held a meeting with the people of the South-South Zone in Yenagoa, where there was visible evidence of neglect by successive preceding administrations. It was a very successful meeting as he obtained the commitment of the youths and their leaders to stop their violent confrontation that had led to a substantial loss of revenue to the nation. When he was eventually elected, Obasanjo kept his word. He increased the revenue allocation to that region from 3 to 13 per cent and followed that up with the establishment of the Niger Delta Development Commission. The Commission was meant to be a Regional Development Authority with resources from both the Federal Government and international oil companies, for the rapid infrastructural and socio-economic development of the region.

One of the hindrances to development in Nigeria and indeed in Africa is the debt burden. Nigeria's case was very bad, with debt servicing alone consuming over 40 per cent of the national budget. Obasanjo spent the first four years of his two-term dispensation canvassing for debt rescheduling or outright cancellation of existing debts. This involved him in several meetings with leaders of creditor nations, international financial institutions, the G8 and other leaders of the European Union, the United States of America and many others. He also worked in concert with other African leaders in order to present a common African front in the quest for the removal of the debt burden. Most of the times, favourable responses were received from these world leaders but at the bureaucratic level of implementation, they often met a stonewall.

He wondered, why the support that his efforts received at the political level of Heads of States could not break bureaucratic walls and produce practical success. The bureaucrats had every reason to be unsympathetic to the Nigerian plea for debt relief. Nigeria was the world's sixth largest exporter of crude oil, which provided a large revenue base that excluded Nigeria from classification as a poor nation. This was an undeniable fact and was the reason, why all the efforts of President Obasanjo to secure debt relief for Nigeria did not succeed.

However, the insight he had gained in the previous four years into the operations of the World Bank made him realise that the concurrence of the political leaders was just the prima facie qualification for debt relief. This was the easiest hurdle but the hard nut was satisfying the conditionality of the bureaucrats in the World Bank, IMF and the Paris Club. President Obasanjo, who was determined to secure debt relief for the country because of its negative impact on development, drew up a strategy that would make it possible for Nigeria to present an acceptable balance sheet to the creditors. He however had to wait until his second term in office to implement the strategy. His strategy was to assemble an economic team that included Dr. (Mrs.) Okonjo-Iweala, Mrs. Oby Ezekwezili, Mallam El Fufai and Prof. Chukwuma Soludo. These were seasoned and high-ranking bureaucrats and technocrats, some of who came from the World Bank. They understood and spoke World Bank language.

When the abundant political will of President Obasanjo was mixed with the expertise of his economic team, it was just a matter of time before he succeeded in obtaining a pardon of about $20 billion Paris Club debt for Nigeria. The success of President Obasanjo in getting debt relief for Nigeria was a landmark and the crowning success of his two-term administration. It gave him the last laugh over those, who had bitterly criticised his incessant foreign diplomatic travels. It also provided the nation with considerable and unusual opportunity to channel the larger bulk of her revenue to national development, particularly to areas bearing on the Millennium Development Goals (MDG).

Perhaps the most intractable socio-economic problem facing Nigeria at the inception of the Obasanjo administration was power. Between 1979 and May 1999, when Chief Obasanjo was inaugurated as President, a period of twenty years, the only investment in power generation and distribution was the completion by the Shagari administration in 1981 of Jebba and Shiroro hydro power plants and the Egbin Thermal Station. These projects were all incidentally started by the Obasanjo military administration. The successive military administrations between 1983 and 1999 thus bequeathed to the democratically elected Obasanjo administration a sixteen-year period of almost total neglect of the power sector. In addition to this was the deep-rooted, overpowering and suffocating corruption in the power sector, which significantly worsened the situation. All these explain why only 1,500MW was being generated for a population of about 150 million in 1999, when Obasanjo became President. It is instructive that at this time, South Africa, with a population of 45 million, was generating 40,000MW.

President Obasanjo tackled the power problem frontally with first, a change of leadership in National Electric Power Authority (NEPA). President Obasanjo brought in an accomplished engineer, Mr. Joe Makoju from the private sector to give NEPA the kind of leadership it needed to accomplish the generation, transmission and distribution of adequate electric power for socio-economic development. President Obasanjo's administration, thereafter shifted its attention to extensive repairs, replacement and maintenance, which started with Afam, where a new thermal unit of 276MW was installed and commissioned.

The Obasanjo administration also invited Oil Companies to participate in the generation of power, which they could also sell to NEPA. Agip responded positively by building at

Okpai a 480MW thermal unit with transmission to the grid system. President Obasanjo himself commissioned this project but unfortunately, there was no such commitment again from any other Oil Company. Notwithstanding the stalled cooperation of the Oil Companies, the Obasanjo administration embarked on the building of four other thermal units at Papalanto, Omotoso, Geregu and Alaoji. These sites were chosen for the projects because they were located in places, where existing gas pipelines were close enough for a reduced cost of gas provision to the locations. The Obasanjo administration had to find a way round budgetary constraints through a loan from China at a concessionary rate to execute these thermal projects. By 2007, when a new government was sworn in, three of the sites, Papalanto, Geregu and Omotosho had been built to commissioning stage.

The Obasanjo administration did not regard any method as sacrosanct. It spent a considerable time during its first and second terms in office to carry out a detailed study of alternative sources of power and energy. This was to identify which one could quickly provide solution to the nation's power problem. The administration went into a detailed study of solar, wind, tide, biomass and thermal from nuclear and hydro sources. The study revealed that the technology for the provision of energy from solar, tide and wind was still too rudimentary for power mass production. This would result in an excessively high unit cost that might defeat the intended ends of the entire project.

These alternatives might however be able to cater for smallholding and domestic needs. In order to encourage recourse to these alternative sources as a limited palliative in private homes and small-scale workplaces, the Obasanjo administration instituted a concessionary policy to make such domestic and smallholding installation and use possible. However, as far as Nigeria is concerned for large-scale power production, there does not for now seem to be any alternative to thermal from coal, gas and hydro.

In 1999, when President Obasanjo was inaugurated for his first term in office, the country could boast of only seven power stations: Kainji, Jebba, Shiroro, Egbin, Afam, Sapele and Delta. All of them were in varying stages of disrepair and obsolescence and they altogether generated only about 1500MW of electricity. The situation had radically improved by the time Obasanjo handed over to a new dispensation in 2007, with an addition, in a period of only eight years, of six new stations at Okpai in Delta (480MW) by Agip, Afam II (276MW), Omotosho (330MW), Papalanto (330MW), Geregu (414MW), Ikot-Abasi-Ibom

(145mw), to which the Federal Government is a partner, Alaoji (545MW); all totalling almost 2000MW.

Besides, the Rivers State Government was also able to produce 300MW and Omotosho, Geregu, Papalanto and Alaoji could each be expanded to produce 1000MW. In addition, the Obasanjo administration took transmission to Bayelsa State for the first time ever and also doubled the transmission from Shiroro to Abuja. The administration further awarded all the transmission contracts to close the transmission loop to ensure that no part of the country would again be thrown into darkness simply because there is a fault or sabotage in another part. Furthermore, the Obasanjo administration introduced the pre-paid metre system to reduce non-payment of bills and eliminate illegal connection. By 2007, when the eight-year dispensation of Olusegun Obasanjo came to an end, monthly revenue generation by the Power Holding Company had moved from about N2 billion to about N7billion.

The most topical symptom of the sick condition of Nigeria by the time Chief Obasanjo was sworn-in as the President of the country, was her pariah status in the comity of nations. Nigeria was a bundle of stench to the international community. Sanctions were heaped upon the country and Nigerians, everywhere were at the receiving end of the negative global perception about Nigeria. Nigerians travelling abroad were subjected to particularly humiliating treatment at airports across the world. Nigeria ceased to have any voice in international forums and its leadership role in Africa had become a thing to be remembered as part of the good old days gone by. Chief Obasanjo as an elected President had to start from the scratch to rebuild Nigeria's image. His knowledge, contact, global reach and experience in the international arena made him his own Foreign Minister; albeit supported by his Foreign Ministers, who projected his ideas and policies on the foreign scene.

President Obasanjo speedily turned the situation around by successfully reintegrating Nigeria into the international community. As a mark of the acceptance of Nigeria into the comity of nations, President Obasanjo was given rousing welcome in all the leading nations of the world that he visited. He in turn played host to many Heads of Government, who paid return visits to Nigeria. Nigeria regained confidence and her credibility was restored as a sub-regional and regional peacekeeper just because of Chief Obasanjo. In the circumstance, Nigeria once again assumed the principal role in the resolution of the crises in Sierra Leone, Cote d'Ivoire, Guinea Bissau, Guinea Conakry, Gambia, Ethiopia/Eritrea, Democratic Republic of Congo, Burundi, Western Sahara, Sudan, Zimbabwe, Liberia and Sao Tome and Principe.

President Obasanjo visited at neck-breaking speed the trouble spots in Africa and the world leaders that were agreeable to Nigeria's peacekeeping role in the region. He mobilised and joined other African leaders to create an environment that was favourable to peace building. Specifically, President Obasanjo facilitated the signing of a peace accord that produced a government of national unity in Liberia. In Sao Tome and Principe, he reversed a coup d'etat by arranging a settlement between the coup plotters and the embattled President.

The New Partnership for Africa's Development (NEPAD), which has become the most significant achievement of the African Union started as an expression of African Renaissance, shared and disseminated by Olusegun Obasanjo, Bouteflika of Algeria and Thabo Mbeki of South Africa. NEPAD is a strategy for achieving sustainable development and the eradication of poverty in Africa. Its significance is in the fact that new partnership with Africa would henceforth be on equal relationship between Africa on the one hand and the development partners and the international community on the other hand.

In 2000, President Obasanjo was elected the Chairman of the G77 plus China, a Group that started with 77 developing countries, with a mandate to present the problems of member nations of the Group before the G8 and the Breton

Woods Institutions. The climax of the successful efforts of President Obasanjo to restore Nigeria to her premiere status in the comity of nations was the readmission of Nigeria to the Commonwealth in 1999. This was crowned with the successful hosting of Commonwealth Heads of Government Meeting in Abuja in December 2003.

In the banking sector, the President first appointed Prof. Charles Soludo, a renowned Professor of Economics, as the Governor of the Central Bank, to implement the banking sector reform. The thrust of the reform was the consolidation of banking institutions through mergers and acquisitions and recapitalisation of shareholders' funds to a minimum of N25 billion. The goals of the reform were first, to create a healthy and secure banking system that would attract depositors' confidence. Second, to strengthen the banks to operate in a way that they would be able to guarantee higher returns to their shareholders. The third was to enable the banks mobilise local and international capital for investment development within our domestic economy. Prof. Soludo had this to say about the reform:

"It became necessary to take pre-emptive measures to avoid the cycle of boom and burst; it is now time to set up a structure that creates a strong base, relative to the kind of economy we are operating where banks become channels to do proper intermediation."

The reform programme was very successful although sadly, within a few years afterwards, the banks were overtaken by corruption. The Central Bank had to intervene again with another reform that saw some bank Chief Executives not only sacked but also made to face criminal prosecution and imprisonment.

The educational sector that happened to be one of the worst hit by the prolonged neglect of the years before 1999, experienced significant revival and recorded notable achievements during the Obasanjo dispensation. The administration introduced the Universal Basic Education (UBE) and the Open University programmes. This programme provided needed opportunity for the poor and those that are otherwise disadvantaged to receive education. The administration did not only encourage, but also actively sought, the participation of the private sector at all levels of the nation's educational development. The outcome is the expansion to which the large numbers of private primary, secondary and tertiary institutions springing up across the country are eloquent witnesses.

Besides, the Obasanjo administration also implemented the Virtual Library Project with the objective of electronically linking Nigeria's tertiary institutions with libraries and information resources in more advanced countries of the world. The education reform of the Obasanjo administration, which covered all areas of the sector, was intended to strengthen the sector to play its expected role in national development.

Another very important aspect of the economic policy of the Obasanjo administration was a private sector driven economy, with the State limiting itself to regulatory roles and the provision of a favourable environment for economic activities. The instrument for the implementation of this policy was privatisation through divestment of government interests from public commercial agencies known as parastatals and quasi-government organisations. While privatisation is a critical instrument of the economic reform agenda of the Obasanjo administration, it was also the only option for a government that was serious about ridding the country of corruption. Successive governments before the Obasanjo administration had pursued a course that was opposite and destructive to the intended role of the parastatals. The latter had inexorably become the bastion of official corruption and a gargantuan drainpipe, through which public funds corruptly flowed into private pockets, at the expense of national development.

The administrations of Nigeria between 1979 and 1998 grew increasingly more brazen in the economic emasculation of the parastatals. By the time Chief Olusegun Obasanjo took over as President, many of the parastatals had been liquidated, while those that remained existed only in name. They had long arrears of unpaid salaries and debts owed to their various clients and could not provide the services they were established to provide. Their pensioners were wallowing in abject poverty and their assets were wasting away as a result of unending disuse. The condition of the parastatals at the time in question was so pitiable that one wondered if the governments that allowed such stage of deterioration were made up of Nigerians. In the circumstance, the only option open to a serious government was privatisation. This was what Obasanjo did.

In spite of the well-known fact that our parastatals had become mere economic carcasses, the avowed undertakers of public institutions stoutly resisted Obasanjo's privatisation policy. They based their opposition on spurious arguments on the ill understood interplay of national security and public wellbeing. In spite of the spirited opposition of the enemies of privatisation, Chief Obasanjo went ahead to implement the privatisation programme. This was not because he enjoyed the controversy it engendered but because he would rather have a controversy in the interest of the nation than trample on the nation's interest in order to avoid a controversy.

At the end of his two-term tenure of eight consecutive years, Chief Obasanjo had successfully privatised 80 public enterprises with a gross proceed of N400 billion. Apart from the revenue that accrued from the privatisation exercise, it provided opportunity for the reform of key sectors of the national economy and also facilitated the resuscitation of the downstream sector of the nation's petroleum industry.

The country's cement industry was also revitalised. This led to a substantial reduction in the importation of cement, consequent job creation and the inflow of foreign investment. The divestment of the interests of the government from commercial banks stood the banks in a good stead for the consolidation of the banking sector. The privatisation exercise saved the country billions of naira, otherwise spent annually in subsidy to corrupt parastatals.

The Communications sector experienced a remarkable advancement during the administration of Chief Olusegun Obasanjo. It established the Nigeria Communications Commission with powers to regulate the telecommunication industry. The initiatives of the administration also saw subscriber levels for fixed lines rise from 473,316 lines in 1999 to 1,027,707 in September 2005, while mobile lines rose from 35,000 in 1999 to 16,078,817 during the same period. The administration further licensed four GSM Operators and a second national carrier.

There was also during this period a significant expansion of the nation's fibre optical transmission and NITEL's CDMA national rollout projects that phenomenally increased fixed wireless lines by about 1.5 million. Furthermore, access to telecommunications facilities such as Telephone, Fax and Internet was provided under the Obasanjo administration's Rural Telephone Programme for over 540 Local Government Headquarters. Direct Access Rural Telephony (DART) was also deployed to another 125 Local Government Headquarters. NIPOST too got a boost as it was repositioned to deliver mails to any part of the country within 72 hours, through the National Mail Route Network System. As a result of the dynamic telecommunications policy of the Obasanjo administration, over $10 billion worth of direct foreign investment was attracted into the telecommunication sector, making it second only to the Oil and Gas sector.

In agriculture, the Obasanjo administration enunciated policies and programmes as well as gave incentives that yielded an amazing 7 per cent annual growth rate in that sector. These included the National Agricultural Policy, the National Rural Development Policy and National Cooperative Policy. In addition, the administration revitalised the National Strategic Grains Reserve and established the Nigeria Agricultural Cooperative and Rural Development Bank (NACRDB) to give loans to farmers at low interest rates. The administration in conjunction with the United Nations Food and Agriculture Organisation began an aggressive National Food Security Programme and implemented a Tuber and Roots Expansion Programme, from which about 5.2 million small-scale farmers benefited.

At the end of Obasanjo's administration, Nigeria had become the world's largest producer of cassava with an annual production of about 50 million metric tonnes, while cocoa production also went from 150,000 tons to 400,000 tons per annum. The ban placed on the importation of frozen poultry in 2003 encouraged so much local production that the country achieved self-sufficiency in poultry production.

There was no area of national life that the Obasanjo administration did not positively touch. In an interview published in Saturday Punch of 20/11/2010, Chief (Mrs.) Opral Benson, reputed as the fashion pacesetter in Nigeria had this to say about Obasanjo and his contribution to the development and popularisation of Nigerian prints beyond the shores of Nigeria:

"For that I give some credit to former President Olusegun Obasanjo because it was during his time that we were given the opportunity to export some of our products in the country and he, as the head of government, started to wear African prints. Then African designers started to make good use of them and now it has come to stay."

There was no area of the nation's polity, upon which his administration did not leave its visibly positive mark; including gender issues. We saw in the administration of Chief Obasanjo the largest participation of women at the highest national decision-making level. The appointment of women to ministerial, ambassadorial and top bureaucratic positions ceased in the Obasanjo administration to be an after thought.

The list is endless but the scope and thrust of this work does not permit exhaustive examination of all the achievements of Chief (Gen.) Olusegun Obasanjo during his two-term tenure as the elected President of Nigeria. He took the country practically from the dunghill and left it well bathed, empowered and beautifully decorated to take her rightful and leadership position in the comity of nations.

The achievements of Chief (Gen.) Obasanjo confounded his detractors, who tirelessly but vainly sought to paint him at best, as a bully and at worst, as an anti-democratic military politician. In one of their attempts to achieve this, they invented what became notoriously known as "the third term agenda". This was an alleged attempt by Obasanjo to obtain for him a tenure extension, which he planned to railroad through the National Assembly in a Constitutional amendment exercise. This accusation, though unsubstantiated, was unmistakably intended to distort Obasanjo's reputation. They were actually very close to achieving that but their stand is considerably weakened by the actual and circumstantial facts of the whole episode, as we know it through the media.

First, nobody can deny Obasanjo's physical and moral courage. His track record from his days as a military commander, through his roles as a military Head of State, farmer, prisoner, to an elected President, attest incontrovertibly to his courage. It is therefore inconceivable that as the President, he would lack the courage to publicly declare that he wanted a tenure elongation, if he truly wanted it. He could not be afraid of anything because it is in any case not an offence to have a desire and seek to realise it within the limits of extant provisions of the constitution.

Second, Obasanjo was a military Head of State from 1976 – 1979, during which time his official decisions and actions were in theory, largely discretionary. His decisions and actions were not subject to any constitutional or democratic moderation. He had at that time wide latitude to give himself, even life tenure but he did not. Therefore, if in spite of the freedom he had at that time to do anything about tenure, he stuck to the original pledge about the time to hand over, it sounds quite far fetched that he would desire it later, when he had the media, the National Assembly, the civil society, the International Community, the Constitution and above all, his reputation and integrity, to moderate his decisions and actions.

Third, nobody has ever come forward to say that Obasanjo told him that he wanted tenure elongation. All the available witnesses to "the third term agenda", who had made public statements about it, including Senator (Mrs.) Florence Ita-Giwa, National Assembly Liaison Officer to President Obasanjo, Alhaji Atiku Abubakar, Vice President, Senator Ibrahim Mantu and a host of others, have consistently said that President Obasanjo did not privately or publicly express any desire for tenure elongation.

Vice-President, Atiku Abubakar, was reported in a newspaper interview to say that President Obasanjo told him categorically that he would leave office at the expiration of his second term in office. In addition, not too long ago, Senator Ibrahim Mantu said publicly that he did not feel ashamed to be identified with the proposed

Constitutional Amendment that contained over one hundred amendment issues, of which term elongation for the President and the Governors was only one. He concluded the press interview thus:

"We have been vindicated even though Obasanjo did not ask us to work for a third term for him."

There is no doubt that Senator Mantu, like the other witnesses mentioned, knew what he was talking about.

Kelechi Anosike also writes:

"Is this not reminiscent of the maddening crowd? In the bid to get a clearer picture of the forces behind the third term, Senator Idris Kuta from Niger State, challenged Ken Nnamani, President of the Senate: "if you have given Baba (President Obasanjo) any commitment that you are going to give him anything in the Constitution, take us into confidence. If you do, we will follow you...(but) if you don't, we will defeat you on the floor of this House." But Nnamani reassured his colleagues that "nobody has asked me for commitment and I have not given any." Kelechi Anosike: Olusegun Obasanjo: The Man, The Movement, The Message, Abuja, 2006. p. 158.

We must also remember that freedom of expression is the bedrock of democracy. Nobody can gag another person, who wants to pursue a wish or desire through democratically established channels. If, therefore, some people wanted tenure elongation for the President and the Governors in a democratic setting, such as we were in at the time, they were absolutely free to pursue it. In the case of the "third term" episode, whoever the protagonists were and whatever their motivation was, they pursued their desire in an appropriate manner by going through the democratic channel. They should in fact therefore be commended or at least, recognised, as democrats in that they subjected their political desire to the democratic grill. When it failed, they acquiesced. They did not attempt any uncivilised or extra-democratic method to force their desire through.

Lastly, This Day, one of Nigeria's most popular newspapers had this to say at that time about the performance of Obasanjo in office:

"By most yardsticks, President Obasanjo has done extremely well, both in Nigeria and on the continent. He is entitled to declare his administration victorious in 2007 and, thereafter, depart the place in a blaze of glory and accolade."

In the face of the witnesses, the facts and a dispassionate examination of the failed Constitution Review exercise in question, as we know them through the news media, one cannot avoid the conclusion that the accusation of

Obasanjo as the instigator of the "third term agenda", was an unfortunate misrepresentation of the latter's character and of his position in the failed Constitution Review exercise.

Figure 15 - Obasanjo with former president Obama

Figure 16 - "Seven Wise Men": Past Heads of State of the Federal Republic of Nigeria

Figure 17 - Obasanjo with former President Clinton of the USA at Clinton Initiative Conference

Figure 18 - At the G8 Sumit

Figure 19 - with Collin Powell

Chapter Seventeen: Transferable Principles of Accomplishment

Once again we saw the hand of God in Olusegun Obasanjo's life. He came out of prison, expecting only to keep his achievements hitherto in an innocuous private life. He did not see himself in any future role in Nigeria beyond making occasional comments on exceedingly vexing public issues but God had a different agenda. When that agenda began to unfold, Obasanjo submitted himself to the Lord and followed His divine direction.

Prison condition in Nigeria at the time of Gen. Obasanjo's imprisonment was enough to ruin an average person's mind. In addition, when such person is coming from the Olympian height of a former Head of State, it is destructive of both mind and body. The first principle, upon which Chief Obasanjo's success as an elected President of Nigeria rested was therefore RESILIENCE.

From the time Chief Obasanjo joined the army, his life had been free, stable, peaceful and vibrant. His army career gave him expected and tolerable challenges that he easily surmounted. The risky and unpredictable part of his career was his participation in the Nigerian civil war and in foreign peacekeeping operations but God saw him through all of them. He came out of the civil war with outstanding success and also returned home from peacekeeping operations without any untoward experience. While yet in the army, he was appointed the Chief of Staff, Supreme Headquarters and later, Head of State. Life as a Head of State might have its own challenges but they were positive and welcome challenges.

Furthermore, the sacrifice he had to make to grow his farm, in whatever form he did it, was self-imposed. It also did not take too long before he began to see the good fruits of the sacrifice and he was happy that he made the sacrifice. However, when this prolonged stability and peace of mind were violently interrupted by a false accusation that was followed by a humiliating arrest, then a phony trial and almost a death sentence, life could not be the same. Some observers thought that he might not survive such assault and the likely disorientation that would follow.

Chief Obasanjo himself was not optimistic that he would walk out of the gulag on his feet but he did. To be in prison is a fatal offensive against the self-worth of the imprisoned person. It is an imputation of irrelevance and utter uselessness. In the case of Obasanjo, the undisguised intention of the powers that sent him to prison was actually to kill him or relegate him to a living corpse, until he physically died. However, to their utter disappointment, he neither died nor become a living corpse.

I came to know through my recent study of eminent persons living in retirement that the real challenge for them and the one that speeds up the death of some of them is not diminished income. The cause of early death in retirement is to a large extent the cloud of irrelevance that covers the lives of retired eminent persons. Obasanjo's prison experience therefore deserves a separate study. This is because most people, who are used to a stable and positively challenging life, do not often survive the opposite but Obasanjo did.

Chief Obasanjo had every cause to be the reverse of what he has been, since he was released from prison. There was enough reason for him to have died physically or mentally. God preserved him and he cooperated with God by protecting his mind with positive engagement and his body with productive physical exercise. Instead of wasting away in regret, bitterness and nihilism, he resorted to studying and writing. He wrote four soul-lifting books of good literary standard, while in prison. Midway in prison, he sought permission to farm, not as an escapist ploy but as a delightful hobby.

By the time he was released from prison, he had learnt new lessons that were, unknown to him at the time, necessary for God's next assignment for him. The lesson in Chief Olusegun Obasanjo's life for those of us going through straits, and we are most likely many in number, is loud and clear. Tough people last, while tough times do not last. We have seen this in the life of Gen. Obasanjo, whose resilience made it possible for him to beautifully and gloriously outlast one of the worst setbacks that can ever befall a man.

The second principle of achievement is the triple element of HOPE, FAITH AND LOVE. The expected attitude of Chief Obasanjo, while in prison and after regaining his freedom was to despair about the present and future of Nigeria. He could lose faith in himself and become passive to whatever might be going on in the country. He could also hate everybody and everything that represented or reminded him of Nigeria and the circumstances of his imprisonment. He then would not have the thought of doing anything beyond keeping the bits and pieces of his own life together. It is amazing that Chief Obasanjo did the exact opposite of all these. The hope he had in Nigeria and the faith he had in God and in himself made him bring the spiritual perspective into what was happening around him. This attitude also encouraged his decision to participate in national politics, even though he knew that it was not going to be easy. He knew that he still had to go through the process of election with its concomitant financial, physical, material and emotional demands that he could ill afford at the time.

After Gen. Obasanjo had been locked up in prison, Abacha did not relent, as he extended his persecution to Gen. Obasanjo's workers. At a stage, some of them had to run to neighbouring Ghana for refuge. During this time, his farm and other investments suffered grave decline and there also arose heartless spurious claimants to his property. These false claimants most probably wished and indeed believed that he would not come out of the prison alive. The point being made is that the problems waiting for Obasanjo by the time he left the prison were gargantuan in nature. If he did not have a more gargantuan hope in Nigeria and faith in God as well as in himself, it would have been impossible for him to think of rendering service to Nigeria again in the capacity of an elected President.

Where does love come in then? The fact that Chief Obasanjo was convicted and sentenced on trumped up and absolutely false charges was well known. It was all a grand conspiracy planned and executed by Abacha and his collaborators to silence him in a very brutal manner. Obasanjo therefore had every natural reason to be bitter against the conspirators and their collaborators, particularly those of them still alive. He however chose to overcome evil with good.

Contrary to the rumours of persecution against Abacha family by President Obasanjo, Abacha's criminal assault against the public treasury was actually discovered by sheer accident. In fact, nobody ever imagined that a Head of State could loot his own country half as much as Abacha looted Nigeria's coffers. As for Obasanjo, his focus was more on the love of God that brought him out of prison alive than on retaliation. He wrote a letter of condolence to Abacha to commiserate with him over the death of his son. He also wrote another to Mrs. Abacha, when Abacha himself died. These letters by Obasanjo clearly shows that he had forgiven Abacha and his collaborators.

He said in a sermon titled "Facing the Future Without Bitterness" delivered at the thanksgiving service held at Abeokuta for his return from prison:

"For me, it (imprisonment) was all a thrilling experience with God in charge and in control. He granted me His peace and joy out of His love and grace. He gave me satisfaction and contentment and kept my spirit high, my conscience free and clear and my hands clean."

He further said in the same sermon:

"Violence destroys, no matter what other message it may send. Let the government take the lead for Nigeria to take the path of peace and dialogue. We need all hands on deck for the work of positive construction and reconstruction that we have ahead of us as a nation. Let the spirit of reconciliation prevail."

Chief (Gen.) Obasanjo gave this sermon immediately after his release from prison, when politics had not at all come into his reckoning as an area, where a role might be waiting for him. It was therefore not difficult for him to insist on an inclusive cabinet, when he eventually became the President. Obasanjo did not resent some known collaborators of Abacha, who had to work with him in the PDP and even directly in government. He operated with love and open-mindedness. This made it possible for him to secure the best performance from many of those who held positions in his administration. Some of them too in turn ended up contributing to his ultimate success.

Without Hope, Faith and Love, it would have been impossible for Olusegun Obasanjo to succeed in his role as President. Hope kept him trying and forging ahead, even in the face of obstacles and distractions. Faith sustained his optimism and Love helped him to quickly forget the past and move ahead in the strength of God.

We can now say categorically that God allowed this to happen to Obasanjo so that both him and the rest of us could learn from it. The Obasanjo story speaks particularly to those, who allow present failures and the weaknesses of fellow human beings around them to push them out of step with God. Let us walk in love and allow God to fight our battles.

The third principle is COMMITMENT. President Obasanjo displayed unalloyed commitment to Nigeria and to his duties as the President of the Federal Republic of Nigeria. Whenever he was tempted to act contrary to his profession of an honest, forthright, purposeful and transparent leadership, he stoutly resisted it. His failure to win the votes from the Southwest, his zone of origin, practically became a political stigma that was often used against him by detractors and opponents within his party, the PDP. He could have seized any slight opportunity to dance to the ethno-centric tune of some influential Yoruba politicians in return for the political support of the Yoruba. He however rejected it for the sake of Nigeria.

In addition, many armchair analysts hurled undeserved criticisms against him but he refused to be discouraged because he had a mission called the Nigeria project. He implemented this project throughout his tenure as President. He travelled to all the continents of the world to promote Nigeria's interest and image. His frequent foreign travels came under scathing criticisms of some people but he did not relent, until he had something to show, in the form of debt relief for those travels. At home, he was ready to take on anybody or group for the sake of Nigeria. While in office, he had no permanent friends or foes because what he decided or did at anytime, and over any issue, was defined and dictated by Nigeria's interest.

There were some of his friends, who for this reason lost out on specific issues of interest to them. They got angry with him on the spur of the moment but they later came back to mend fences. They ended up praising him for his forthrightness and commitment to the Nigerian cause. There were also a few of his political associates, who most probably believed that their relationship with the President would shield them, even if they ran foul of the law. Some of them learnt the truth too late as those of them, who were caught with corrupt practices, were arrested and properly prosecuted. Some of them were even convicted and jailed.

Success is to a large extent a function of the degree of commitment brought into one's endeavour. President Obasanjo succeeded as much as he did partly because he was deeply committed to his role. There are bound to be varying degrees of obstacles, distractions and setbacks in the course of any endeavour. There is no amount of preparation that can permanently shield a person from the challenges of life but a committed person will always bounce back after every setback to finish what he started.

The fourth principle is HARD WORK. To say that Chief (Gen.) Obasanjo is hardworking is an understatement in that he works as if tomorrow would not come. He slept for only a few hours in the evening and night put together. In a typical day, he attended to all his numerous files and held formal and informal meetings with various interest groups and individuals, from morning till far into the night. He read his files and memos painstakingly. He also travelled extensively, and when he did, he kept his hosts on their toes. His reaction was comprehensive to whatever was placed before him. His hard work kept him familiar with the various projects being executed by his administration and also made coordination less tedious for him.

Many people fail out of sheer laziness. Hard work on the other hand, helps one to persevere, to be proactive, to be resourceful and be creative. Laziness is a kind of lameness that restricts a person to a low level of achievement or to outright failure. It takes hard work to offer an effective leadership and set the right standard. Laziness breeds mediocrity that in turn breeds poverty. It also stifles growth. An enterprise is like an organism that begins to die when it can no longer grow. It takes hard work to sustain the growth of an enterprise to enduring prosperity. Laziness on the part of the man at the helm of affairs gives room for the distortion and ultimate destruction of organisational vision and goals by errant subordinates or opportunistic competitors.

The fifth principle is COURAGE. In a developing polity like ours, where people are moved more by primordial loyalty and immediate personal gratification than by national interest and long-term benefit, courage is one of the most important qualities a leader needs in order to succeed. Some analysts prefer to call it political will but political will is also the consensus of the political elite. The snag here is that such consensus is usually secured through bargaining, at the expense of some other vital principle. The administration of President Obasanjo, however demystified the so-called political will; not by being dictatorial but by showing us that a lot depends upon the courage that an incumbent President, as a person, is willing to bring into governance.

The laws setting up the EFCC and the ICPC would have remained paper tigers but for the teeth that were given to their implementation by Nuhu Ribadu and Justice Akanbi respectively. They derived their motivation and daring from President Obasanjo's total support, which was itself a reflection of the latter's courage. This explains why the public lamented the absence of Obasanjo, when Nuhu Ribadu was removed from the EFCC by Obasanjo's successor, President Umaru Yar'Adua,. The friends of Nigeria too, who lent a helping hand to Nigeria in building these anti-corruption agencies were miffed by the removal of Nuhu Ribadu from EFCC. Late President Yar'Adua, as a person was not in any way corrupt. One can therefore not resist the conclusion that his unimpressive handling of the fight against corruption was a sign of the absence of courage.

In addition to the fight against corruption, the privatisation policy of the Obasanjo regime was very unpopular with the political hangers-on, who were nothing but worms, feeding fat on the economic apparatus of the nation. They opposed the privatisation policy with all their political influence and even feigned sympathy for the workers. It was the courage of President Obasanjo that drove the programme into the success it achieved. Today the public can compare the effectiveness of public enterprises that were privatised then and those that are not yet privatised. The performance of the telecommunication sector can be compared to that of power. The difference is very clear.

Courage is a virtue that is applicable in all walks of life. The opposite of courage is fear; fear of the outcome of the decision or action that we are about to take. God has not given us the spirit of fear. We must forge ahead and take whatever decision we consider right in our situation. If a decision or action leads to failure, it only shows that there is yet another decision that will lead to success. We only need to continue to explore until we get there. On the other hand, when we refuse to act for the fear of what the outcome would be or the fear of the likely reaction of people, we might never make any progress. Obasanjo was never afraid of doing what he believed to be right, even when it might attract criticisms. The result of the courageous leadership that he gave to the nation is the huge socio-economic progress the nation experienced under his administration.

The sixth principle is PROBITY. The anti-corruption initiatives of President Obasanjo, while in office speak encyclopaedic volumes about his probity and transparency. His anti-corruption stance so encouraged some friends of Nigeria and the international community that they committed large resources to support the relevant agencies in the area of training and provision of equipment. There were however some people, who just did not believe the professed probity of Chief Obasanjo. Such people, though with vindictive avidity went round the whole world, as far as they could go, searching meticulously for one little skeleton, in the form of laundered money or some other secret illegality, in the cupboard of Obasanjo. They found nothing.

The barrage of petitions, though unsubstantiated against Obasanjo to the Economic and Financial Crimes Commission (EFCC) prompted it to carry out its own covert investigation within and outside Nigeria but it found nothing against him. The outcome of the investigation of EFCC was officially submitted to Obasanjo's successor.

Furthermore, Late Senator Abubakar, who was Deputy Senate President, confessed that he spent $250,000.00 to hire a forensic accountant to fish out 'Obasanjo's money' laundered in any foreign account. When nothing of such was found, he regretted and came back to apologise to Obasanjo.

Shortly after Chief (Gen.) Obasanjo left office in 2007, the House of Representatives' Committee on Power alleged that he did not act appropriately in the management of the budgetary allocation to power during his regime. The Committee therefore wrote a letter inviting him to give evidence before it. The discourteous manner in which the letter was written was suggestive of their belief that the opportunity to ridicule Obasanjo had finally come.

Notwithstanding the departure of the House of Representatives' Committee from protocol in their manner of invitation, Chief Obasanjo sent a humble reply containing a detailed account of the actions and decisions he took over power during the period in question. The facts and figures presented by Chief Obasanjo in his reply confounded and silenced the Committee. Besides, the Chairman of the House Committee probe, Ndidi Godwin

Elumelu, was arrested and put in State detention, while awaiting trial on allegations of corrupt practices during the probe. Those who inspired and goaded the House of Representatives Committee into chasing the shadow of skeletons in Obasanjo's cupboard speedily fizzled out, without a trace.

Chief Obasanjo's enemies did not for the reason of the failure of their power probe stratagem relent. They soon came out with another allegation of the involvement of the former President in the well-publicised Halliburton bribe scandal. The detractors of Chief (Gen.) Obasanjo again felt that they had finally got him, when for some time he did not respond to the malicious publications linking him, without any evidence at all, to the bribery scandal. When the vilifying publications would not cease, he sent a personal letter, published in Guardian Newspaper, to the President, Dr. Goodluck Jonathan. He detailed in the letter his efforts that led to the recovery of US$100 million from Halliburton into Nigerian Treasury. Once again the enemies were silenced!

Part, and a very significant part, of the success of President Obasanjo in office and his victory over his detractors, was due to his characteristic probity in the handling of public affairs. Any skeleton in his cupboard would not have ended in hushed tones. It would have been blown open by his enemies in order to render him fake and mar his hard earned reputation. This is natural because promotion, accomplishment, breakthroughs, success and the like, will forever attract jealousy and hatred. The only effective shield is characteristic transparency and probity.

Some people are today putting up with the irreversible punishing consequences of their corrupt past, when they were in office. They learned too late that power is transient and the tracks of the corrupt cannot be forever covered. Time will roll by and the dark places that hide the evil deeds of corrupt men will give up their secrets. Then the social and legal repercussions will take their full course and the corrupt put to shame.

The seventh principle is KNOWLEDGE. Chief (Gen.) Olusegun Obasanjo held many public appointments, including military appointments during a period spanning the greater part of his whole adult life. He was General Officer Commanding, Inspector of Army Engineers, Federal Commissioner (Minister) of Works and Housing, Chief of Staff, Supreme Headquarters, Head of the Federal Military Government, farmer and prisoner, before his election as President of the Federal Republic of Nigeria. He had seen the highest, the middle and the lowest points of Nigeria. He was for that reason a carrier of an undeniable wealth of knowledge and experience in governance. However, in spite

347

of the enormous wealth of knowledge and experience that he had accumulated from his previous callings, he never at any time felt that he had known enough.

He was in the habit of inviting his friends, who were not in public office for informal discussions. In these discussions, he explicitly sought their dispassionate comments on various issues bearing on any government policy. Wherever relevant knowledge was, Obasanjo would fish it out. He was always ready to bring into whatever he was doing or hoping to do anybody, regardless of age or position, who could give him any helpful information about it. He did not mind waking his friends up in the night to find out something as commonplace as the price of a particular foodstuff, just to ascertain the effectiveness of an official agricultural policy.

His first child, now Senator Iyabo Obasanjo-Bello jokingly attributed the President's frequent calls to his friends during late hours of the night to a bout of insomnia. The truth however is that President Obasanjo did not see himself as a reservoir of knowledge and he was therefore ready to draw from the experience and knowledge of others. In fact, there is nothing that Obasanjo enjoys more than the opportunity to exchange ideas with others on any issue for the purpose of gaining relevant knowledge. He does not mind at all if an argument, in the process turns into a heated debate. He may even part angrily with a friend he invited to give him advice. That however does not inhibit him from calling the same person the following day, if there arises another issue he believes that the person can make useful contribution to. He did not allow any situation or consideration to hamper him from seeking knowledge and useful information from anybody or any quarters at any time, even if it meant waking up somebody at night.

Unfortunately, the public did not know this. Those who saw Obasanjo as a short-cut to their selfish ends too did not know that he possessed enough information that put him in close touch with the realities of the Nigerian political and socio-economic situation at any given time. This enabled him to quickly see through any jaundiced information or advice and dismiss it with a wave of the hand, no matter how well cloaked it was. It is understandable then that those, whose pieces of advice or information he glibly rejected because they were useless for his purpose or because they harboured selfish motives, left to disparage and label him self-opinionated. The truth is that Obasanjo did not run the affairs of the Nigerian State as if he knew it all but he also did not give in to the misleading advice from those, who wanted to cash in on his not being omniscient. He consciously sought relevant information from both official and unofficial quarters and from people in different walks of life to enrich or correct his own tentatively held ideas.

Moreover, shortly after his inauguration as the President of the Federal Republic of Nigeria, he instituted the Saturday Forum, to which he invited all manners of professionals, technocrats, public officers and ordinary people to discuss various issues bearing on official policies and their effects on the citizens, as well as the performance of his administration. These regular gatherings provided him and his administration the opportunity to discover and examine the various perspectives on specific issues and thereafter evolve well-reasoned policy positions on such issues. The outcome was the consistently sound, relevant and sustainable policy decisions characteristic of the Obasanjo administration.

This aspect of President Obasanjo's approach to management and policy formulation reminds all of us that knowledge is a sine qua non of right behaviour and it is inexhaustible. Many people fail in their enterprises for lack of appropriate knowledge, upon which they can build their actions. Nobody can at anytime cease to require knowledge. With the certainty and endlessness of change, only knowledge of the changing phases of life and the factors of change can sustain human life and improve human endeavour on earth. Evolutionists call this 'natural selection'.

The eighth principle is PASSION. This is the attribute that activates and sustains other attributes and ensures good success in any endeavour. It is more than commitment in that it is the column that holds other attributes for the success of any pursuit. Without passion, other attributes will fall flat, when they are challenged by unexpected pressure and storms. Passion provides the strength to weather storms and move on towards an expected goal. Passion is perhaps the most effective antidote to failure as there can be no turning back from a pursuit, cause or endeavour that is birthed and sustained by passion.

Passion, passion for Nigeria, is written large in all the roles of Chief (Gen.) Obasanjo, from the war to his presidency. His passion attracted to him highly talented men and women, who under his direction worked for the advancement of Nigeria and ipso facto, his own success. As a military commander, a military Head of State and an elected President, his passion for the unity and greatness of this country cheered him on in the face of pressures, mischief, cynicism and wanton attacks. It was in his farming career that he displayed most his passion for whatever he was handling. Many of his friends, who saw what he had committed into his farm, felt that he was either sub-normal or just eccentric. His success in farming has however proved to them that he is neither sub-normal nor eccentric. The truth is that passion burns in his bones for whatever he lays his hands on.

Passion breaks the bounds of failure and success, as vividly seen in Gen. Obasanjo's story. In spite of the challenges that he had faced and the present prodigious success of the Obasanjo Farms, he continues to explore and break into still wider frontiers of farming. Unfortunately today, many people lack passion for their endeavours. Such people easily become rolling stones that gather no moss in that on facing the slightest challenge, they run from one endeavour to the other. They are therefore known for nothing and they achieve nothing.

There are bound to be daunting challenges in any endeavour but passion makes mountains look like a field for innovation and creativity instead of a barrier to success. This is because passion never gives up on its object. Let us therefore stop trying this or that, expecting to blunder into right. We can be in the right place from the very beginning, if we pursue the things for which we have the passion.

The ninth and highest principle of all is GOD. In the course of my interviews with Chief (Gen.) Obasanjo, when I was working on this book, he repeatedly and thankfully affirmed the grace of God in his life, as the Giver of all gifts, the Enabler and the Provider of the opportunities for the gifts to manifest and function. Chief (Gen.) Obasanjo received a Christian upbringing through the Baptist Schools that were available at Abeokuta, when he was growing up. In the course of life, he had also become persuaded that only God works, while all other things work only at the command of God.

While he was incarcerated in Yola prison, he was referred to as the chaplain because he conducted the prison Christian fellowship. He eventually built a place of worship there. He also in the same Yola prison identified a notorious armed robber, whom he led to Christ. When both of them were released, he sponsored the reformed young man in the Seminary and he is today a preacher of the Gospel of Jesus Christ. Apart from his fervent and daily personal devotions, he also held morning fellowship for his household everyday without fail. He did this throughout his eight years of office as the President of Nigeria and he continues to do it in Abeokuta even now.

Right from his youth as a subaltern, Chief Obasanjo had learnt to trust God to order his footsteps. He therefore never sought any undue advantage, except what was required to make him perform well wherever God put him. When the plot against him was very thick, the arrowhead of the plot boasted that he had the party executive, the majority of the members of the National Assembly and the majority of members of the Federal Executive Council behind him to fight Obasanjo. He proudly asserted that he had finally nailed Obasanjo. The person, who came to report this to Chief Obasanjo was flabbergasted, when instead of panic Obasanjo relaxed and sent for his ADC to play a game of squash with him.

When the man regained composure, he wondered if Obasanjo thought that he was lying. Obasanjo smiling, replied with one disdainful remark. He said:

"No. I don't think that you are lying but I cannot be moved by boasts and plans that exclude God. The man you talked about might have, as far as he is concerned, made a good plan but I know that he left God out of his plan. For that reason, the plan will certainly fail. Why should I be bothered by a Godless plan?"

The plan actually failed woefully and the man in question is still wallowing in the morass of the consequences of his godless political contrivance.

Many of Obasanjo's political enemies came in the end with apologies to confess their failed perfidy and atrocities against him. Obasanjo keeps wondering, who else could make one's enemy fail in his evil plan and also make the enemy scamper like a puppy to confess and ask for forgiveness? It is only God, who can do that. Chief

Obasanjo knew this so much that he refused to bow to any man or be frightened by the boasts of his enemies. He held on to God. The result was that in spite of the seeming political weakness of Chief Obasanjo, when he was in office, God consistently gave him victory over his enemies.

We can from Obasanjo's life see that it does not matter, whether we are talented or not. It also does not matter what man is saying or doing. It is God who changes the times and the seasons and He has the final say over all the affairs of our lives. Should we not, then like Obasanjo, make God the Pillar of all our plans and endeavours?

Figure 20 - Welcoming President Bush and Wife Laura Bush to Nigeria

Figure 21 - African Heads of State at African Union Summit

Figure 22 - Obasanjo with Colleagues at an African Union Summit

Figure 23 - Obasanjo and Bouteflika of Egypt at African Union Summit

Figure 24 - Obasanjo with Bill Gates of the USA at Economic Summit

Chapter Eighteen: Still Pressing Forward

When Gen. Obasanjo handed over power to Alhaji Shehu Shagari and left the State House in 1979, one of the things he did not leave behind in the State House was Africa and her problems. He did not forget that all his efforts and those of his colleagues made little or no difference in the face of the plethora of crises that bedevilled the Continent. He ruminated over this for a long time and came to identify leadership recruitment as one of the fundamental problems of Africa. At that time, Africa had a grave leadership recruitment problem with incessant and widespread coups, sit-tight rulers and the general absence of strong democratic institutions capable of promoting rapid political and socio-economic development across the Continent. Sitting down and bemoaning the problem would not in any way help the situation. Gen. Obasanjo then came up with the African Leadership Forum (ALF).

Gen. Obasanjo himself stated the objective of the Forum as follows:

"To bring together young, potential African leaders to enhance their knowledge and awareness of current issues, provide an environment for interaction between experienced world leaders and emerging young African leaders and diagnose, understand, and search for informed solutions to local, regional and global problems."

The Forum regularly holds seminars and conferences, which attract prominent world leaders as participants or facilitators. The issues examined at the conferences were topical political, social and economic matters. These included Democracy, Leadership, Poverty Eradication, Agriculture, Food Security, Human Development and Disease Eradication.

The ALF had at its inception an Advisory Board, made up of notable world leaders such as Simeon Adebo, former Permanent Representative of Nigeria to the United Nations, Takeo Fukuda, former Prime Minister of Japan, Winnie Mandela of South Africa, Julius Nyerere, former President of Tanzania, Leopold Senghor, former President of Senegal, Helmut Schmidt, former Chancellor of now defunct West Germany, Robert McNamara, former US Secretary of Defence and President of the World Bank, Jimmy Carter, former President of the USA and Jim Callaghan, former Prime Minister of the United Kingdom.

The highpoint of the relevance and achievement of the ALF was the Conference on Security, Stability, Development and Cooperation in Africa (CSSDCA), which took place in

Kampala, Uganda in May 1991. The Conference hosted over 500 delegates from all over the world including Yovweri Museveni of Uganda, Joachim Chissano of Mozambique, Kenneth Kaunda of Zambia, Hosni Mubarak of Egypt, Julius Nyerere of Tanzania and many others. The Conference produced what came to be known as the Kampala Document, which contained far-reaching decisions and recommendations on the strategies for achieving rapid socio-economic development in Africa. Gen. Obasanjo expressed his satisfaction with the meeting and described the document as one that "we can hand over to incumbent African leaders...that they can now take, endorse, adopt and make to form the basis of inter-governmental negotiations."

In addition, Chief (Gen.) Obasanjo believes rightly that while God gave him the gifts and talents for his achievements, his society too made varying degrees of sacrifice for the opportunity and scope to use these talents. He therefore decided to give back to his society something similar to what he had received from it. This was the raison d'être for the founding at Ota by Chief (Gen.) Obasanjo of The Bells Comprehensive School made up of a Nursery, Primary and Secondary School. The fees charged by the school are among the lowest charged by schools of similar standard and quality in Nigeria. He did not stop there, as he lately founded Bells University of Technology. Apart from satisfying the yearning for social responsibility, the institutions are also a desirable and timely contribution to our nation's inadequate educational facilities.

It is difficult to deny the multi-disciplinary achievements of Chief (Gen.) Olusegun Obasanjo. As a soldier, he received from the rebel army the Instrument of Surrender that ended a thirty-month-long fratricidal war in Nigeria. He was Head of the Federal Military Government and Commander-in-Chief of Nigerian Armed Forces. He thereafter started poultry farming from the very scratch and he is now the largest poultry farmer in Africa. He served time in prison and came out with an alert mind and a stable personality. He was democratically elected as the President of the Federal Republic of Nigeria, the most populous black nation in the world for two consecutive terms. He is the founder of the African Leadership Forum and the proprietor of The Bells Comprehensive School and Bells University of Technology.

Olusegun Obasanjo was also at various times Member of the UNESCO Commission for Peace in the Minds of Men, Member of the World Health Organisation Committee of Experts on the Effects of Nuclear Weapons, Member Independent Commission on Disarmament and Security Issues, Member Inter-Action Council of Former Heads of

State and Government, Member Committee on the United Nations Population Award, Member UN Secretary General's Advisory Panel on Africa, Member The Carnegie Commission on Preventing Deadly Conflict, Director and Member of the Board of Trustees of Ford Foundation (the first black man to occupy that position and he held that position for 12 consecutive years), Member Board of Directors University of Peace Costa Rica, Member Independent Group on Financial Development Commission (Schmidt Commission), Member United Nations Panel of Eminent Persons on the Relationship between Disarmament and Development, Chairman Expert Group on Military Expenditures by Developing Countries, Co-Chairman Commonwealth Eminent Persons Group on South Africa, Chairman Hearings on Namibia of the World Council of Churches Washington, Chairman Advisory Council of Transparency International, Director Better World Society, Chairman G77 plus China and lately, Representative of the UN Secretary General to the Democratic Republic of Congo and the Great Lakes.

The life of Olusegun Obasanjo is eventful and bedecked with such an array of inspiring multi-disciplinary accomplishments that one cannot resist calling him God's unique blessing to Nigeria in particular and to Africa and the world in general. His life is also a proof of God's loving kindness towards all, regardless of parentage and environmental circumstance. If a person like Obasanjo, who set out in life with the shackles of absolute poverty could achieve so much in a world of loveless competition, why should you, dear reader of this book, accept failure? No, you dare not. This is surely because God is no respecter of persons.

God has enough gifts to go round and right now, everybody has one or more innate gifts and talents. There are many Obasanjo's among us but some are, sadly, languishing in the throes of the exact opposite of what God intended for them because they either cannot discover the God-given treasures lurked in them or they succumb too early to the inclemency of their environment. God said through Prophet Isaiah:

"Shall I bring to the birth, and not cause to bring forth? saith the Lord: shall I cause to bring forth, and shut the womb? saith thy God." Isaiah 66: 9 (KJV).

God, who gave the gifts will surely also give the opportunity to use them but we have to seek before we can find. We must labour and apply principles that will, all other things being equal, move us in the path of progress to our goal. This may along the line call for varying degrees of sacrifice but 'all is well that ends well.'

The story of Olusegun Obasanjo is an eye opener and also a message of hope to those, who are overwhelmed by the hostility of their environment, those, who have fallen in one way or the other and those, who are aspiring to greatness in their field. What God is saying to you through the life of Obasanjo is not to give up but to be constantly renewed and press forward.

Figure 25- Nigeria on his mind

Bibliography

Adinoyi Ojo Onukaba   Olusegun Obasanjo In the Eyes of Time, Ibadan 2007.

Kelechi Anosike   Olusegun Obasanjo: The Man, The Message, The

Movement, Abuja 2007.

Tunde Olusunle   On the Trail of History, Ibadan 2006.

Olusegun Obasanjo   My Command: An Account of the Nigerian Civil War

1967-70, Heinemann 1980.

Olusegun Obasanjo   Not My Will, Ibadan 1990.

Olusegun Obasanjo   Nzeogwu, Ibadan 1987.

Keith Panter-Brick, ed.   Soldiers and Oil: The Political Transformation

of Nigeria, London 1978.

Bola Akinterinwa, ed.   Nigeria's Foreign Policy Thrust: Essays in Honour of

Ambassador Oluyemi Adeniji, CON, Ibadan 2004.

David Akpode Ejoor — Reminiscences, Lagos 1989.

Yar'Adua Foundation — Shehu Musa Yar'Adua: A Life of Service, Abuja 2004.

Maj. Gen. J. N. Garba, CFR — Revolution in Nigeria: Another View, London 1982.

Maj. Gen. J. N. Garba, CFR — Diplomatic Soldiering: The Conduct of Nigerian Foreign Policy, 1975-1979, Ibadan 1987.

Philip Efiong — Nigeria and Biafra: My Story, Princeton, 2004.

Ken Post & G. D. Jenkins — The Price of Liberty: Personality and Politics in Colonial Nigeria, Cambridge 1973.

Shakespeare — Julius Caesar

Oluremi Obasanjo — Bitter-Sweet: My Life with Obasanjo, Lagos 2009.

J. J. Oluleye, p.s.c., CFR — Military Leadership in Nigeria 1966-1979, Ibadan, 1985

Ken Saro-Wiwa   On a Darkling Plain: An
Account of the Nigerian

                         Civil War, Port Harcourt 1989.

Ben Gbulie   The Fall of Biafra, Enugu 1989.

Alexander Madiebo   The Nigerian Revolution and
the Biafran War,

                         Enugu 1980.

Patrick Anwunah   The Nigeria-Biafra War (1967-
1970), Ibadan 2007.

Maj. Gen. H. B. Momoh, ed.   The Nigeria Civil War 1967-
1970, Ibadan 2000.

Federal Ministry of Information   A March of Progress:
Collected Speeches of

                         H. E. Lt. Gen. Olusegun
Obasanjo, Lagos.

Federal Govt. Printer   Report of the Political
Bureau, Lagos, 1987.

Presidential Comms. Unit   A New Dawn: Selected
Speeches by Olusegun

                         Obasanjo, President of the
Federal Republic of

                         Nigeria, Abuja 2000

Ad'Obe Obe Collection of Speeches of

A New Dawn (Vol. II): A

President Olusegun

Obasanjo, 2001.

Snr. Sp. Asst. to the President Achievements of the Obasanjo

Steady Steps of Progress:

Administration

Newspaper publications, Interviews and Unpublished Articles and Speeches.

About The Book

Nigeria is sadly a country that exhibits bad governance and poor leadership at almost all levels. On the other hand, it is also a nation that has given birth to great men and women, who took the name of Nigeria to higher heights through their exemplary achievements in their different callings. The gap that exists today between our inspiring past and our disheartening present is partly created by the absence of a leadership culture that can be passed from one generation of leaders to another. This author believes that we can build a leadership culture only if we consciously document the uplifting achievements of our past citizens and expose present and future generations to the same through teaching. This is the way to redirect our feet to the path of national greatness.

It is in line with this scenario that this book looks at the extra-ordinary multi-disciplinary achievements of a contemporary Nigerian, Chief (Gen.) Olusegun Obasanjo, to challenge those that are aspiring to leadership positions in Nigeria and those, who are thirsty for success and greatness in their calling. His accomplishments are a torch of progress, worthy to be passed on to the present and future generations.

About The Author

Albert G. P. Omotayo, MFR, is an alumnus of the University of Lagos, Nigeria, the University of Manchester, United Kingdom and L. I. F. E. Theological Seminary, Ikorodu, Nigeria.

Albert was a career Federal civil servant. He served in various capacities, including serving as Nigeria's High Commissioner to the Republic of Mozambique with concurrent accreditation to the Royal Kingdom of Swaziland, the Republic of Madagascar and the Republic of Mauritius. He also thereafter further served as Commissioner for Environment and Chief of Staff to the Governor in Ekiti State, Nigeria before retiring from public service. He is a recipient of the National Honours Award of Member of the Order of the Federal Republic (MFR).

Albert now lives in Lagos, Nigeria.

www.ingramcontent.com/pod-product-compliance
Lightning Source LLC
Chambersburg PA
CBHW061334280526
45784CB00001B/10